MW00424841

WE DARED TO FLY

WE DARED TO FLY

Dangerous Secret Missions During the Vietnam War

WILLIAM REEDER JR.

Essex, Connecticut

An imprint of The Globe Pequot Publishing Group, Inc.
64 South Main Street
Essex, CT 06246
www.globepequot.com

Distributed by NATIONAL BOOK NETWORK

British Library Cataloguing in Publication Information available

Library of Congress Cataloging-in-Publication Data
Names: Reeder, William, Jr., author.
Title: We dared to fly : dangerous secret missions during the Vietnam War / William Reeder Jr.
Other titles: Dangerous secret missions during the Vietnam War
Description: Essex, Connecticut : Lyons Press, [2024] | Includes bibliographical references and
    index.
Identifiers: LCCN 2024013087 (print) | LCCN 2024013088 (ebook) | ISBN 9781493085309
    (cloth) | ISBN 9781493085194 (epub)
Subjects: LCSH: Reeder, William, Jr. | United States. Army. Surveillance Airplane Company,
    131st. | Vietnam War, 1961–1975—Reconnaissance operations, American. | Helicopter pilots—
    United States—Biography. | Helicopter pilots—Vietnam—Phú Bài—Biography. | United
    States. Army—Officers—Biography. | Vietnam War, 1961–1975—Aerial operations, American.
    | Vietnam War, 1961–1975—Personal narratives, American.
Classification: LCC DS558.8 .R44 2024 (print) | LCC DS558.8 (ebook) | DDC 959.704/348—
    dc23/eng/20240405
LC record available at https://lccn.loc.gov/2024013087
LC ebook record available at https://lccn.loc.gov/2024013088

In memory of our commander, Major Gary Alton, and to all the brave "SPUDs" who survived the war and to those many others who gave their lives in the skies over Southeast Asia.

When you go to war as a boy, you have a great illusion of immortality.

ERNEST HEMINGWAY, *MEN AT WAR*

This is the true story of my experience flying OV-1 Mohawks on my first tour of duty in the Vietnam War. It is an account of actual events and real people. I use dialogue in telling the story. I've crafted that dialogue from my best recollections and those of the others involved. The conversations are faithful renditions drawn from our memories. This is our story.

Contents

CONTENTS

MAPS

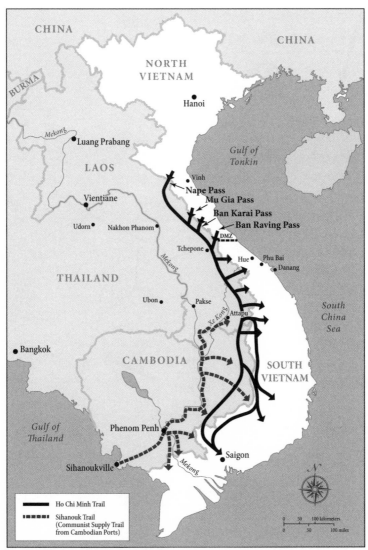

CHINA

CHINA

NORTH
VIETNAM

Hanoi

Mekong

Luang Prabang

Gulf of
Tonkin

LAOS

Vientiane

Vinh

Nape Pass

Udorn   Nakhon Phanom

Mu Gia Pass

Ban Karai Pass

Ban Raving Pass

DMZ

Tchepone

Hue   Phu Bai

Danang

Mekong

THAILAND

Ubon   Pakse

South
China
Sea

Attapu

Bangkok

CAMBODIA

SOUTH
VIETNAM

Gulf of
Thailand

Phenom Penh

Saigon

Sihanoukville

Mekong

N

Ho Chi Minh Trail

Sihanouk Trail
(Communist Supply Trail
from Cambodian Ports)

0   50   100 kilometers
0   50   100 miles

Ho Chi Minh and Sihanouk Trails

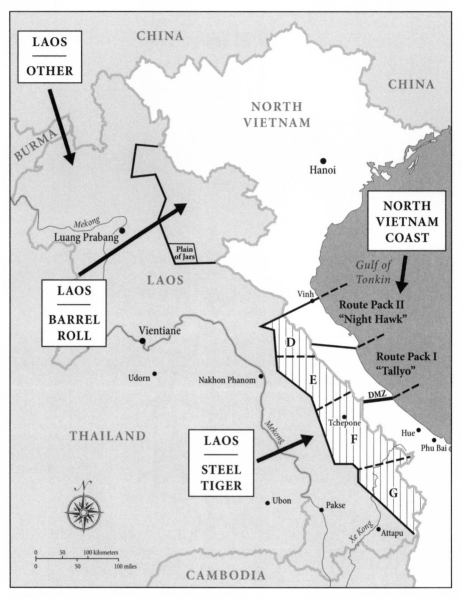

Our Areas of Operation

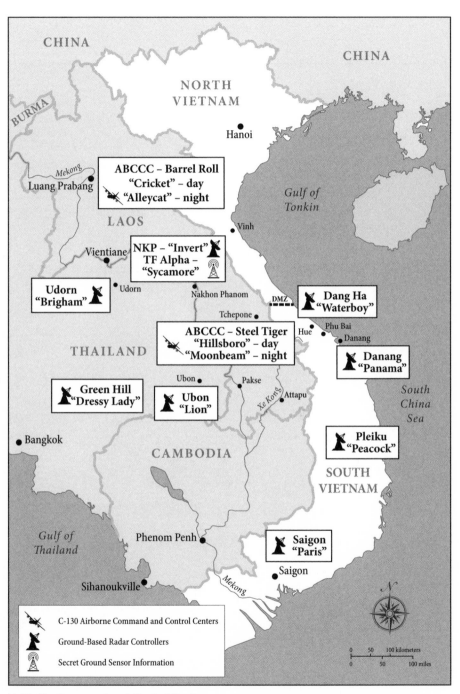

CHINA

CHINA

NORTH
VIETNAM

BURMA

Hanoi

Mekong

Luang Prabang

**ABCCC – Barrel Roll
"Cricket" – day
"Alleycat" – night**

*Gulf of
Tonkin*

LAOS

Vinh

Vientiane

**NKP – "Invert"
TF Alpha –
"Sycamore"**

Udorn

**Udorn
"Brigham"**

Nakhon Phanom

DMZ

**Dang Ha
"Waterboy"**

Tchepone

Phu Bai

**ABCCC – Steel Tiger
"Hillsboro" – day
"Moonbeam" – night**

Hue

Danang

THAILAND

**Danang
"Panama"**

Ubon

Pakse

**Green Hill
"Dressy Lady"**

**Ubon
"Lion"**

Attapu

Xe Kong

*South
China
Sea*

Bangkok

CAMBODIA

**Pleiku
"Peacock"**

SOUTH
VIETNAM

*Gulf of
Thailand*

Phenom Penh

**Saigon
"Paris"**

Saigon

Mekong

Sihanoukville

N

C-130 Airborne Command and Control Centers

Ground-Based Radar Controllers

Secret Ground Sensor Information

0   50   100 kilometers

0   50   100 miles

Air Traffic Command and Control Centers

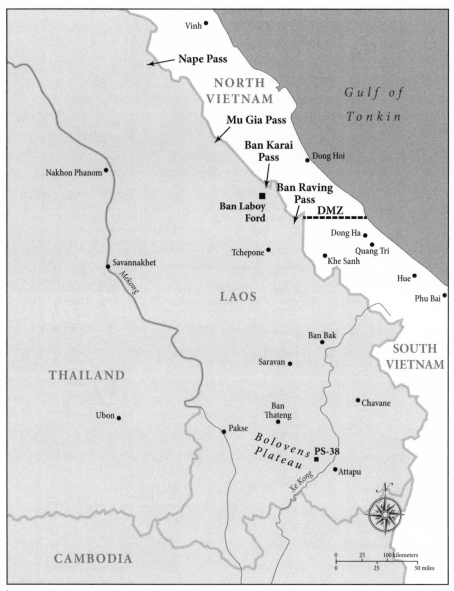

Southern Laos

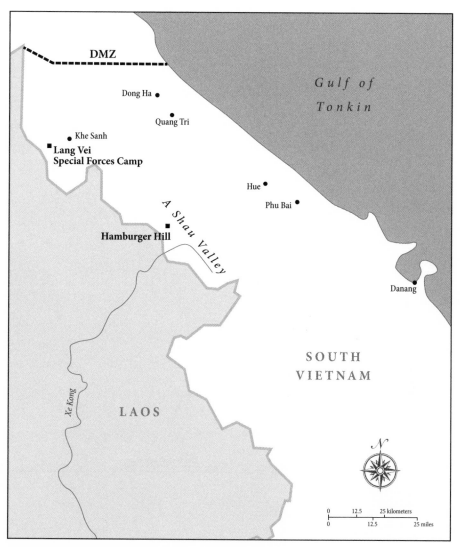

DMZ

Gulf of
Tonkin

Dong Ha

Quang Tri

Khe Sanh

■ Lang Vei
Special Forces Camp

Hue

Phu Bai

A Shau Valley

Hamburger Hill ■

Danang

SOUTH
VIETNAM

Xe Kong

LAOS

N

0   12.5   25 kilometers

0   12.5   25 miles

I Corps—The Northern Portion of South Vietnam

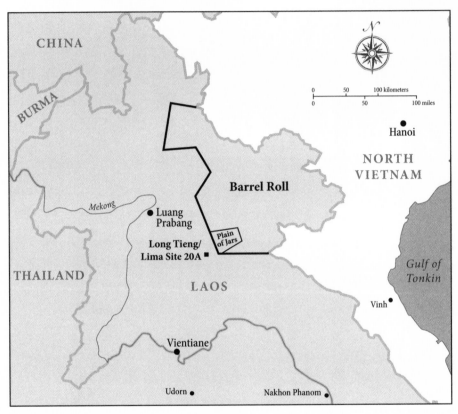

Northern Laos

III Corps—The Saigon Area

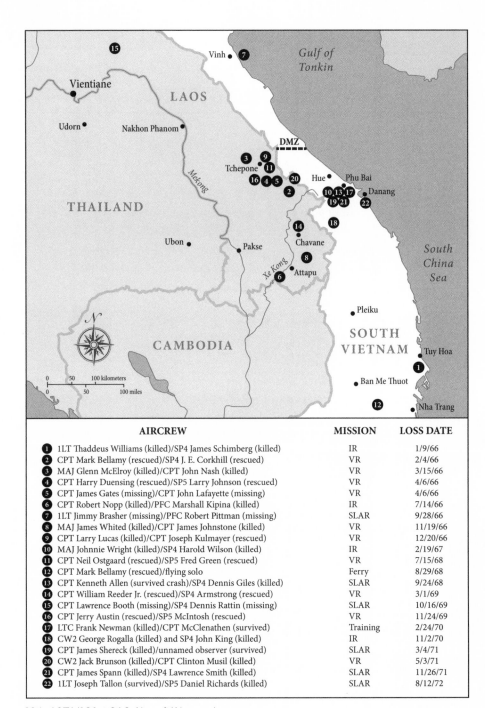

AIRCREW	MISSION	LOSS DATE
❶ 1LT Thaddeus Williams (killed)/SP4 James Schimberg (killed)	IR	1/9/66
❷ CPT Mark Bellamy (rescued)/SP4 J. E. Corkhill (rescued)	VR	2/4/66
❸ MAJ Glenn McElroy (killed)/CPT John Nash (killed)	VR	3/15/66
❹ CPT Harry Duensing (rescued)/SP5 Larry Johnson (rescued)	VR	4/6/66
❺ CPT James Gates (missing)/CPT John Lafayette (missing)	VR	4/6/66
❻ CPT Robert Nopp (killed)/PFC Marshall Kipina (killed)	IR	7/14/66
❼ 1LT Jimmy Brasher (missing)/PFC Robert Pittman (missing)	SLAR	9/28/66
❽ MAJ James Whited (killed)/CPT James Johnstone (killed)	VR	11/19/66
❾ CPT Larry Lucas (killed)/CPT Joseph Kulmayer (rescued)	VR	12/20/66
❿ MAJ Johnnie Wright (killed)/SP4 Harold Wilson (killed)	IR	2/19/67
⓫ CPT Neil Ostgaard (rescued)/SP5 Fred Green (rescued)	VR	7/15/68
⓬ CPT Mark Bellamy (rescued)/flying solo	Ferry	8/29/68
⓭ CPT Kenneth Allen (survived crash)/SP4 Dennis Giles (killed)	SLAR	9/24/68
⓮ CPT William Reeder Jr. (rescued)/SP4 Armstrong (rescued)	VR	3/1/69
⓯ CPT Lawrence Booth (missing)/SP4 Dennis Rattin (missing)	SLAR	10/16/69
⓰ CPT Jerry Austin (rescued)/SP5 McIntosh (rescued)	VR	11/24/69
⓱ LTC Frank Newman (killed)/CPT McClenathen (survived)	Training	2/24/70
⓲ CW2 George Rogalla (killed) and SP4 John King (killed)	IR	11/2/70
⓳ CPT James Shereck (killed)/unnamed observer (survived)	SLAR	3/4/71
⓴ CW2 Jack Brunson (killed)/CPT Clinton Musil (killed)	VR	5/3/71
㉑ CPT James Spann (killed)/SP4 Lawrence Smith (killed)	SLAR	11/26/71
㉒ 1LT Joseph Tallon (survived)/SP5 Daniel Richards (killed)	SLAR	8/12/72

20th ASTA/131st SAC Aircraft/Aircrew Losses

PREFACE

This is the last volume of what has become a Vietnam War trilogy. I never intended a trilogy, but here it is, three books written about a war that left an indelible mark on my soul and so molded my life thereafter.

Chronologically, this book is the beginning; but it comes as the last that I wrote. My first book, *Through the Valley*, recounts my trials and tribulations as a prisoner of war, a captive of the communist North Vietnamese for nearly a year. My second, *Extraordinary Valor*, chronicles one of the most significant, yet little known battles of the war, focusing on the bravery of the two heroes of the fight, US advisor Major John Duffy and South Vietnamese paratroop officer Major Le Van Me. In 2022, President Joe Biden presented a much belated Congressional Medal of Honor to John Duffy for his actions in that battle. I was proud to have flown a Cobra attack helicopter in support of those brave men, just over three weeks before I was shot down and captured.

And now I've written the story of my first tour of duty, my introduction to combat. This story is as much about a legendary unit and the courageous men who flew its perilous missions as it is a journey along my road to manhood as a twenty-two-year-old, newly minted aviator, facing war for the first time.

CHAPTER 1

Into the Cauldron

THE WAR RAGED. IT HAD BEEN RAGING FOR SOME TIME. I ARRIVED IN the country in the middle of the night, on Halloween 1968. I was young, a twenty-two-year-old newly promoted US Army captain, eager to find my manhood, to learn what I was made of. I was anxious over the explosive light displays I'd seen in the distance as our World Airways flight abruptly dropped into a steep spiraling approach for landing at Bien Hoa Airbase, just outside Saigon, the capital of South Vietnam.

As I walked toward the military bus there to pick us up, I noted, with some concern, the heavy-gauge wire mesh across the windows. Our escort told us it was to prevent anyone from throwing grenades through the windows as we drove down narrow streets on our way to Long Binh Army Post, a few miles northwest. *Welcome to the combat zone*, I thought. Little did I know how far this was from the reality of war I'd soon come to know.

I cooled my heels on the Long Binh base for a few days awaiting my assignment. Once I had orders in hand, I flew for hours in the belly of a C-130 cargo plane and disembarked in the late afternoon at Marble Mountain Airfield, near Danang, a city along the coast in the northern reaches of South Vietnam.

I checked into the aviation battalion headquarters there and was told my unit was sending a plane to fly me to our base near the town of Phu Bai, some distance further north. I stood on the ramp waiting, my duffle bag on the ground beside me. Raindrops began hitting my head and shoulders, one plop at a time. A single-engine airplane appeared in the traffic pattern, landed, and shut down only feet away. The plane was classic, not at all like the aircraft I'd been sent here to fly. It was a clunky-looking beast. Reminded me of Charles Lindberg's *Spirit of Saint Louis*. The Army called it a U-6 *Beaver*. A large radial engine powered its big propeller. It looked like a relic from before World War II.

The pilot got out. He wore a black flight suit, evidence of his membership in a special fraternity of aviators. I'd heard the unit I was going to, the 131st, flew special, highly classified missions—some of the most hazardous in Southeast Asia. Many of its aircraft had been shot down far behind enemy lines, only a few crew members ever recovered. General Westmoreland, the commander of all the forces in Vietnam, authorized the black flight suit for the aviators, the only Army unit in Vietnam given that honor.

The pilot greeted me. "Hi, I'm Barry Taylor. They call me 'Black Eagle.' That's my nickname. Throw your shit in the back and jump in the right seat. You're my only passenger. You'll be co-pilot."

The sun had set, the sky turning grey. Sheets of rain pelted the windscreen as we rolled down the runway for takeoff. We flew northward and stayed at a low altitude. We made our way across the mouth of a large bay, skirting a mountain on our left, its massive shoulder jutting down into the sea.

Barry noted, "The road from Danang to Phu Bai crosses that mountain. Goes over Hai Van Pass. Dangerous place. Lots of ambushes on our trucks. The railroad tracks were blown up a while ago. The train doesn't run anymore."

We continued, out over the ocean. The plane flew a couple thousand feet over the waves, bumping along through a now driving rain. As we turned toward land, I could barely make out a few scattered lights through the deepening darkness as the wipers swished across the windscreen. Barry was busy on the radio, setting up our approach for landing. Dead ahead, I saw it—the runway lights on the Phu Bai Airfield. And then we were down, a nice three-point landing.

After we parked the airplane and turned it over to the ground crew, Barry took me to my "hootch," a simple wooden structure raised a couple feet off the ground. I couldn't help but notice the heavily sandbagged bunker pressed just against the left side. The hootch was big enough to comfortably fit four standard Army-issue beds: narrow metal frames with thin mattresses and funky pillows. Mine was the first on the left. It was neatly made with clean sheets and an olive drab Army blanket. A wooden footlocker sat on the floor at the foot of the bed, and a tall metal cabinet stood against the wall. My new home for the next year.

Lots of guys had it far worse. I had a crummy bed inside a shabby hootch while so many others lived in holes dug in the dirt on small firebases scattered around the country. And my infantry brothers were out in the jungle, sleeping in the rain and mud, enduring the full wrath of Vietnam's heat and humidity and crawly creatures. As I looked around, counting my blessings, I noticed an air conditioner on the right hand wall, blowing a cool mist across the space. *This will do*, I thought.

"Drop your stuff and come with me. Major Alton, the CO, is waiting for you at the club."

I dutifully set my duffle bag on the bed and followed. We turned right out the door and headed down a wide dirt lane along the row of like hootches. As we walked, we were paralleling the runway, a couple of hundred yards to our left. Heavily sandbagged workspaces, shop vans, and hangars occupied that side of the road. At the end of the row of hootches was a nondescript, squat building on the left. It was made of plywood with a metal roof.

"That's our officers' club," Barry Taylor announced.

The building was painted a dull grey. Fifty-five-gallon barrels, stacked two-high and filled with sand, lined the outside, save an opening for the entry door in the front and two other exit doors, one on the far side and another onto a small concrete patio in the back. The sand-filled barrels were there to provide some protection from the frequent mortar and rocket attacks that pounded the base. Our enemy lurked close by.

I stepped through the door to see a couple dozen people standing in front of the bar. These were the pilots not out flying missions that night, along with the intel officers and civilian tech reps supporting the unit. Many of the aviators wore black flight suits, others standard jungle fatigues. They all smiled. I saw three familiar faces straight ahead, Jon and Joe Lowdermilk, identical twin brothers, and Billy Wood. We were flight school classmates. The three of us were among the six top graduates in our class picked to go directly into the qualification course to learn to fly the Grumman-built OV-1 Mohawk, the most sophisticated and expensive aircraft in the Army, the airplane I'd now come to Vietnam to fly. The Lowdermilks and I had carpooled together every day for the first half of flight school. We were close—good friends.

The group faced me in a crescent, my friends in the middle. They sported the biggest grins. Jon put out his hand. I began raising mine as I walked toward him. I'd only taken a few steps when everyone began to chant.

"He's on the Hawk, on the Hawk! New guy stepped on the Hawk." I heard the bell over the bar ring loudly. "He's buying the bar!"

I looked down. My feet stood squarely on top of a large black hawk inlaid into the club's tile floor, right in the center of the room. You'd only miss stepping on it if you knew it was there and understood the penalty imposed on all who dared tread upon the sacred image. (Or, as I would learn later, were thrown on it.)

"Welcome aboard, Wild Bill," Jon said, laughing. "You're paying for drinks. That's what it costs when you step on the Hawk."

"Wild Bill?" I inquired.

"Yes, Wild Bill. We remember your antics in flight school. So gave you that nickname. Everybody's got a nickname here. That one is quite appropriate for you."

"OK, Wild Bill it is."

"Yeah, and I'm Sour and Joe is Sweet. Since we're twins, they branded us with that right away. Joe's married, so he got Sweet. I'm not, so I'm Sour."

Billy Wood piped up. "And I'm Sack Rat. They think I sleep a lot."

I said, "I had no idea you'd been assigned to the 131st. When did you guys get here?"

Joe answered, "Only a few days ago. We weren't far ahead of you."

A tall bald major walked over, looking particularly sharp. I'm not sure if I was more impressed with his rank, height, or shiny head. Smiling, he offered his hand. Joe made the introduction. "Major Alton, this is our classmate, Bill Reeder. Bill, Major Alton, the CO."

"Hi. I'm Gary Alton. Spud 6. Welcome to the 131st." He gave me a good close look. "We've got a hell of a mission and a great bunch of guys. Happy to have you here with us." He added, "Report to my office in the morning to officially sign in and get your in-processing done."

As we shook hands, Joe added, "Major Alton's nickname is Mr. Clean."

The analogy was immediately clear. He had a strong resemblance to the Mr. Clean genie in the popular cleanser adds of the day. He would turn out to be the most outstanding commander I would ever have.

As Jon introduced me around, Joe asked, "What are you drinking? You're buying."

"I'll have a scotch and soda if they have it."

"How about Chivas Regal? It'll cost you all of twenty-five cents a shot. The cheaper stuff is a nickel less."

"Chivas it is, then."

The bartender, an off-duty sergeant named Jac Belet, opened beers and poured drinks. I put ten dollars on the bar. That would cover things for a while.

We drank the evening away. My classmates celebrated my arrival, and I chatted with strangers who would soon become my brothers. It got late. I got drunk, and I went to bed.

CHAPTER 2

First Missions

BEFORE I COULD FLY MISSIONS, I HAD TO RECEIVE A CHECKOUT FROM A 131st instructor pilot. Mine was with Captain Ed Paquette, the infrared platoon leader and one of the unit's most competent and conscientious pilots. Every Mohawk unit in Vietnam had three types of aircraft: A, B, and C models. The As sported a suite of cameras. They flew daytime visual reconnaissance and photo intelligence missions. Because of the high threat they faced, they were armed with dozens of rockets for self-defense. They operated in flights of two. The Bs mounted a side-looking airborne radar system, or SLAR, capable of detecting moving targets at distances of more than thirty miles. They stood apart from the other airplanes because of the long cylindrical radar mounted below the cockpit on the right side. Some called the appendage a "donkey dick." The C model Mohawks flew at low altitudes in the night to capture the heat signatures of enemy activity on their infrared equipment; dangerous, stressful missions. That was Ed Paquette's forte, infrared, or IR. He still flew some of the SLAR missions, but he was the company's IR guru.

We met at the aircraft. I was still in awe every time I looked at a Mohawk. It was unlike any other airplane. It was fast by Army standards, 180 knots at cruise (over 200 miles an hour), and 386 knots in a dive (444 miles per hour). The plane was acrobatic, capable of loops and rolls and any number of other sleights of aerial ballet. It was strong, able to sustain punishing G-forces* and keep on flying through battle damage that would bring other airplanes out of the sky. The Mohawk was built by Grumman Aircraft whose Long Island factory was popularly known as "The Grumman Iron Works" because of its long-standing reputation of building nearly indestructible military airplanes.

Some said it was not a pretty airplane. They likened it to a bug-eyed pregnant guppy. I found it beautiful. I'd seen my first Mohawk a year earlier while in flight school at Fort Stewart, Georgia, about forty miles southwest of Savannah. I'd just finished a training flight and landed a small single-engine airplane on the airfield when my instructor said, "Look!" and pointed to the sky.

I spied an airplane approaching at traffic pattern altitude. The pilot lined up with the runway for landing but did not descend. He stayed high at a thousand feet and kept his airspeed fast, much faster than we could ever fly our T-41 Cessna trainers. When the plane was straight overhead, it banked sharply left into a steep spiral turn, slowing and descending rapidly as the pilot reduced power and activated hydraulic pistons that opened panels on each side of the fuselage, the aircraft's aerodynamic speed brakes. Next came wing flaps and landing gear in time for the plane to finish 360 degrees of turn and squeak its tires onto the white painted numbers at the approach end of the runway. The propellers went into reverse pitch as the two turbine engines whined to full power, stopping the airplane in a few feet. I was impressed.

A studly young pilot got out, wearing the orange flight suit and white helmet of a test pilot. He answered questions of the flight students gathering around.

One student pilot bragged, "That's what I want to do. I want to be a Mohawk pilot."

A classmate snidely jabbed, "You'd better worry about graduating from flight school first, Bosco Breath."

---

* G-force is the force of gravity exerted on an object (human body included). One G is what we feel as we go about our normal routine on earth. Two Gs is twice that force. In other words, if we weigh 180 pounds, at two Gs it is as if we weigh 360 pounds. Most pilots lose consciousness at around 5 Gs. The Mohawk can handle 7 Gs.

The test pilot heard and proclaimed to all, "Only a few of the very best ever get to be Mohawk pilots." He turned and pointed at the three vertical fins at the back of the aircraft. "It takes quite a superb aviator to be able to handle three pieces of tail so close together." That was a wise-crack about the Mohawk I'd hear often over the years.

I asked the pilot if I could step forward and touch the side of that marvelous thing. He nodded. "Sure." I walked over and put my hand against its olive-drab metal skin. I fell in love.

A shop in Thailand still had my flight suit for dying and embroidery, so today I flew in jungle fatigues, sleeves rolled down. I'd completed the exterior preflight inspection of our airplane, one of the A-model gun-ships. Those had dual controls, which allowed each pilot to fly. We needed that for my checkout. As Ed approached, I put on my parachute harness and survival vest. I had a black leather gun belt already fastened around my waist with my Army-issued .38-caliber Smith & Wesson revolver holstered, à la cowboy style. With my flight helmet and gloves in hand, I was ready for my ride.

I took off and demonstrated my flying skills in the traffic pattern and at altitude. Ed then had me fly around the local area as he pointed out the prominent landmarks I'd need to know for the various departure and arrival patterns at the airfield. I also gained an appreciation for the lay of the land and how features on the map looked on the ground. My famil-iarity with our actual operating area would have to wait, though. I'd have to learn that terrain through the experience I'd gain flying unit missions.

Ed offered, "You know you will only see South Vietnam for takeoffs and landings, don't you?"

"I'd heard something like that."

"Yeah, our missions are all out of country, over the border into North Vietnam and Laos. We don't have a mission inside South Vietnam. Those are for the other four Mohawk companies. There is one in each corps tactical zone. The battlespace in South Vietnam is broken up into four sectors, four corps. There is one Mohawk company for each corps. And then there is us."

We flew a bit more before he continued, "We are the fifth company, the bastard company, the special unit. We're assigned directly to the highest headquarters in the land MACV, that's Miliary Assistance Command, Vietnam. Their intel section owns us, MACV J2. All our operations are classified at least SECRET, and our mission results are sent not only to headquarters here in the war zone but also to the Pentagon, State Department, and other national agencies. This is important stuff we're about."

He paused, before adding, "But there's been a cost for what we do. We've had a lot of airplanes shot down. Lost too many aircrews. You be careful!"

"I will."

I thought on that for a moment, on what these guys in the 131st had been through, on what I might face. That sparked a random question. "Where's the call sign 'Spud' come from?"

"Not sure, exactly. An iron spud is supposed to be some sort of heavy construction tool used on the railroad. That's our official call sign, 'Iron Spud.' We use just 'Spud' on the radio. It's a good call sign, brief, unique, and easy to understand. You won't find any unit prouder than us. We're all Spuds."

It was time to head back to Phu Bai. "Tune in TACAN Channel 69. That'll take us home." TACAN, or Tactical Air Navigation, was a system in wide use in Southeast Asia. The station at Phu Bai was on channel 69. I tuned it on the control head and followed the needle pointing back to our base.

"Two things to remember," Ed said. "Phu Bai is alright! And, the wind never blows there, it always sucks." (Two joking adages I'd hear often during my tour of duty.)

I could see the airfield in the distance. Suddenly the airplane lurched to the right. *Engine failure!* I retained control, put in a whole lot of left rudder and reached for the right engine prop lever to feather the number 2 (right-side) engine. As I did, I could see that the power lever for that engine was already pulled back. I looked at the smirk on Ed's face as he announced, "Simulated engine failure. Take us home."

As I cleaned up the aircraft and recited the emergency procedure checklist, Ed reiterated the importance of knowing the Mohawk emergency procedures, absolutely. "No mistakes, no hesitation. Know them by heart. Your life depends on it."

He continued, in earnest, "We had an accident a few weeks ago. B-model lost an engine on takeoff. You went through the emergency procedures perfectly. That pilot didn't. He failed to jettison his drop tanks.* They were full of fuel. Very heavy. Had he jettisoned them, the aircraft would have flown fine, and he could have made it around for a safe landing. With those heavy drop tanks still on his wings, he could not hold altitude. Just before impact, his right seat observer, Specialist Dennis Giles, ejected. The pilot stayed with the airplane. The sad irony is that the pilot survived the crash, riding the aircraft in, all the way to the ground. Giles ejected but did not have the speed or altitude necessary to separate from his ejection seat. He died with his face in the muddy water only a few hundred yards from the runway. Specialist Giles was a good young man. He'd just celebrated his twenty-first birthday days earlier. Everybody liked him. He died because his pilot screwed up."

Ed let that settle in. "That's why I pulled your engine to make a point. Know your emergency procedures. Your reactions must be instinctive, locked into your brain to do exactly the right things when situations present themselves, because here, in this unit, with the missions we fly, situations will present themselves, bad things will happen."

I completed the approach, landed, and taxied to our parking revetment. We got out and Ed shook my hand, looking up at me. Ed Paquette was short. His nickname was Tom Thumb. With his strong New England accent, he said, "Congratulations. You're good to go."

Phu Bai combat base was a large military complex. Through the middle ran a five-thousand-foot east-west airstrip. Engineers had constructed the runway of prefabricated aluminum sections and used perforated steel planking, known as PSP, for the taxiways and parking ramps. Daily drips

---

* Large cylinders holding up to 150 gallons (over one thousand pounds) of fuel, each. One hung under each wing.

of aircraft fuel, oil, and hydraulic fluid turned the PSP into a greased sheet in the rain, and oh it did rain in Phu Bai.

Our unit area was on the southern edge of the runway toward the eastern end. We had our own barber shop, mess hall, and of course, our small officers' club, the Spud Club, where we could drink, share stories, act stupid, and generally decompress after flying stressful combat missions. A short walk to the west of our area brought us to a nearby military post office, PX*, and aviation medical clinic.

Eighteen OV-1 Mohawks parked in U-shaped protective revetments; ten-foot-high wooden frames filled with sand. These shielded our aircraft from damage by enemy rockets and mortars. Of course, if one exploded right on top of an airplane, it would be toast. But as far as I know that never happened to one of our birds. The well-constructed revetments had only recently replaced sand-filled fifty-five-gallon drums stacked high on three sides of each airplane.

I'd arrived at the dawning of civilized life at Phu Bai: new revetments, wooden hootches instead of tents, and a covered shower area on a concrete slab. We even had electricity throughout our area. We endured a six-hole latrine though, an outhouse where you'd sit over one of six holes cut in a wooden board to defecate into fifty-five-gallon drums. Each morning, a Vietnamese laborer pulled the drums out, poured in a quantity of fuel, and torched each one. When the wind was right, the pungent smell of burning crap wafted across the company area.

We got a lot of use out of the fifty-five-gallon drums the Army used to ship all forms of lubricants and other materials to the war. That included the shitter barrels, rocket and mortar protective barriers, and our barbeque grill out back of the Spud Club.

Besides our 131st Surveillance Airplane Company, Phu Bai was home to other units. The 220th Reconnaissance Airplane Company was just to our west. They flew two-seat, single-engine O-1 Bird Dog light observation airplanes on their own risky missions in the northern reaches

---

* A PX, or post exchange, is equivalent to a department store on larger installations or a convenience store at smaller facilities. The Phu Bai PX was small, but stocked some top-shelf, high-demand items such as high-end cameras and stereo equipment. Soldiers could also order new cars at discount prices for delivery to a stateside dealership of their choice.

of South Vietnam and into the Demilitarized Zone, or DMZ, separating North and South Vietnam at the 17th parallel. There were US Army and Marine Corps helicopters of all shapes and sizes, airplanes rigged to listen to enemy communications, an infrequently used civilian air terminal, two Army hospitals, several field artillery units, an Army corps headquarters overseeing all military operations across the northern provinces of South Vietnam, and a launch site for special operations missions into Laos. Camp Eagle, home to the massive 101st Airborne Division, sat only five miles to the northwest. We lived in a busy place.

Our namesake, the adjacent village of Phu Bai, straddled the country's main north-south road, Highway 1. Local families struggled to survive through subsistence farming and running small stores, food stalls, and repair shops; the town's young men had gone to military service. Work on the combat base gave old men and women the welcome chance to supplement their families' income. Daily job-seekers stood in line at the base employment office near the entry gate. Those already hired showed their passes to be escorted to their job sites on base.

Only eight miles to the northwest was the ancient imperial capital of Hue, boasting a magnificent walled citadel and palaces, home to the long line of Nguyen Dynasty emperors who ruled Vietnam from 1802 to 1945, ruling under the thumb of French colonial administrators after 1883. Earlier in 1968, Hue had suffered the worst of the fighting during North Vietnam's Tet Offensive. The communists launched their attack on January 30th during an agreed Lunar New Year ceasefire. The North declared the fighting a spontaneous uprising of local Viet Cong* insurgents. In fact, regular North Vietnamese Army (NVA) units planned and supported most of the attacks and outright led several, including the battle for Hue.[1]

US and South Vietnamese forces eventually won the day, but not before weeks of brutal combat destroyed 80 percent of the city, severely damaged the historic citadel, and cost the lives of 605 allies killed in action and 3,164 American and South Vietnamese soldiers wounded. More than five thousand South Vietnamese civilians were killed in the

---

* Viet Cong translates to Vietnamese Communists. The term refers to the irregular guerrilla forces drawn from the local population inside South Vietnam, often led by cadre from North Vietnam.

battle or rounded up and summarily executed by communist forces and
buried in mass graves. The enemy took several American prisoners of war
in Hue, including the technicians operating the armed forces radio and
television station, military intelligence operatives, civilian contractors,
and a senior State Department official. The Tet battles touched Phu
Bai Combat Base, but never breached its perimeter. Nonetheless, the
danger was real, and the 131st evacuated all flyable aircraft to airbases
in Thailand during the upheaval. The carnage of Tet '68 weighed on the
Americans at Phu Bai as months passed and yet another Tet lurked not
so many weeks ahead.[2]

Despite the scars of war, the region remained majestically beautiful.
Lagoons and rice paddies stretched to the east of Phu Bai Airbase—a
broad carpet of wetland that swept below us as we approached Runway
27 for landings. Only a few farmsteads sat atop rice paddy dikes. An
occasional small fishing village pressed onto the sand along the coastline, and fishmen's boats pulled onto the beach, clear of the ebbing and
flowing tide. Directly south, mountains towered over five thousand feet,
rising still higher as they stretched northwestward, cloaked in foliage,
like a green blanket tucked into the deep black folds of the jungle below.

That's the world we lived in.

I flew my first tactical mission a day after my new-guy checkout with Ed
Paquette. I was assigned a morning side-looking airborne radar run up
the coast of North Vietnam into Route Packages I and II.* Operations
paired me with our most experienced SLAR operator, Specialist 5 Ed
McCarthy, nicknamed "Ichabod." He'd be in my right seat. McCarthy
got that nickname because of his tall, slender appearance. Our enlisted
right-seaters had all earned the military specialty of airborne system
operator. We referred to them all as TOs (technical observers). They
trained to operate all three Mohawk systems—side-looking airborne
radar (SLAR), infrared (IR), and the visual reconnaissance (VR) suite
of cameras. Each specialized in one specific system after arrival in the
131st; some able to manage two. Specialist McCarthy was the best SLAR

---

* The United States divided North Vietnam into seven Route Packages, or Route Pacs. The 131st
flew into RP I and select missions into RP II. See map 2 (page xiv).

TO in the unit. His expertise in operating and maintaining the SLAR equipment was unmatched. He could use the rolling in-flight imagery to precisely track the aircraft's position. If the system failed in flight, he was able to quickly fix it.

McCarthy was the TO of choice to accompany new pilots on their first flights to show them the ropes and keep their flight paths on track. Once I took off, all I had to do was check in with the combat air traffic controller, call sign "Waterboy," climb to an altitude of 5,500 feet, switch on the autopilot, and turn to whatever heading McCarthy directed.

We flew along the North Vietnamese coast to our assigned turn-around point abeam the city of Vinh, the largest city in the central part of North Vietnam and almost halfway to the communist capital, Hanoi. The United States placed critical importance on our North Vietnam SLAR missions. Only days before my arrival at Phu Bai, President Johnson declared a bombing halt in all North Vietnam. That was on October 31, 1968. He hoped to energize peace talks.[3] No one flew in that airspace after that. Only us, as far as I knew—alone, unarmed, and scared shitless, as we'd say.

My classmate, Joe Lowdermilk, flew that first mission along the coast of North Vietnam after the bombing halt. Gary Alton asked if he'd volunteer. He'd be the only one up there. There'd be no help if he got into trouble. Joe thought better of it but said "Yes." He felt he couldn't live with himself if he said "No" and someone lost their life in his place. He worried he might not come back and told his brother, Jon, what to say to their parents if he didn't. It was an unnerving flight but ended without incident.

More missions followed. We became the principal source of intelligence to track North Vietnamese convoy movements as they pushed men, supplies, and equipment southward toward the demilitarized zone and across key mountain passes into Laos, onto the Ho Chi Minh Trail network, destined for the war they waged in South Vietnam.

With our Side-Looking Airborne Radar, we could look well into North Vietnam, penetrate jungle foliage, and see vehicles moving more than three miles per hour. The imagery was captured on an eighteen-inch-wide band of film, automatically processed by the equipment inside the cockpit, and displayed to the right-seat technical observer in near real time, within two minutes, as the film rolled up over a small light table protruding from the observer's instrument panel. The split imagery showed terrain features on the left and moving targets over a subdued terrain background on the right. This enabled the TO to plot the exact location of movers, determine the number of vehicles, and calculate their approximate speed on subsequent passes. Importantly, it also allowed him to accurately track the aircraft's position.

Our surveillance proved the enemy was taking advantage of the bombing halt to surge supply convoys. The North Vietnamese did not accept the gesture as a sign of goodwill and lean more fully into peace talks. Our flights showed string upon string of moving vehicles. Where they'd previously driven only at night, using small, nearly invisible blackout lights, they now rolled defiantly with bright headlights burning—even making daylight runs with impunity.

"Turn right to one three zero," McCarthy commanded.

I turned the autopilot knob and set us on the new course, heading back down the coast. As the wings leveled, the ECM came alive. (That's electronic countermeasures, a system designed to give us warning of surface-to-air missile launches.) It consisted of a round four-inch scope with a rectangular box lying across the top of it.

A rattlesnake-sounding audio alerted me. At the same time, a dashed strobe appeared on the scope. One of the blocks on the rectangular box lit up. I sat up straight. McCarthy glued his eyes to the ECM.

"You know the drill?" he asked.

"I do."

I remembered back to my training flights in the Mohawk course at Fort Rucker. My instructor pilot, Major Max Davison, crammed so much into my head so that I might survive my combat tour in Vietnam. Max was tough. He was demanding, oft times demeaning. His intentions were always clear, though. Make me the best pilot I could be. Mold me into what I needed to be to live through a tour with the 131st, should I be assigned there. He pounded the procedures and flight skills into my mind and muscle memory. Drilled me over and over again. Max had served in the unit. He knew the risks. But he loved the Spuds. He spoke so reverently of the unit and its classified mission that there was no doubt that's where I wanted to go. I sought assignment to the 131st because of Max. And now I was there. I'd made it.

Yes, I remembered the drill. Max had described the ECM gear. The escalating series of warnings. First a dashed strobe with a rattling sound and a yellow warning light on the box. That yellow warning light indicated that you were being tracked by enemy radar. Next, a solid strobe with a continuous tone and an orange warning light on the box. That orange warning light meant the enemy locked their missile to the radar track, ready to fire. Finally, the bold solid strobe with a screaming tone and red warning lights on the box. They'd launched a SAM and it was coming at you.

If the ECM went through the sequence and showed a launch, the drill was to immediately push the stick down and dive in the direction of the strobe, go straight toward the missile that was coming for you, and gain as much speed as possible. Strain your eyes, looking ahead, searching for the telephone pole-sized object hurtling toward you to blow you to pieces—at night, hoping to see the propellant flame at its tail. The instant you saw the thing, roll left and pull back hard on the stick, making the highest-G turn you could bear. The theory was that the missile could not match that tight of a turn and would tumble harmlessly out of control and crash to the earth.

Our strobe stayed dashed, the warning lights didn't advance, the sound never went beyond a rattle. In a few minutes, all fell silent again. No missile launch. I relaxed and lit a cigarette. Specialist McCarthy picked up the Coke he'd brought along and took a sip. He breathed deeply and said, "You know we had a crew shot down up here a while back."

"No, I didn't. I heard several 131st crews have been lost, but nothing specifically about a Route Pac mission."

"It was about two years ago. Right off the city of Vinh. Lieutenant Jimmy Brasher and Bobby Pittman. They'd flown the same track as us, but a late-night mission. Waterboy saw several missiles fired in this area. Announced warnings on guard. Called Spud 09, Brasher and Pittman.

No reply. Never found the aircraft or the crew. A SAM missile got 'em. Right here."

He fell silent for a moment, remembering their fate. "We get lit up here a lot. Some crews encounter MIGs. No one else has gone down on a Route Pac mission since then, though. Now we stay mostly below the North Cape in Route Pac I. There's more SAMs as you get up into Route Pac II, closer to Vinh. We only come up here, anymore, when they really need that intel, when specifically tasked, like our mission today."

I finished my Marlboro and lit another. We flew down to the South Cape, turned back north, and repeated the track. No SAM warnings on our second lap. Nothing but the humming of the two big Lycoming turbine engines just beside our ears. Time droned on, the Martin-Baker ejection seat felt harder and harder on my butt. As I tuned the Armed Forces Vietnam station on one of the radios, McCarthy looked at me and smiled. "They say these Route Pac missions are hours and hours of boredom, interrupted by moments of stark terror."

After nearly four hours of flight time, I set up our approach for Phu Bai, TACAN Channel 69.

"Waterboy, this is Spud 20 headed home. Request frequency change to Phu Bai approach."

"Roger, Spud. Frequency change approved. Have a good one!"

I switched the radio and made the call, requesting a ground-controlled radar approach, a GCA, where a radar operator talks you down a glide path to landing. In bad weather, a good GCA operator can bring you to within a hundred feet of the ground. At that point, you will hopefully have broken below the clouds and be able to complete a landing.

I didn't need the help. The late morning weather was fine for a relaxed visual approach, but I wanted the practice. Max had drilled that into me. I could hear his voice in my head, *You can never have too much practice. Take every opportunity to hone your flying skills. Keep pushing yourself to be better.* I did. Max had affixed himself to my conscience. He spoke to me on every flight.

On landing, McCarthy and I walked through the operations office into the intelligence section just behind. Specialist McCarthy delivered the SLAR film, going over it with the analysts. I ran through a mission debrief for the intel chief and the company operations officer, Major Linus "Blanket" Fiely. I guess I impressed Major Fiely because later that day the company clerk handed me orders. I was the new assistant operations officer—something to keep me busy when not in the cockpit flying daily missions.

That night, like most, I spent in the Spud Club.

I'd done well on my first mission. I'd performed as expected in piloting the OV-1 Mohawk on a tactical mission. I'd dealt with the stress of mortal danger in combat, at least the potential of mortal danger. I'd taken another stride into the cauldron of war, a bigger step than when my commercial flight landed near Saigon. Way back then, less than a week ago, I'd been naively anxious over distant artillery strikes that presented no danger at all. Today I'd been tracked by a North Vietnamese surface-to-air-missile crew who could have launched a SAM, but didn't. I could have been blown out of the sky, but wasn't. *Now I've been to war.* But there was a lot more to war as I would come to know it; a much closer look was still to come.

"Jac, I'll have a Chivas and soda, if you will."

"Right, 'Wild Bill.' Comin' up."

Jac poured a double. I quickly downed it and asked for another.

A voice behind me spoke. "So, how'd it go?"

I turned around. Ed Paquette stood there, beaming.

"Good, I think. We flew the coast and the TO got some good imagery. ECM showed us being tracked by a SAM radar for a while, then nothing for the rest of the mission. Mostly just quiet. My butt aches from sitting on that hard ejection seat for over four hours."

"Well, you popped your cherry. You're now officially a 131st combat aviator. You're a Spud." He added, "You know what that means?"

I raised my eyebrows.

"You buy the bar."

That cost me another ten dollars.

I shared stories with my Mohawk classmates and new pilot friends in the unit. They listened to my first mission account. I learned lessons from the tales they told. I noticed a small cluster of black-suited guys standing separate from the rest of us, at the right side of the bar. They appeared a little older, more seasoned, with battle-hardened furrows on their brows and a slightly crazed look in their eyes.

Joe Lowdermilk caught me staring. "That's the VR Platoon," he said. "They fly the daytime visual reconnaissance missions and take aerial photographs over the Ho Chi Minh Trail, across the border in Laos. They fly in pairs of old A-models, all armed with rockets for self-defense. That's the most dangerous mission the 131st has. A lot of aircraft have been shot down. They've lost many crews over the past couple of years. Some killed outright, others missing in action. Very few ever recovered."

Max Davison had told me about the unit's VR missions, about the dangers involved, and about the pride and camaraderie this tight-knit group shared together. That's what I wanted, to fly armed OV-1 Mohawks, to become a Spud VR pilot. I looked at those studs at the bar and could only hope that one day I might be good enough to be one of them.

After my mission the next day, I reported to Major Fiely to begin my duties as assistant operations officer. I'd help in the scheduling of air crews, pairing observers with pilots and putting them against the A-, B-, and C- model aircraft that the maintenance officer gave me as mission ready for the VR, SLAR, and IR missions that came to us from MACV, through 7th Air Force in Saigon. We kept a white tag for each crew member in operations, with their rank, name, and nickname. There was a big board on the wall with a section for each of the three types of missions. The left-hand column listed the available aircraft, by model type. We'd hang the name tags next to the aircraft at least twelve hours before a mission was to be flown.

I also helped oversee the work of the flight records clerk, documenting the hours and missions each pilot flew. I collected lessons learned for submission through higher headquarters and ensured the close coordination between ops and intel on both target priorities and keeping up with the enemy anti-aircraft threat throughout our area of operations. Important work.

Major Alton popped in that afternoon to let me know that a new pilot was inbound from Marble Mountain. He was First Lieutenant Cook Waldran. I jumped up and grinned.

"Cook Waldran? Cook M. Waldran?! Mitch Waldran! He's another classmate from flight school and Mohawk qualification. That makes five of us here in the 131st. Amazing."

Mitch was a good friend. We'd known each other for over a year and had become especially close during Mohawk training. We were both artillery officers and counted our blessings as being the only two artillerymen selected to go directly from flight school into the Mohawk program. Mitch was six years older than me, but we were about the same rank. I'd been recently promoted to captain, and I knew Mitch was due to pin on within days. We were both married, I for less than three years, Mitch for almost ten, and we each had young sons.

I asked Major Fiely's permission and rushed down to the hootches to pass the good news to the Lowdermilks and the Sack Rat, Billy Wood. We gathered in the Spud Club, ready to greet our buddy. Others joined us to help sustain the unit welcoming ritual.

We formed a similar gauntlet to what had greeted me; Sweet and Sour, Sack Rat, and me, all at the apex. Mitch walked in, moved gleefully toward us, and stepped on the Hawk. Another raucous evening at the club ensued. It was good to have the five of us together.

More coastal SLAR missions followed. After a few days, I flew my first night mission. I liked flying at night. I also came to enjoy the flights into bad weather. The solidly built Mohawk handled the conditions fine. I took pride in my ability to fly precisely in the thickest muck, relying solely on instruments. It was a special feeling to break through the clouds, not far above the ground, catch a glimpse of the runway or even just the runway lights, and make small control adjustments to put the airplane down safely on a soaking wet airstrip. I guess I just enjoyed the challenge and doing something quite well. Thanks again, Max. We spent the last day of the Mohawk qualification course shooting multiple instrument approaches to the Montgomery, Alabama, airport in absolute abysmal conditions. I gained total confidence that day.

I got into a daily pattern of work and flying coastal SLAR missions. Restrictions soon came down limiting us to Route Pac I. We'd only proceed farther up the coast on specially authorized missions that required intelligence on communist movements further north. Route Pac I still presented a potentially dangerous SAM missile threat, along with the worry of long ranging MIG fighters.

I'd wake up in the morning at 7:00, shower, and grab breakfast, or at least a foul cup of well-doctored coffee. At some point, I'd hike over to the six-hole latrine for my daily constitutional. I'd get as much work done as I could, before launching on whatever mission I'd scheduled for myself that day. Almost always, I'd choke down dinner and head to the club. If I wasn't flying later that night, it was Chivas and soda. If I was flying, it was coke until I'd landed and then Chivas and soda if I got back to the club before it closed. And always, camaraderie with my brother aviators as war stories and shenanigans became more brag worthy as the evening, and flow of beverage, progressed.

If I flew very late at night, I'd sleep in a bit in the morning. That meant hitting the showers after the hootch maids had arrived. As part of the civilian employment plan, the Army hired local Vietnamese as laborers on the combat base, or to perform essential services such as cooking in the mess hall, cutting hair, and doing maid work in our hootches. One maid was authorized for each hootch. Ours was a kind, hard-working young woman whose husband was off fighting in the South Vietnamese Army. She made our four beds, swept, washed our dirty laundry, and polished our boots. If you didn't get to the showers early, the hootch maids were in there washing clothes. I was totally embarrassed the first morning I slept in after a late-night mission and walked down to the showers to stand naked, washing, with half a dozen young women squatting, scrubbing clothes around me. I never really got over it, but adjusted somewhat over time.

I never thought much of our mess hall, the company's dining room. I recall cold scrambled eggs in the morning, nothing particularly memorable for lunch, and most often dry tough roast beef (we called it Phu Bai steak) and mashed potatoes with a barely warm squishy canned vegetable for dinner. The coffee demanded heaps of sugar and milk. The milk was reconstituted from some foul powder substance. Some thought I was overly critical, but one day things were so bad that I bolted from the dinner table after spotting dead flies in my potatoes. I swore I'd never eat there again. That lasted until hunger set in the next day.

Our Beaver pilot had the standing order to see what he could procure on his supply flights to Danang to supplement our meager food rations. Most of the time he struck out. On rare occasions, he'd snatch some steaks from the Navy in Danang. On rarer instances, he was able to scrounge a tub of ice cream that had just come off a supply ship there. It was soft by the time it got to Phu Bai, but always celebrated when it arrived. One day, a package came for our Grumman tech rep, Joe DiMaggio. His mom had sent all the ingredients for pizza. Joe spent an afternoon crafting several fine Neapolitan pies and cooked them for our dinner that evening. Those were all happy meals. The rest of the time, the mess hall food sucked.

I ate one particularly lousy breakfast on a malaria pill day. We took the mandatory pill once a week, sometimes with unsettling side effects. This day was one I'd not soon forget. I forced down my made-from-powder eggs then took my pill with a glass of fake milk. I grabbed a cup of coffee and headed for my desk at ops. I worked for a few hours then headed to the airplane. After a thorough preflight, we launched on what had become yet another routine SLAR mission up the coast. We were well past the South Cape on our first run when it hit me. I turned to my TO and said, "I've got a problem."

"Waterboy, this is Spud 21. I am aborting the mission. I need immediate vectors to the nearest friendly airfield."

"Are you declaring an emergency? Is Phu Bai close enough? Do you need crash rescue waiting?"

"Negative Waterboy, Phu Bai is too far. Is there anything closer? Yes, emergency. No, no crash rescue needed."

"Spud, turn to one three five degrees. I'll turn you into Dong Ha Airfield as soon as you clear the DMZ. Descend at your discretion. I'll get you tower clearance for an immediate landing. No crash rescue, right?"

"Roger, no crash rescue."

The minutes passed. Finally, "Spud 21, turn to heading 270, contact the tower on one, eighteen, eight; one, one, eight point eight. They have cleared you to land."

"Roger, thanks for the help. So long Waterboy."

A quick turn of the radio knobs, then, "Dong Ha tower, this is Spud 21. Understand cleared to land. Request taxi to the closest latrine to the runway."

"Roger, Spud. You are cleared. Land short, as close to the numbers as possible. You'll see a latrine just to your left side. Go ahead and shut down on the runway. We have no other traffic."

I landed inches short of the numbers, pulled the power levers into full reverse and stopped on a dime. I put the engines in idle, set the brake, and shut 'er down. I safed my seat, released my lap belt and ejection seat connections, opened my canopy, and jumped out, being careful to stay in front of the still spinning propeller. I tore off my survival vest and para-chute harness as I ran. I bolted into the stinky hut, unzipped and pulled down my spiffy new black flight suit, and plopped on the foul seat—just in time.

I'd had about enough of these long, boring, uncomfortable coastal SLAR flights. I craved more excitement, something more challenging.

CHAPTER 3

Deeper in Darkness

MY GOAL REMAINED VISUAL RECON. I WANTED TO JOIN THE VR PLA-
toon and fly armed A-models. It was more dangerous. The missions
demanded better piloting skills. But that's where I needed to be. Max
Davison instilled that dream in my heart. I saw it as the ultimate rung
for a Mohawk pilot. But I knew it was too soon. I wasn't quite ready yet.
I needed more experience.

There was some good news, though. Major Fiely, the operations officer and my boss, put me on the schedule for our western SLAR missions,
radar surveillance flights over the Ho Chi Minh Trail. They'd be across
the border, in Laos—a bit more challenging than the dull coastal orbits
I'd been flying these past days.

Over Laos, I'd no longer worry so much about rare incidents of SAM
missiles or enemy MIG fighters. Instead, I would face more frequent
and intimidating threats, flying directly over deadly enemy anti-aircraft
weapons, ranging from .51-caliber to high-reaching 23, 37, and 57 mm
guns. Recent reports included big 85 mm and 100 mm guns as well.
Scores of our aircraft had taken devastating hits over the years. The
enemy downed many of our Mohawks, killed far too many of our crews.
At least on SLAR missions, I'd be at a reasonably high altitude, improv-
ing my odds. That would no longer be the case if I ever got my wish and
made it to VR.

Once again, Major Fiely crewed me with Specialist Ed "Ichabod"
McCarthy. He'd be my right seat TO for this mission across the border
into Laos. He'd kept me straight on my first flight into North Vietnam.

Now he'd do the same for this, my initial foray into Laos. It was all bad-guy territory out there, at least in the eastern part of the country where we flew surveillance of the Ho Chi Minh Trail. Thousands of enemy soldiers occupied that turf. Many more thousands of North Vietnamese combat troops moved along the route. It would not be a good place to go down.

The Ho Chi Minh Trail was much more than a trail. It was a heavily defended network of roads and footpaths crossing the Annamite Mountains from North Vietnam into Laos and stretching southward over a wide geographic swath before reaching into South Vietnam along multiple infiltration routes. The network delivered logistical and manpower support to North Vietnamese Army and Viet Cong forces fighting there.

Another trail, leading from the south coast of neighboring Cambodia, the Sihanouk Trail, formed a complimentary communist network running from the port of Sihanoukville, northward, to infiltration routes feeding the war in the central and southern parts of South Vietnam. The two trail networks kept the enemy supplied with men, equipment, and ammunition.[1]

Others flew over Laos as well. They had for some time. Indeed, the US Army was a minority player. The Air Force flew the most, then the Navy and Marines. The Air Force codenamed this part of the Laotian panhandle *Steel Tiger*. They called their interdiction bombing campaign *Commando Hunt*. More than six hundred daily air strikes pounded the zone with a variety of aircraft.[2] Ground radar sites and high-flying airborne command and control centers (ABCCC) orchestrated the campaign, while forward air controllers, or FACs, flying small O-1, O-2, and OV-10 spotter planes, directed fighter aircraft onto the ground targets. Call sign "Covey" FACs flew from South Vietnam, "Nail" FACs from bases in Thailand. A few "Misty" fast FACs flew F-100 Super Saber jets for the same purpose. Several clandestine "Raven" FACs directed airstrikes from vulnerable, slow-moving O-1 Bird Dogs based out of towns in dodgy locales in western regions of Laos.*

---

*See table 3.1 for a partial list of the different aircraft and their call signs.

Table 3.1. Crowded Laotian Skies—a Sampling

TYPE	CALL SIGN	SERVICE	MISSION
PROPELLER AIRPLANES			
A-1 Skyraider	Sandy	US Air Force	CAS/SAR
A-6 Intruder	*Various*	US Navy	Precision all-weather air strikes
A-26 Invader	Nimrod	US Air Force	Strike
C-45/Beech 18 Expeditor	*Various*	Air America/ CASI	CIA/Royal Lao support
C-46/CW-20 Commando	*Various*	Air America/ CASI	CIA/Royal Lao support
C-47/DC-3 Skytrain	*Various*	Air America/ CASI	CIA/Royal Lao support
C-119 Flying Boxcar	Shadow/Stinger	US Air Force	Gunship
C-123 Provider	Ranch Hand/ Candlestick	US Air Force	Agent Orange spraying/Flare-ship
C-130 Hercules AC-130	Ally Cat	US Air Force	Night ABCCC— Northern Laos
	Cricket	US Air Force	Day ABCCC— Northern Laos
	Hillsboro	US Air Force	Day ABCCC— Southern Laos
	King	US Air Force	Rescue Coordination Center
	Blind Bat	US Air Force	Flare-ship
	Spectre	US Air Force	Gunship
O-1 Bird Dog	Catkiller	US Army	FAC—Northern South Vietnam
	Raven	US Air Force	FAC support to CIA and Royal Lao
O-2 Skymaster	Covey/Nail	US Air Force	FAC from Danang, SVN/NKP, TH
OV-1 Mohawk	Spud	US Army	Reconnaissance/ Strike capable

(continued)

Table 3.1. *Continued*

TYPE	CALL SIGN	SERVICE	MISSION
PROPELLER AIRPLANES (*continued*)			
OV-10 Bronco	Covey/Nail	US Air Force	FAC from Danang, SVN/NKP, TH
PC-6 Porter	*Various*	Air America/CASI	CIA/Royal Lao Support
T-28 Nomad	*Various*	USAF/R-LAF/RTAF/AA	CIA/Royal Lao Support/Air Strike
JET AIRPLANES			
A-7 Corsair	*Various*	USAF/USN	Air Strike
B-52 Stratofortress	*Various*	US Air Force	Heavy bombing
B-57 Canberra	*Various*	US Air Force	Recon/Bombing
F-4 Phantom	*Various*	USAF/USN/USMC	Fighter/Air Strike
F-100 Sabre	Misty	US Air Force	Fast FAC
F-105 Thunderchief	*Various*	US Air Force	Fighter/Air Strike
HELICOPTERS			
AH-1 Cobra	*Various*	US Army	Special Ops Insertion
H-34 Choctaw	Kingbee	SVN Air Force	Special Ops Insertion
HH-3/53 Stallion	Jolly Green	US Air Force	SAR
UH-1 Iroquois / Huey	*Various*	Air America/CASI	CIA/Royal Lao support
	Knife/Pony Express	US Air Force	Special Operations
	Various	US Army	Special Operations Insertion

LEGEND: AA, AIR AMERICA; ABCCC, AIRBORNE COMMAND AND CONTROL CENTER; CAS, CLOSE AIR SUPPORT; CASI, CONTINENTAL AIR SERVICES INC; FAC, FORWARD AIR CONTROLLER; RLAF, ROYAL LAOTIAN AIR FORCE; RTAF, ROYAL THAI AIR FORCE; SAR, SEARCH AND RESCUE; USAF, US AIR FORCE; USMC, US MARINE CORPS; USN, US NAVY.

Search and rescue teams, consisting of large HH-3 "Jolly Green" helicopters and vintage A-1 "Skyraider" close air support propeller planes stood ready to launch as needed to attempt rescues of downed aircrews. Four-engine AC-130 "Spectre" gunships trolled the skies at night, using advanced targeting and weapons systems to wreak devastation from above. A slew of other aircraft pummeled the ground with rockets and bombs. These ranged from antiquated A-26 propeller airplanes to B-57, A-4, A-6, and F-4 jet bomber/attack/fighter aircraft. And then the B-52s. They operated in flights of three, far above the fray, pulverizing broad sections of jungle with hundreds of bombs released simultaneously in "Arclight" strikes. C-123 "Ranch Hand" twin-engine propeller cargo planes sprayed Agent Orange. Secret entities such as Air America and Continental Air Services flew there as well. The clandestine operations of MACV-SOG* also touched into Steel Tiger with low-flying support from lift and attack helicopters.**

No, we were not alone in Laos. Not at all. At times, it was a crowded sky. We were only a small fragment of the daily flow of aircraft. But we provided some of the most critical information, fed directly to national authorities in Washington, DC, as well as the staffs, planners, and decision makers conducting the war in Vietnam.

We flew slower than some and faster than others. That put our SLAR radar missions in a risk environment on par with what most others faced. Only our infrared and visual reconnaissance flights dared go so low as to amp up their risk significantly as they collected information critical to the US war effort.

My TO, "Ichabod" McCarthy, met me in operations. We received the pre-mission brief together, making special note of the most menacing anti-aircraft locations. We stopped by the E&E shack next door to pick up our flight gear and escape & evasion kit. We found the appropriate hook on the wall with our name above it and donned our assigned

---

* MACV-SOG, Military Assistance Command, Vietnam—Studies and Observations Group. Special operations reconnaissance teams of three American Special Forces with eight to ten indigenous tribal fighters, supported by US Army or Air Force transport and attack helicopters. The teams conducted road watch, raid, and prisoner snatch missions along the Ho Chi Minh Trail.
** See the glossary for details on all these aircraft.

harness and survival vest and grabbed our helmets.* We stepped over to the counter, took an emergency radio, and signed for and holstered a .38 pistol before heading to the aircraft. On arrival, we found other members of the SLAR Platoon standing by. They'd completed the radar system runup and confirmed all was operational and ready to go. The crew chief stood near them.

He greeted us and confirmed he'd checked the aircraft. He highlighted a couple of non-mission-critical discrepancies noted in the logbook and then watched as I walked around and climbed over the plane, conducting a thorough pilot's pre-flight inspection. The night was dark. No moon. The overcast sky opened in pouring rain just as I finished my task.

"Let's go," I yelled above the downpour.

I put one foot on the step and pulled myself into the cockpit. McCarthy got onto the long cigar shaped SLAR boom on the other side of the airplane and stepped in. We both hooked up to our ejection seats. He handed me a small towel to wipe my rain-soaked face.

"Thanks. Much appreciated."

"Yes sir, nice night for flying," he said.

I toggled the battery switch to "on" in time to see the wry sarcastic smile on his face in the dim red glow of the cockpit lights.

"You bet," I answered.

I started the engines and went through the flight control checks as the crew chief signaled. Water streamed off the hood of his rain jacket. Once he removed the wheel chocks and waved us out, I pushed the power levers forward a bit and rolled from the revetment. We taxied to a pullout near the end of the runway where we were to perform our pre-takeoff runup. One task required me to advance the power levers to check the propeller governors. When I did, the airplane slipped on the wet taxiway surface and began to slide. I pulled the power levers back to idle. That

---

* Ejection seat harness. Just like any parachute harness, but with attachment fittings for clipping to the ejection seat parachute risers. Each harness was fitted individually and donned carefully to ensure your private parts rode not too uncomfortably during the long hours of flight and would not be squashed painfully by the crotch straps should you have to eject from the airplane in an emergency. Survival vest. A netted fabric vest with pockets for our emergency radio and an assortment of survival gear. See glossary for list of contents.

part of the runup would have to wait until we got onto the runway. That different surface had better traction. I'd ask the tower for a short delay in our takeoff position to complete the check. It would only take a moment.

We got clearance onto the runway, completed the runup checks, and armed our ejection seats. I reported, "Ready to go."

"Spud 9, you are cleared for takeoff."

"This is Spud 9. Roger."

I pushed the two power levers all the way forward to take off. We quickly gained speed. I pulled back on the stick. I raised the landing gear as soon as the wheels came off the ground. Next the flaps. We were flying! I never got over the joy of bringing a plane into the air—even on such a dark miserable rainy night as this. *Ah, the magic of it all*, I thought.

I kept my focus, though. The engine failure emergency procedures were foremost in my mind. Takeoff and initial climb-out were the most critical times to lose an engine in a Mohawk. Only the immediate completion of emergency actions would keep the aircraft from living up to its ominous nickname, "Widow Maker." McCarthy sat with his hand on the wing-stores jettison handle ready to release the heavy fuel tanks under the wings at my command. We gained a safe altitude and reduced power to continue climbing through the clouds, up to our mission altitude of 7,500 feet.

We headed west "in the soup." I relied totally on the instruments in the cockpit. Outside was blackness. Heavy rain pounded the windscreen. I'd become quite comfortable with instrument flying. I learned the basics quickly in flight school. In the Mohawk qualification course, Max Davison ensured I got plenty of practice there. After arriving at Phu Bai, I racked up instrument experience flying the less challenging SLAR missions off the North Vietnam coast. Now I was quite comfortable in all types of weather as I headed into Laos for the first time. Here, I'd get a closer look at the face of war. I'd also have to deal with several other aircraft plying the same skies.

I checked in with the ABCCC controllers. They flew high overhead, maintaining a semblance of control over the sometimes-intense activity below. Their airplanes, lumbering four engine turbo-prop C-130 cargo planes, had been considerably modified and specially crewed for the airborne command-and-control role.

"Moonbeam, this is Spud 9. Crossing the fence, approaching checkpoint Delta Forty-Five. Understand we'll be working area Golf tonight. We'll be at seventy-five hundred feet, that's seven thousand five hundred feet." That altitude would keep us between two to six thousand feet above the terrain and clear of mountaintops en route. It also put us within desired SLAR system parameters.

"Roger, Spud. You are cleared into Golf. Right now, we've got fighters working with a FAC, Covey 375. Talk to him on 126.2. There is also a Spectre gunship working farther north. He may come down your way later."

"Roger, Moonbeam. Thanks."

The weather improved after we got a way into Laos. The clouds became scattered, but we still couldn't see much. It was so very dark and there was not a light to be seen across any of the broad stretch of earth below us. In the distance, I could make out explosions from the strike Covey was putting in. That ended, and all was dark again, save the red rotating beacon of the FAC aircraft.

Like flying off the coast of North Vietnam, these were tedious missions tracing long oval tracks in the sky. Ichabod busily monitored his SLAR equipment as the imagery rolled up across the illuminated screen. For night missions, the TO fit an accordion-style hood over the apparatus to eliminate any glare in the cockpit. It had an opening just large enough for him to hold against his eyes and peer through at the imagery. The film, with radar images of terrain and blips of any moving vehicles, took about three minutes to process and roll up onto the lighted screen.

That allowed McCarthy to accurately track our position on his map and determine the map coordinates of the trucks we spotted moving along some segment of the Ho Chi Minh Trail network. I passed those along to Covey 375 who worked a flight of F-4s from the 497th Fighter Squadron "Night Owls" out of Ubon, Thailand. We watched them blow things to kingdom come as we orbited for a few minutes before continuing our mission track. We also provided inflight reports of particularly significant targets to Moonbeam, hoping they might use them to entice Spectre into the area later that evening.

It only seemed right that on this first mission into Laos I should be baptized by fire. A stream of tracers reached toward us through the dark sky. I snatched the controls off autopilot and slammed the stick hard right.

Pushing the intercom switch, I said, "Taking fire, ten o'clock." I surprised myself with the calmness in my voice. This was the first time I'd ever been shot at in my life.

McCarthy simply replied, "Roger," as he pulled his face away from the screen and glanced at the fireworks show. Obviously not his first time.

The enemy fire continued like beads of water streaming from a hose, bending in arcs as the gunners moved the tracers, searching for us.

"Hard for them to see us at night, sir." McCarthy sounded only somewhat anxious. "They just shoot at the noise and see if they hit anything." He paused, then added, "There are some radar-controlled guns out here, but we got nothing on our ECM*, and he wasn't that close. Not radar controlled, or at least he wasn't using it."

I took a deep breath, double-checked that the position lights on our wingtips and tail were off, so the enemy would not see them. Yep, only the red rotating beacon atop the Mohawk was on, so other aircraft could see us. Hopefully, it was not visible from the ground. I resumed the desired heading for our mission, McCarthy looking for more movement on the SLAR.

After four hours of flight time, we landed back at Phu Bai. The crew chief welcomed us home and began his maintenance tasks after I completed my post-flight inspection. I always respected our crew chiefs. They worked hard to maintain their assigned airplane, toiling all day and long into many nights to be sure their plane would be ready for missions. They pulled their share of duty as well, manning our portion of the Phu Bai base perimeter whenever their name came up on the guard roster.

SLAR technicians serviced the system and took the mission imagery to the intel shop for analysis. McCarthy and I walked to the E&E shed,

---

* ECM. Radar-detecting electronic countermeasure equipment, as discussed in chapter 2.

dropped our gear, and went next door for our mission debrief. Once that was done, I headed straight to the Spud Club. It was a welcome sanctuary after missions.

Somebody asked, "How'd it go out west? You get shot at tonight?"

I answered, "Yeah, not that close though."

"Well, you know what that means, don't you? The first time you take fire?"

Here we go again. Drinks on me, of course. I smiled with a dumb look on my face. Jac, our bartender, rang the bell. The guys all cheered. Another ten dollars on the bar. Jac poured my Chivas and soda. We had a grand time.

For the next several weeks, I flew that same mission or the later one, the after-midnight run. I relished the change of pace Steel Tiger gave me. Yes, it involved more risk. But we were doing something tangible. In addition to providing badly needed information about the Ho Chi Minh Trail to analysts and planners at high levels, we were also contributing directly to the cause in that moment. On a good night, we acquired targets that were immediately struck by attack aircraft or deadly Spectre gunships. Every night, as I journeyed further into war, I caught glimpses into my being, discovering a bit more of myself.

I sat at a table in the Spud Club one afternoon, chatting with friends and drinking a Coke before heading to the mess hall for dinner. I was scheduled to fly that night, so Coke was it. In my sober state, I looked around, taking it all in, the stone-fronted bar with the requisite row of stools, the shelves of alcohol behind, a refrigerator full of beer, tables and chairs around the room leaving a big open space in the center for the black tile image of our sacred hawk on the floor. I peered into the large side room to the left, where we'd hold meetings and watch Armed Forces Television Network programming on a small TV or enjoy a movie projected onto the back wall. Artwork, plaques, and posters hung on all the other walls of the club.

The two most prominent pieces were a framed picture of an armed Mohawk firing five-inch Zuni rockets at night and a large board with several small brass plates affixed to it. The picture was a striking image of the awesome firepower that could hang under the wings of our birds. I noted, however, that we never carried those large Zunis. Instead, our A-models loaded many smaller 2.75-inch rockets, a little over half that size. We could strike more targets that way.

I'd already had a close look at the engraved brass plates on the board. Each was about two by four inches. There was one for every pilot who had served in the unit. Those going home ceremoniously nailed their plate to the board the night before they left. The commander nailed a plate for anyone who was killed or missing in action. Each plate had the pilot's name and dates of service in the 131st. For those lost, the plate listed the date of loss and KIA or MIA.

Jon Lowdermilk came into the club, his eyes wide open. He went to the bar without as much as a hello and ordered a Chivas and water. He drank it down, spilling some down the front of his black flight suit. He wiped his mouth, looked around at me and said, "Fuck me."

"What happened to you?" I asked.

"MIGs, two MIGs came after me." He turned back to Jac, tending the bar. "Another."

I stepped up beside him as he grasped his second drink.

"Just landed. Christ!" He looked right at me. "We were in Route Pack II, all the way up the coast, headed north, almost to Vinh. It was another boring SLAR mission and my thoughts were elsewhere. All of a sudden, my TO starts pounding my shoulder and pointing. I don't think he could speak. I looked ahead and saw two fast-moving aircraft approaching from dead ahead. At the same time, I hear Crown* on guard announcing bandits north of Vinh, heading south.

"I grabbed the stick and did a quick 180. There was a big fluffy cloud a bit below. I dove into it and kept barreling south as fast as that Mohawk would go. I knew I couldn't outrun them. I just hoped for a miracle.

"I got a brief strobe on my ECM gear, then it stopped. Crown came back up on guard and said the MIGs had turned north. It was over.

---

* Crown. "Red Crown" was the call sign of the Combat Information Center (CIC) aboard a US Navy ship off the coast of North Vietnam. CIC personnel continuously monitored radar screens watching for enemy MIG activity that might threaten American ships or aircraft, issuing warnings as threats arose.

"We got to the South Cape, turned around and made a second run up the coast. My TO was not happy about continuing the mission. I think he about shit his pants. I know I was ready for a drink when we landed." *So that boring SLAR mission off the coast of North Vietnam had its moments.* I gave Jon a knowing look, a nod, and a reassuring smile. "Sorry I can't have a drink with you. I'm flying tonight."

That mission went without major incident. So did the next few. I found that enemy gunners sprayed rounds into the air anytime they heard us in the night sky. Normally, they didn't come close. A quick turn or two got us out of any immediate danger. Combat pilots called it "jinking." We made a point of not flying directly over areas we knew harbored concentrations of the big radar-controlled stuff, places like Tchepone and the major passes over North Vietnam's mountainous border. Normally a few "jinks" moved us safely away from the sting of anti-aircraft tracers and exploding shells.

A few nights later, I was out on still another Steel Tiger mission when the radio crackled.

"Spud, this is Moonbeam. Wondering if you could look in the vicinity of the intersection of Routes 23 and 9. Sycamore has indications of activity there that they'd like to confirm."

"Roger, Moonbeam. Can do."

My TO that night was a young man I'd never forget, Specialist 5 Steve Easley. He was eager, always game for whatever any mission held. At eighteen, he was one of the youngest soldiers in the 131st. Still, he knew the SLAR system at a level few could match. He was able to get the most out of its operation, both in finding moving targets and his ability to relate the system's ground imagery to the map and, in fact, be my navigator. He had become expert in analyzing bright spots on his film and assessing the legitimacy of the target as a moving vehicle or a false indication.

In less than a minute, Spec 5 Easley came on the intercom. "Sir, heading 310 will take us on a good track to get coverage. We should be there in about ten minutes."

I turned to the new heading and keyed the mic. "Moonbeam, this is Spud 19. We should have something for you in another ten minutes or so."

Easley asked, "Why's Sycamore think there's something there? And who are they?"

I knew the answer. "I'm sure Igloo White is detecting something. Have you heard of it?"

"No."

"OK. Igloo White is a highly classified program run out of Nakhon Phanom, Thailand, by an outfit called Task Force Alpha. It's part of McNamara's Wall." They drop sensors along the Trail then scatter mine-fields to stop trucks and people. The sensors detect and the mines kill. The data is transmitted in real time to orbiting aircraft and relayed to Task Force Alpha for analysis. Their radio call sign is 'Sycamore.' They pass targets to strike aircraft through their radar control site, 'Invert,' or through ABCC. Good in theory, but usually doesn't work too well."

We got to the area and ran one track, imaging the intersection from the southeast, and another in the opposite direction from the northwest. Our radar scanned a broad swath to our side on each pass. We'd covered the area from two sides. Nothing.

"Moonbeam, this is Spud 19, negative movers around the intersection of Routes 9 and 23. The only movement we see is known rapids on the river nearby. Sorry to disappoint. Heading back south."

"Roger, Spud. Be advised we've got Spectre 07 working Area Golf. You can talk to him on uniform 275.8."

Specialist Easley kept his eyes on the SLAR imagery, every so often noting the locations of a moving vehicle or two. I routinely relayed reports to Moonbeam. Then my TO's tone picked up. "I've got movers along Route 92, a bunch, maybe a dozen. Stand by for the grid."

---

* Robert S. McNamara, US secretary of defense, 1961–1968. One of the first systems analysts, he had a penchant for details and efficiency, reducing operational decisions to statistical analysis. His self-assurance oft times manifested as arrogance. McNamara's Wall or Line, was his vision for sealing South Vietnam from Northern infiltration with physical barriers and strong defensive points along the Demilitarized Zone (DMZ), extending westward across the Laotian panhandle as an impene-trable electronic fence (Igloo White) bolstered by minefields and air strikes.

Easley worked diligently for a moment, then announced, "Grid X-ray Charlie 850 620. If you'll give me a tight 180, I should be able to give you direction of movement."

As I turned, I called Spectre 07 with the location and description, possibly a dozen vehicles. He was interested.

Spectre was an awesome AC-130 gunship. The Air Force modified several four-engine turboprop C-130 cargo airplanes into flying battleships. Each sported an array of 7.62 mm miniguns and 20 mm Vulcan Gatling guns, both firing six thousand rounds a minute. He also had 40 mm Bofors cannons with a rate of fire of 140 rounds per minute. Both the Vulcans and Bofors fired devastating exploding shells. Spectre utilized a state-of-the-art infrared target acquisition system to find and lock his weapons onto any target giving off heat, such as a vehicle or human body. His system was limited to his immediate vicinity, though. We, on the other hand, could pick up movers over a much wider area, up to thirty miles away. This let us pass lucrative target locations to Spectre for him to move to and engage. It was a good partnership.

On our second pass, Easley was able to determine the direction of movement: south. I passed that to Spectre. The enemy unleashed sporadic anti-aircraft fire at us. We moved away and waited.

"Spud, this is Spectre 07. We've flown into your target area and picked up several trucks on our system. We'll engage momentarily. Are you clear?"

"Roger, Spud is clear to the east."

Weapons fire streamed down from the sky. I thought I could make out the grey hulk of Spectre's fuselage against the black of the night. Anti-aircraft fire answered, reaching up at him. Looked like 37 mm. Some close, bursting in yellowish-white blasts just behind his wing. But Spectre held his orbit and continued shooting. His rounds hit with precision. A series of small explosions erupted on the ground. A line of smoldering fires remained.

As I looked on, I thought, *If you don't pay attention to what's really going on, it's kind of beautiful.*

"Thank you, Spud. We can confirm ten trucks destroyed. Good work. We always appreciate the help."

We completed the rest of the mission without incident or any more enemy fire. We flew home to Phu Bai. It was late. When we contacted approach control all was quiet. In his boredom, the controller asked, "Hey Spud, are you a turtle?"

I keyed the intercom, asking Easley, "You have any idea what that's about?"

He responded, "Sure, sir. Tell him 'You bet your sweet ass I am.'"

I paused. Easley said, "Go ahead." I did. The air traffic controller laughed and said, "Welcome home Spud. What kind of approach would you like this evening?" It was a lovely clear night, so I asked for a handoff to the tower for an unaided visual approach. Easley smiled from the right seat. "Well sir, welcome to the Ancient and Honorable Order of Turtles.* Now you are one."

As had become my norm, I headed to the Spud Club right after our mission debrief. I stepped into the club to find everyone gathered around singing bawdy and irreverent songs. Leading them on was a pilot who'd been in the unit a while longer than me, Buick Bingham. He wore his black party flight suit and was playing a guitar.

We all had party suits, as we called them. A nice black blended material, custom made for us by a tailor in Ubon, Thailand. Every suit had a white hawk with the word *SPUD* embroidered high on the right breast. On the left breast, the tailor stitched white aviator wings above the words *US Army* with the pilot's name just below. Each person's suit sported an assortment of patches representing their identity in the unit. Most everyone had the standard Mohawk patch, signifying qualification in the aircraft. Others might include patches indicating countries flown, platoon affiliation (SLAR, IR, or VR), or some statement of pride such as "Yankee Air Pirate" or "Over 200 Missions" in Southeast Asia. Many suits became full patchworks of stuff over the entire front and both sleeves. We'd wear them frequently in the club for special occasions, or just because. Tonight seemed to be, just because.

---

* Ancient and Honorable Order of Turtles. Originated as a casual drinking club among pilots during World War II and continued through subsequent conflicts, even spreading to fraternal organizations and college campuses. I'd just never heard of it.

Everyone was well into a good drunk by the time I arrived off my mission, Buick more than most. I found my way to the bar, weaving through what had become a small crowd. Ah the harmonies, off-key voices blending into the larger chorus; the inebriated slurred cacophony sounding somehow delightful at the end of my long day. Lyrics ranged from absurd sexual limericks to tunes irreverently mocking the death of pilots. Many of the latter focused on local, Southeast Asian hotspots such as "dirty, deadly, Tchepone" or catastrophic flying mistakes as in "He got below glide slope on the Phu Bai GCA." The guys had accumulated dozens of these songs, and Buick led them through the whole playlist that night.[3]

I got my usual Chivas and soda, turned, and found myself facing Major Kennedy. He was having as good a time as anyone. Major Joe Kennedy had been in the Mohawk class ahead of mine. He'd arrived in the unit a few weeks before the Lowdermilks. Our paths had crossed only briefly during training before he graduated and moved on. Now in the 131st, with the rank of major he was one of the handful of field-grade officers in the unit, and like the four other majors, he was on his second tour of duty in Vietnam. He had my respect.

I'd never spoken to him much before. That evening, we got to talking over several drinks. He liked to drink and raise hell, but he always retained a steady look in his eye, one of contemplation and focus, always thinking, always in control, always ready for what this war might throw at him.

Joe Kennedy had a reputation as an outstanding Mohawk pilot. He'd begun gunnery training on his way to flying visual recon missions. He shared that he'd flown Caribou airplanes on his first tour, twin-engine cargo planes that the Air Force wrangled away from the Army. Our brothers in blue complained the Army was stepping into their mission set by hauling its own cargo on the battlefield. The dispute resulted in the Army relinquishing the Caribou to the Air Force in 1967. In exchange, the Army got free rein moving forward with its helicopter ambitions. One good outcome of losing the Caribou was that Major Joe Kennedy became a Mohawk pilot. Though he was an OV-1 novice, he readily applied his Caribou experience to the new aircraft, already showing superb aviation skill in the airplane.

As we listened to the singing, I had a question. "How did Buick get that nickname?"

"It's a good story. You should ask him."

"I will."

I had a strong urge to pee and used Buick as my excuse to step away. I started toward the side door when Major Kennedy added, "Looks like I'm your new boss. Major Alton is moving Linus to company headquarters to be his executive officer. That opens ops. I'm the new operations officer. I'll see you at work tomorrow."

I looked back, composed an expression of sincere interest, and said, "That's great, sir," before dashing to the door. Only a few steps outside the club, I stopped at the edge of a steep gully where we all went to piss into Pfeiffer's Gulch. The gully got its name from Captain John Pfeiffer, an infamous VR pilot in days of yore. In fact, Pfeiffer had been in the unit the same time as my instructor, Max Davison.

John saw horrendous things during his tour of duty with the 131st. The unit originally came to Vietnam as the 20th ASTA Detachment (Aerial Surveillance and Target Acquisition) in the opening days of 1966. They brought six Mohawks. Within three months, five of those six aircrafts had been shot down. Replacement birds arrived after each loss. On June 1, 1966, the Army enlarged the unit dramatically. The 20th ASTA became the 131st Surveillance Airplane Company. The number of aircraft increased to eighteen. By year's end, enemy gunners downed four more Mohawks. Nine aircraft lost in one year with thirteen pilots and observers killed or missing in action (remains never recovered). Only five crew members rescued.

John had been on some of the hairiest missions the unit would know during his tour of duty. He flew wingman to a Mohawk he watched "take fire and smash into the ground like a dog being snapped when it comes to the end of a leash."[4] It was no wonder he, like many other Spuds, took to heavy drinking.

John Pfeiffer was already special when he got to the unit in 1966. He arrived as an aerial gunnery expert. Even before he started flight school, he had been part of the earliest efforts to exploit the armed potential of the Mohawk. The Army sent him to the Navy base at Patuxent River, Maryland, to join Major Cliff Johnson in drawing from the Navy's experience and techniques to learn how to best mount armament systems on the airplane. Together, they developed the first Mohawk aerial gunnery program run out of the Naval Air Station in Jacksonville, Florida. Add to that his nickname, "Tree," that he earned for returning from a 131st mission with branch pieces stuck to both wings, and you have the makings of a true legend.

As the story of Pfeiffer's Gulch went, one night at the club, John was particularly soused. He was taken with the urge to pee off the edge of the yet-to-be-named gully. He stumbled out the side door but never returned. After a time, his mates wondered where John was. With some concern, they launched a search. No one could find John. Panic rose as their concern grew. Finally, two wobbly drunk pilots discovered him, unconscious at the bottom of the gully, his flight suit still unzipped. John said that while he stood, unsteadily, at the edge of the chasm pissing, the nearby explosion of an incoming enemy rocket threw him off balance. He rolled all the way to the bottom. After his cries for help went unanswered, he passed out and laid fast asleep until he was found. Thus, the name, Pfeiffer's Gulch, remained with that gully until American forces departed Phu Bai, long after my tour of duty—and John Pfeiffer became a legend.

When I came back into the club, I positioned myself closer to Buick's seat at the center of festivities, waiting for him to take a break. He stopped playing, set his guitar down, and took a long chug of his beer. He relieved himself in the gulch, came back to his chair, sat down and said, "I'm done. Bring me another beer, barkeep!" Jac kindly obliged with service to the table for our happy minstrel.

I started, "That was great, Buick."

"Thanks."

"You play a mean guitar. And what a voice. I love your jokes, too."

"Thanks."

"Say, how'd you get that nickname, Buick, anyway?"

His eyes brightened. He looked right at me, smiled, and began a story.

"Shortly after I got here, I was trying to join in, to truly become a Spud. Didn't want to be outdone at the bar, so I was really throwing them down one night. I did OK for most of the evening. But once I felt the room starting to spin, I figured it was time for this good Mormon boy from Utah to head for bed. I made it out the door and stumbled a few steps before falling face down on the muddy road. I got up on my hands and knees, crawled a few more steps, and began to retch. What I didn't realize was that some of the guys had followed me out of the club, wanting to ensure I made it back to my hootch. They stood there while I puked my guts out."

He bent over and made audible imitations of a puking sound. After a few iterations of the "huu eck" noise, I could detect something like "Buu eck."

He looked back up, smiled, and proclaimed, "And that's how I got my nickname, 'Buick.'"

Bingham was proud of that nickname, and no one ever called him John again. He had become, forevermore, Buick, our Spud minstrel and jester.

CHAPTER 4

A Dream Come True

IT HAD BEEN A BUSY MORNING IN OPERATIONS. I GLANCED UP FROM MY work to see Major Hank Brummett, the VR platoon leader, standing in front of my desk. I stood up. "Yes, sir."

He looked at me for a moment and said, "I've had my eye on you, Wild Bill. Let's start your gun checkout. Not every pilot is cut out for this. You are and you're ready."

My heart raced. My expression laid bare my excitement. I tried to regain my composure before blurting out, "Now?"

"No, not now. We'll fly tomorrow. We'll start with some basic skills and go from there. For today, I want you to read up on the armament system. Here's some stuff to go over."

He handed me a small stack of relevant gunnery materials.

"I talked to Major Kennedy and Major Alton. They're good with this. Let's meet here at 0800 and go do some shooting."

"Yes, sir!"

Of the five OV-1 companies in Vietnam, only one flew armed Mohawks, the 131st Spuds.* That's because of the high-risk missions we flew. All our VR work was daylight, out-of-country, across the border into Laos, well

---

* Other units, including the 23rd Special Warfare Aviation Detachment and the 73rd Surveillance Airplane Company, had flown armed aircraft earlier in the war. Directives ordered them to remove their weapons after the Joint Air Force/Army McConnell-Johnson Agreement in 1966. After that, only the 131st retained armed Mohawks for our special high-risk daytime visual reconnaissance missions.

WE DARED TO FLY

behind enemy lines. We flew there in extremely high-threat anti-aircraft environments. We needed armament for self-defense. We conducted our reconnaissance/photo missions in flights of two aircraft. That way, one could provide supporting fire for the other. The MACV leadership acknowledged that need and approved our continued use of armed aircraft despite Air Force objections. They also recognized our special mission status by authorizing our wear of black flight suits as our duty uniform, the only US Army unit allowed to do so.[1]

It had been my dream to come here and become a visual recon gun pilot. Our airplanes had been armed with both rockets and a .50-caliber machine gun mounted on the under-wing pylons. The .50s were great weapons, but repair parts were hard to come by. In time, they'd become impossible to maintain and had to be removed. Now we only had rockets, but those were terrific. Depending on the type of the rocket pods installed, we could carry anywhere from twenty-four to sixty rockets per airplane.

Major Brummett was a gunship guru. He had been in the Mohawk program since the early days. Five years earlier, back in 1964, he'd flown in the 11th Air Assault Division at Fort Benning, Georgia. That's where the Mohawk first joined the Army. The airplane came into service as part of a large-scale test the Army ran there for two years. The tests involved training exercises with ground forces, helicopters, and airplanes. The Army's new OV-1 Mohawk played a significant role in the Division tests. The air assault exercises utilized the aircraft in both reconnaissance and attack roles. The division boasted a Mohawk battalion of three companies for a total of thirty aircraft. Brummett's company, C Company, used the call sign "Spud."[2]

The 11th Air Assault Division experience produced the concepts the Army later embraced in bringing air mobile operations to the battlefield. The whole idea of helicopter warfare that came to the fore in Vietnam had its birth in the exercises run at Fort Benning, Georgia.[3]

Hank Brummett arrived at Fort Benning in 1964, right after finishing flight school and the Mohawk qualification course. He helped develop the tactics and gunnery techniques that would later be used by Mohawk units in Vietnam. The 131st was his second combat tour. His first was flying Mohawks in the 1st Cavalry Division. I was in awe of this aviation warrior.

The next day, we spent a good deal of time talking about the Mohawk as a gunship. Major Brummett tested my knowledge of every aspect of the aircraft as we walked around our assigned A-model. As we looked over the rocket pods, he told me every detail about the pods and 2.75-inch folding fin aerial rockets they carried. Once in the cockpit, he went over the switches on the armament panel and the firing controls on the pilot's stick. He emphasized safety every step of the way. We flew out to our gunnery range, a small, deserted valley in the mountains several miles south of Phu Bai. Once there, another safety briefing was followed by a hands-on tutorial on setting the switches. Then Major Brummett made a couple of demonstration runs using a splintered bridge across a ravine as our target.

"OK, now it's your turn. First a dry run. Leave the armament switch safe."

Our initial runs used something close to a standard airport traffic pattern, just compressed into a much tighter box. Major Brummett had me do two dry runs, then told me to go hot. I turned on the master armament switch and focused my senses in anticipation.

"That's good. Just keep your thumb away from the firing button until you have the target in your gun site. The other day, one of your buddies launched a rocket off to who-knows-where before we were even in a dive toward the target. Last I saw the rocket, it was arching over that ridge. I don't think it hurt anyone, at least no friendlies, or we'd have heard about it."

The target bridge passed by my wingtip. I turned the plane left and then left again to line the nose up with the bridge. Then I pushed the stick forward until the target entered the site. When it hit the center, I pushed the firing button. Two rockets left the tubes with a swish, accelerating ahead of the airplane, missing the bridge by a wide margin.

"The rockets will seek the relative wind. Get the nose steady on the target before firing, not moving up or down, left or right."

He took the stick. "I've got the controls. Let me show you one more."

"Roger."

He talked me through everything he did, explained the final maneuver in detail as he rolled steeply onto the wing, letting the nose fall naturally toward the earth, then leveling the wings at a point with the nose pointing right at the bridge. He held that for just a moment before firing a pair of rockets. They hit right on target. He pulled the stick back hard. I felt my cheeks sag under the increased force of gravity, my whole body heavy like a bag of sand, my vision darkening at the edges.

"That's a 4-G pullout. That's what I want to see." He emphasized the point. "Target fixation will kill you as quick as enemy fire. Pilots fly right into the ground, focused on hitting a target. You've got to pull up in plenty of time. Pull at 4 Gs. Get away from the ground and back to altitude quick."

Controls back to me. I tried to duplicate his pattern exactly. The final roll-in felt a little stiff, but it worked. I was much closer that time. I pulled up hard. There was an accelerometer in the cockpit to record G forces. On my pullout, it touched 4.

"Good, Wild Bill. Let's take a break from this and go have some fun with the airplane. Fly east and climb to seven thousand feet."

On the way, he asked, "Have you ever done much acrobatics with the airplane?"

During my first ride in a Mohawk, Max Davison had spent a good part of the flight demonstrating several acrobatic maneuvers. He started with a roll, where he pushed the stick hard to the side, rotating the wings around the long axis of the airplane. A loop followed as he dove to gain airspeed, then pulled the nose up and over the top, careening down the back side, in the pattern of a giant vertical donut. After a couple of other impressive gyrations, he said, "So there you go. The airplane is fully acrobatic. Just no sustained inverted flight. The engine oil system is not designed for that."

I don't know if Max's demonstration was more to show me what the airplane could do, or let me witness Major Davison's superb skill, or to see if I'd get sick. Probably all three. But I survived and quite enjoyed the thrill of it all. Days later, he let me have a go and I was able to perform the maneuvers successfully if not completely to his satisfaction. That was the end of acrobatics during the Mohawk qualification course.

Major Max Davison was quite an aviator, and it was my good fortune, if oft times painful experience, to have him as my instructor. Max had been a US Marine Corps fighter pilot. He was so good he'd been invited to join the Navy's precision flight demonstration team, the Blue Angels. At the time he was stationed in Japan and had fallen in love with a local girl and wanted to get married. His command refused to support him and sent him back to the States. His response? He resigned from the Marine Corps, went back to Japan, got married, and brought his bride, Sam, back home.

He enlisted in the Army. One day, while standing formation, an officer stopped, looked at him, and asked accusingly, "What are you doing wearing Navy pilot wings?"

"I was a Marine fighter pilot, sir," Max answered.

That encounter led to a US Army commission and the award of Army flight wings.

I keyed the mic and answered Major Brummett's question about acrobatics. "Yes, sir. But only a couple of iterations in the Mohawk course."

At altitude, Hank Brummett took the controls and demonstrated a few maneuvers to refresh my recollections. He turned the controls back over to me. "Go ahead, do whatever you want. Have some fun."

I started slowly with a couple of rolls and one big loop. The A-model Mohawk was a bit underpowered compared to the B- and C-models, and it had shorter wings than the Bs. It could still do all the maneuvers. You just had to build a bit of airspeed before starting each one and then execute it with a bit of finesse. Once I got the feel, I did fine. As I progressed, I turned that bird upside down and inside out. I had a ball, loving every minute of it.

When we returned to the gunnery practice area the next day, I brought the Mohawk's left wing alongside our target bridge, flew just a bit past, and then did a steep smooth arching turn, letting the airplane's nose fall through the horizon, pointing toward the ground. I rolled the wings level with the gun site lined up on the target. Holding steady for a moment, I fired two rockets. They hit right on target. I pulled up and repeated my performance, making shallow, medium, and steep (sixty-degree dive angle) runs, until all our rockets were gone. We flew home to Phu Bai.

On the third day of gunnery training, as we flew out to the practice area, we spent time discussing some of the challenges I might face on the visual recon missions I'd have in Laos, the losses we'd experienced, and lessons learned. We talked through the anti-aircraft threat at the low levels I'd have to fly and the techniques that would help maximize my chances of survival. He warned me to use extreme caution when flying near the most heavily defended sites, the enemy communications and logistic center at Tchepone and the major mountain passes out of North Vietnam.

"If you get hit and the aircraft won't fly anymore, get out. Eject. Don't hesitate. That'll get you killed."

I remembered more of Max Davison's counsel. "We had a bird get hit, slammed out of control. The co-pilot, Joe Kulmayer, ejected immediately and was rescued. The pilot, Larry Lucas, never got out and was killed in the crash. Kulmayer remembered seeing Larry's hand reaching up for the canopy release handle. He was trying to jettison the canopy before ejecting. Don't do that. The top of the seat will break right though the canopy plexiglass. Don't waste time with it. If you have to go, pull the ejection handle and get out. Don't fuck around with the canopy."

We fired more rockets, then shifted focus to the aircraft camera systems, a principal task on VR missions. Unlike the rolling imagery, automatically developed in the cockpit on SLAR flights, we used KA-30 and KA-60 aerial cameras with standard photographic film for our VR photo missions. The cameras were not accessible from the cockpit. On landing at Phu Bai, ground crews retrieved the film for processing and analysis.

We practiced some camera runs, with me setting the approach to the photo target and Major Brummett operating the camera on my command. On missions, that would be the duty of the technical observer. Brummett gave me pointers on how to ensure a good photo run for vertical shots, directly below the airplane, and oblique shots, angled to the side. He also offered suggestions on using the forward-looking panoramic camera. I flew several runs that set him up for a bunch of photos. The imagery interpretation shop developed the film when we landed and

Major Brummett used the images for a helpful post-mission critique to refine my process.

As we wrapped up late in the afternoon, Brummett said, "I run this as a five-day gunnery checkout. This is only the end of Day 3. But you're done. Ready to go. The rest you'll pick up on missions. You've got a pass for your VR-gunnery checkout. I'm putting you on the flight schedule starting day after tomorrow."

For my first few VR missions, Major Brummett paired me with one of the experienced VR pilots in my right seat. I learned the ropes of the missions into Steel Tiger in the daylight, of navigating without a SLAR TO continuously tracking our position from his near-real-time imagery. My aerial observer and I had only paper maps and our eyes. I became familiar with the terrain and learned the key landmarks. I soon memorized the checkpoints that served as common ground references between aircrews flying over Laos. It was a whole new world out there in the daylight. I could see. But the enemy could also see me.

I honed my formation flying skills. I'd done a little in the qualification course, but none since. Now I was flying daily two-ship missions, a lead aircraft and a wingman. The most experienced pilot flew lead. I'd be flying wing for a while. As such, I needed to get damned good at formation flying. We did everything in synchrony, from getting into the cockpit, to engine start, and taxi. We took off with only a short separation and formed into a tight flight as soon as we were airborne. We flew a looser formation en route to the mission area. Coming home, we formed up nice and tight several miles out on final approach. We kept that tight formation and held a thousand feet above the ground until we came over the runway numbers. Lead called our break on the radio. Together, in rapid sequence, we'd bank hard left, pop speed boards,* and lower the landing gear, all the while descending in a steep left spiral, rolling wings level just in time for our wheels to squeak onto the runway. On lead's command, we pulled the power levers back to reverse thrust and taxied off the runway together once we slowed. My thoughts raced back to the

---

* Speed boards, or speed brakes, were drag-increasing panels located on both sides of the fuselage halfway between the wing and the tail. They were hydraulically activated using a thumb-switch on the power levers in the cockpit to rapidly reduce the aircraft's speed.

lone airplane I'd seen make that same dramatic 360-degree overhead approach while I was in flight school—when I'd first set my eyes on an OV-1 Mohawk, fell in love, and began to dream. Now that dream had come true.

The missions were dangerous. I got shot at almost every day. The first time I came home with bullet holes in my aircraft, I felt I'd passed another milestone. Strange, I know, but a feeling I had, nonetheless. I'd been shot at. The sting of death came close enough to hit my airplane, only feet away from me. The threat was real. It was personal. Still, I was ready to go out again the next day. Injury and death occurred, sure, but always to the other guy. I got shot at. Yes. But it was other guys who got wounded and killed. Not me. That sense of invulnerability bolsters some young men in war. I guess it needs to, for them to do what they must do, over and over again. I found I was one of them. I never hesitated. I was never bothered. Good thing for me, now facing the perils of these VR missions that had taken so many Spud lives. Of course, nightly doses of alcohol at the Spud Club helped, as well.

A typical VR mission involved a good deal of eyeballing the land, looking for enemy activity along the roads, footpaths, and rivers that made up the Ho Chi Minh Trail. Much of that activity happened under thick jungle canopy. That meant we needed to get low and slow to be able to see much of anything.

Our missions came from MACV J2, the intelligence section of the highest headquarters in the land. They passed along their areas of interest for our reconnaissance. They also requested photographs of specific locations. Our flights were then integrated into the overall air tasking order, the plan for all air operations over Laos, published daily by 7th Air Force, the air boss in Saigon. MACV used the photos to assess the level of activity along portions of the trail, as well as the amount of damage recent bomb strikes caused to narrow road sections, fords, truck parks, and logistic hubs. The intelligence analysts also determined how quickly and effectively the North Vietnamese made repairs.

On our low passes for photos and visual reconnaissance, one bird stayed at altitude, ready to pounce with suppressive rocket fire if the enemy shot at the low bird on his run. It was important for the high bird to keep his buddy in sight and maintain the best relative position to allow him to immediately engage any enemy threat. The low Mohawk was exposed and vulnerable in what often became dicey situations.

I loved VR missions, the excitement, the joy of flying airplanes to their limits, the satisfaction of being a highly skilled practitioner plying his trade with his consciousness centered on piloting skills or focused into the narrow, concentrated world that was the view through the gun site on rocket runs. I felt I was born to be a Spud VR pilot with the intensity it brought to living. My life was today. I had few cares for tomorrow or thoughts of yesterday. Today was my moment and now was my story. I was alive in this instant. And that was what this war, horrible as it was, was like for me.

My sense of invulnerability was tested from time to time. That struck home on one of my early VR missions. I flew as wingman to Captain Frank Griswold. Frank had only recently arrived in the unit but was a senior captain and a second tour OV-1 aviator with gunship experience. He was a Mohawk pilot extraordinaire. He had flown armed Mohawks on his first Vietnam tour with the 73rd Surveillance Airplane Company down south, in Vung Tau. He was also one of the instructor pilots in our Mohawk qualification course. Frank Griswold brought the skills and experience needed to step right in as one of the VR flight platoon stalwarts.

On this mission, Frank completed the initial photo runs while I stayed high, covering him. He climbed up and had me go low to finish the final two. On my last run, I took heavy fire. As was our practice, after I climbed back to altitude, Frank flew close to check me over for damage. I held a steady heading and altitude as I watched him carefully slide his Mohawk cylindrically around me, giving my airplane a good look.

"You took some hits there, Wild Bill. I see holes under your right wing. There's some fluid there as well. Let's head home. You lead, I'll follow."

"Roger. Hydraulic pressure is low."

We weren't going to do anything fancy on this approach. Just a long straight-in to the runway. I had some concern about losing my hydraulics. The Mohawk had two hydraulic pumps for redundancy, but they fed one common system. If one pump failed, I'd be fine. If the system had a leak and we lost too much fluid, I'd have my hands full.

Frank made the radio calls. After the appropriate controller hand-offs, he called for landing. "Phu Bai tower, this is Spud zero five. We are two OV-1 Mohawks for landing. Lead has battle damage and requests a straight in. I'll follow with a low pass and pitch up for downwind. Copy?"

"Roger Spud flight. You are cleared for approach and landing as requested."

I established a steady descent toward the end of the runway. I slowed and put the landing gear handle down. The gear should lower in about five seconds. More than ten seconds passed, no gear. I could see in my side mirror that the main wheels were part way down but stopped. The hydraulic gauge showed no pressure on either side. I was in a pickle. But that's what emergency procedures are for. So, I mentally opened the checklist in my mind.

HYDRAULIC FAILURE: Flaps—UP (They are). Perform a no-flap approach and landing (I'm set up—but no landing gear). LANDING GEAR SYSTEM FAILURE: Hydraulic pressure—check (It's zero), Gear—recycle (Done), Gear—check (Checked). Still no landing gear.

I went to the final backup procedure. *EMERGENCY GEAR EXTENSION: Airspeed—reduce (I have), Gear—DOWN (The handle is), Emergency landing gear release handle—PULL, Gear indications—check.*

I reached across the central cockpit pedestal, took hold of the yellow-and-black-striped T-handle and pulled, hoping the emergency backup system would work as advertised. I drew comfort, knowing if that failed, I still had the option of making a wheels-up landing on the long ten-thousand-foot runway at Danang Air Base, forty miles southeast. We had the fuel. An added benefit was that the Air Force could cover the runway with foam. Odds were, my observer and I would walk away fine.

I glanced over at him. He sat stoic, calm, not overly concerned with the situation. He trusted me. He had confidence in my ability to deal with the situation and bring us both down safely. I was always moved by the faith our technical observers had in us. No matter the mission, no matter the circumstances, they strapped into the right-side ejection seat and did their duty, oft times in the face of daunting enemy fire. I felt the weight of my responsibility to him and his loved ones. Indeed, I did always, with every observer I flew.

The emergency backup high-pressure air cylinder worked. The landing gear clunked down. The warning light went out in the gear handle, the indicator showed all three down and locked. I could see the left main solidly down in my left-side mirror. My observer confirmed the same in his right-side mirror.

Without hydraulics, I had no wing flaps available, so I had to make a somewhat faster approach than usual. Still, we touched down right by the numbers. On rollout, I knew that without hydraulics, the brakes would be limited and nosewheel steering would be tough. I relied on the reverse thrust of my engines to slow down and the asymmetric application of power to clear the runway and taxi to the Spud ramp. What a day!

Steve Ward, our new unit maintenance officer, was there to meet us. Steve was the sixth member of our Mohawk qualification course to join us in the 131st. We had six graduates from our flight school class go to the Mohawk course. Amazingly, all six of us were now assigned to the same unit in Vietnam, the 131st—all six of us, Spuds. We'd only recently welcomed Steve into the unit with the standard new guy protocol: enter the Spud Club, step on the Hawk, and buy the bar. Steve deployed later than the rest of us after his graduation from the aircraft maintenance officer course, qualifying him for a critical role in keeping airplanes flying.

Now, as our maintenance officer, he looked at the bird full of holes and no hydraulics, imagining the hours needed to complete the necessary repairs. Steve was not happy. In a very short time, he'd built a fine reputation for the number of airplanes he kept in flyable, mission-ready condition. His percentages were the best of any Mohawk unit in Vietnam. I'd just ruined his day. I knew I was in for it.

Frank Griswold landed and rescued me. "Come on. Let's get our debrief done and hit the club. I'll buy you a drink."

"Sorry, Steve," I said with a sad smirk as I turned and walked away, catching up with Frank and our two observers. Steve wasn't smiling.

Inside the club, I made a beeline for the bar. Jac poured my Chivas and soda. I looked at Frank and said, "He's buying."

Frank smiled. "Gladly. This young Spud had a hell of a mission today."

We shared a couple of drinks and told stories of our adventure to the small group of guys who were there after flying their day's missions. Major Alton heard of my battle damage and came over to the club to hear my account. I was hungry. Several of us headed to the mess hall for chow.

Later that evening, I returned to the club for a usual evening of raucous fun and camaraderie. I walked in to find the club full of folks in varying degrees of inebriation, a songfest already underway. Jac stayed busy handing up beers and pouring drinks in rapid succession.

My newly arrived classmate and unit maintenance officer, Steve Ward, was there as well. He gave me a warm greeting, and we talked for a while. Though I was not forgiven for letting North Vietnamese gunners badly damage his airplane, he'd certainly not let that stand in the way of our friendship. That dated to our first days in flight school together, over a year earlier. Steve did not have a drink that night. He never did. He didn't drink and he didn't smoke. Steve Ward was both a loving husband and a good Mormon. He was the most ethical and well-behaved person I knew in Vietnam.

I scoped out the room. The old VR veterans gathered at the end of the bar like seasoned gladiators, reflecting on contests past and imagining the tranquil days ahead that awaited their approaching return home. I was only a recent addition to their brotherhood and revered their status in the 131st. These old guys exuded swagger, bravado, and mystique. I was new and still had so much to experience and learn. These guys raised hell with the best of them, but at the same time, there was something about the look in their eyes. Their shenanigans were tempered by having survived months of daring combat missions and far too many near-death experiences. A few days more and that would all be behind them. They'd be home.

Our two Grumman Aircraft tech reps, pizza-making Joe DiMaggio and his cohort, Charlie Caputo, sat quietly at a table taking it all in. Without warning, two small groups of pilots assembled behind them. With a wink from the instigator, they grabbed them both and dragged them each onto the Hawk. Cheers erupted. Everyone thought the civilian tech reps were raking in the dough while serving in Vietnam. That was far from the truth, but they were always good sports about laying their cash on the bar.

I should comment about the "cash." We did not have greenback dollars. Our pay in Vietnam came in the form of MPC, or military payment certificates. The certificates equated dollar for dollar but looked like some of the play money we had as kids. Denominations went down to paper five-cent certificates. The purpose was to keep an influx of American dollars from inflating local economies. However, the Vietnamese working on base accepted them for payment for services rendered directly to soldiers.

The US military compensated formal contract work in Vietnamese currency, but soldiers paid their Vietnamese barbers and hootch maids in MPC. MPC spent fine on the local Vietnamese black market economy. The dread was that, on occasion, the military converted to new series MPC, so that the certificates themselves did not sustain an inflated black-market economy. The conversions were done on a single day throughout Vietnam. You'd stand in line at designated facilities on base and change the MPC in your pocket for the new issue. The next day, the old series was worthless. Anyone still holding those certificates had nothing. The black market convulsed. Those Vietnamese workers receiving pay from soldiers were devastated on conversion days. We were always happy to help out and exchange a reasonable amount of the certificates for them if we could link up on a conversion day.

So, Joe DiMaggio and Charlie Caputo laid money on the bar and the pace of party picked up with the flow of free drinks.

"Night carrier landings!" Somebody shouted.

The singing stopped and people started moving tables, assembling several in a long row, extending from just inside the front door all the way to the bar, right up against its stone front. Someone doused the tabletops with quantities of beer while others placed lighted candles along the edges. On command, the lights went out and the fun began. The idea was to stand just outside the club, get a running start and do a belly dive onto the end table, sliding the full length along the slick glistening beer, all the way to the bar without knocking candles off and potentially burning down the club.

My classmate, Mitch Waldran, was up to being first that night. He stepped outside, wailed a "yeehaw" and sprinted through the door. He hit the table with a splash and slid more than halfway down the "carrier deck." He got a muffled cheer. Others followed, some making it farther down the deck, others not quite so far. Joe Kennedy careened all the way, the full length of the tables. Everyone screamed, "Hurrah!"

My classmate, Jon Lowdermilk, grabbed my arm. "Let's go, Wild Bill."

Jon got a good run and launched onto the table, freshly doused in beer, with a good head of steam. He careened down the surface like an arrow, his hands down by his side. He slid and slid, barely slowing at all. At the end, his head hit the bar's stone front. Jon stood up smiling, tenderly touching a rising bump beneath his scalp.

Normally, the civilian tech reps refrained from our more insane stunts in the club. But tonight, Charlie Caputo was game. Charlie was not a tall man. In fact, he and "Tom Thumb" Ed Paquette were of similar statures. By this point in the evening, Charlie was drunk, flat drunk. He staggered outside, looked at the row of tables ahead of him, pawed his right foot like a bull ready to charge, and set off in a sprint—of sorts. Just as he launched into his dive, he stumbled, never rising to the level of the carrier deck, smashing his head smack into the edge of the first table. He flopped onto the ground, laying there in a growing pool of blood.

A couple of guys applied pressure with a bar towel while others got a jeep and took him to the dispensary, only a few hundred yards away. They rousted one of our flight surgeons to tend to our wounded friend. Charlie got seven stitches that night. The doc commented that he treated more trauma from accidents in the Spud club than wounds from combat missions. I guess we did have a few casualties from time to time, from throwing guys on the Hawk, or carrier landings, or tumbling into Pfeiffer's Gulch. Ah, what fun we had!

That night was still young, though. After Charlie's injury, the carrier landings stopped for the evening. The songfest erupted again. One poor guy, who declared a "health night" to catch up on some much-needed sleep, was rousted from his bunk and escorted to the club. His buddies deposited him on the Hawk for more money on the bar. As the evening progressed, singing drifted to off-key mumbling, flying stories swelled like fishing tales, and friends boosted the fortitude of friends just by being together. A good time was being had by all.

In the club door walked Buick Bingham, dripping wet, wearing a poncho. He walked up to the bar and sat down next to Major Kennedy. How had we even had a party without him?

Buick had just returned from a SLAR mission. The weather had worsened through the afternoon. It was a rainy, drizzly night. A solid layer of clouds came almost to the ground. Buick made a ground-controlled radar approach to minimums, barely identifying a couple of runway lights, and landed. Only then did he learn that most other flights that evening had diverted to Thailand because of the horrible weather around Phu Bai and Danang. After his mission debrief, he came to the club, ready for a drink.

When he walked into the club, a frog about three inches long followed him in the door. As Buick threw down a drink, talking with Major Kennedy, someone stepped on the frog and dropped it in Joe Kennedy's glass. Kennedy fished it out, put it on the bar, and continued drinking.

A black-suited Spud nearby said, "Oh my God. You're not going to drink that now, are you?"

Another pilot chimed in. "You'll make Buick sick. He's a SLAR pilot."

Buick took offense. He was an aspiring VR pilot. He wanted it badly. His Mohawk instructor pilot, Burwin Reed, had been a visual recon pilot in the 131st two years earlier. Just as Max Davison inspired my desire to become a 131st gun pilot, so Burwin planted that seed with Buick. He wanted to get on with his gun checkout as soon as they would have him. Meanwhile, he was still flying SLAR missions.

Buick's action was immediate. He picked up the frog and said, "To Spud!"

With that, he threw the creature in his mouth, crunched him between his molars and swallowed him with some difficulty. The noisy room full of drunks fell silent. After a few seconds, someone yelled, "He ate it. Buick ate the frog!"

About that time, the frog started to come back up. With one of the best one-liners I've ever heard, Buick calmly said, "Excuse me, I've got a frog in my throat." With that, he picked up his beer and washed the little amphibian down. For his feat, Harry Durgin, an Army ranger and senior VR pilot, presented Buick a special Spud Ranger patch to sew on his party flight suit.

Buick would complete his VR checkout shortly afterward, becoming one of the best visual recon pilots in the unit. He would also eat frogs whenever guests came to the club, especially US Marine helicopter pilots from across the airfield. Invariably, someone would shout, "Find Buick a frog," and the club would clear while men in black flight suits scoured Pfeiffer's Gulch for a suitable morsel. Buick ate three frogs before he finally declared, "I'm done. No more frogs until someone else eats three. Then I'll eat another to keep my record intact." No one ever rose to the challenge.

Luckily, Buick never encountered a poison frog. There were plenty of those in Vietnam. Oh, the insanity of it all.

Turned out Buick, like so many Spuds, had good reason to take a drink now and then. He'd already had some harrowing experiences, even before seeking admission into the brotherhood of visual recon. He shared one.

"Shortly after the bombing halt in the North, must have been like two days before you got here, I was flying a daytime SLAR mission, flight following with Waterboy. After reaching Vinh, I made a 180-degree turn and headed south. I was 'feet wet' about a half mile when Waterboy notified me of a 'bandit, six o'clock closing.' About that time my ECM gear started squawking and a strobe pointed off my tail. Waterboy called again, 'Spud 8, bandit three miles and closing.' I asked if he could give me the altitude. He said he appeared to be at 5,000 feet. I was at 5,500 feet.

"I gave a quick refresher course to my TO about ejection, life raft, and emergency radio procedures as I turned east to get away from the coast. I maintained my slow 140-knots speed, not wanting to aggravate him. Meantime, Waterboy kept me advised of his position until he was right on me. I could not get a visual. He had climbed high to dive down onto me. I turned upside down and dove straight for the top of the ocean. I headed for home, skimming the water. I figured if he made another pass, the waves might interfere with his radar."

Buick was one of the bravest pilots in the 131st. He'd earned his spot in the VR platoon.

Over the next weeks, there was a passing of the guard. The old-time VR pilots rotated home. Major Brummett, the platoon leader, "Big John" Kelly, Harry "Shorty" Durgin, Jim "Traveler" Parish, and Mark "Smilin' Jack" Bellamy. Neil "Uncle Nils" Ostgaard and Larry "Fox" Hower had departed shortly before my arrival.

Neil Ostgaard had been shot down on a VR mission over Laos just over three months before I got to Phu Bai. A 37 mm gun hit his airplane. The Mohawk rolled wildly out of control. He and his observer, Specialist 5 Fred Green, both ejected. Neil landed in a tree, hanging about forty feet above the ground. He made radio contact with his wingman, Jim Parish. Jim got the rescue ball rolling. Soon an Army Huey showed up to make the rescue. Problem was, Neil was hanging in a tree. Neil radioed the helicopter pilot and asked if he had a jungle penetrator to recover him from his aerial predicament. The Huey pilot's response, "No I don't. I've got fifteen minutes of fuel left. If you want to go with us, you better get your ass out of that tree right now."

Ostgaard swung back and forth in his parachute as best he could until he was able to get a precarious hold on the tree trunk. He uncoupled his risers and started down. He slipped and fell the last thirty feet, crashing to the jungle floor on his back. With adrenaline pumping, he got up and ran to the sound of the helicopter. Specialist Green was already on board, waiting.

The Huey took heavy fire from enemy soldiers only feet away. Ostgaard and Green had both been only moments from being killed or captured. The rescue helicopter took multiple hits. The pilot called out, "We've been hit. We're going down." The engine sputtered and the aircraft yawed. The crew struggled and somehow maintained enough control to get across the border and make a controlled crash onto the first secure landing zone back inside South Vietnam. After a twenty-minute wait, another Huey took them on to Phu Bai.

Meanwhile, Major Brummett got word back in Spud operations. He dashed to the flight line and launched in an armed A-model to lend assistance. By the time he arrived on scene, the rescue was complete. Brummett knew of a big anti-aircraft gun in the area that had been shooting at Spuds. He suspected it was the very gun that blew Neil out of the sky. Hank Brummett rolled in and fired all his rockets on the bastard in one pass. He said later that he was no hero that day, he was just damn mad. No Spud ever took fire from that site again.

Another departing old timer was Mark "Smilin' Jack" Bellamy. "Smilin' Jack" had been my hootch-mate, sleeping directly across from me. He knew he snored and encouraged me to throw a boot at him in the night if he disturbed me. A kind offer, but I never did. I've always been a sound sleeper, even sometimes sleeping though rocket and mortar attacks. His snoring never woke me.

Mark Bellamy was the only Mohawk pilot I ever heard of who ejected out of a Mohawk twice. He was shot down flying an armed OV-1 on a VR mission over Laos on February 4, 1966, shortly after the unit's arrival in Vietnam as the 20th ASTA Detachment. He and his observer both successfully ejected and were promptly rescued.

Several weeks before I showed up in the 131st, Mark was flying a Mohawk solo, a maintenance ferry flight, bringing it back to Phu Bai from an airfield far to the south. After sunset, he encountered a violent storm that battered the airplane, causing heavy damage that made it tumble out of control. The last thing Mark remembered was seeing his instruments show a rate of descent more than six thousand feet per minute and his altimeter spinning down through three thousand feet. He pulled his ejection handle, and all went black.

He regained consciousness in the daylight, lying in the rain-soaked jungle, water still dripping from glistening leaves. As he opened his eyes, he looked into the face of a tiger staring at him. He remembered holding that glance for a moment before the tiger turned and walked away. Mark shuddered and released the parachute risers from his harness. He pulled out his emergency radio. Couldn't raise anyone. He moved with much difficulty to a bald hillock and made contact. A US Air Force Huey helicopter picked him up early that afternoon and took him to the Army hospital in the coastal city of Nha Trang. Within a few days he was back in Phu Bai ready to resume flight duties.

So those were some of the adventures of the outgoing crew. Now, it was time for us new guys to take over. Major Joe Kennedy replaced Hank Brummett, becoming our beloved VR platoon leader. His team of pilots included me, Mitch Waldran, "Sweet" and "Sour" (the Lowdermilk twins), Buick Bingham, and Frank Griswold, who became my boss, replacing Joe Kennedy as the operations officer. And of course, our company commander, Spud 6—"Mr. Clean," Major Gary Alton—would continue to take his share of the riskiest missions flown. Together, we'd carve out our own legacy over the months ahead.

CHAPTER 5

Dirty, Deadly Tchepone

TCHEPONE REPRESENTED THE WORST OF THE WAR IN LAOS. IT MOCKED us, like a beast lying in wait, a serpent coiled, ready to strike and kill in an instant. Communist anti-aircraft positions dotted the landscape. Sand-bagged and cleverly camouflaged, they hid among thousands of bomb craters, the pockmarks of incessant American airstrikes. More airplanes had been shot down there than any other place in Laos.[1]

Since ancient times, Tchepone had been a Laotian settlement, a quiet farming and trade community. The town site sat in a two-and-a-half-mile-wide valley at six hundred feet elevation. Key trade routes intersected there at the juncture of two major rivers. For much of history, its strategic position was central to commerce throughout the region, playing a crucial socioeconomic-political role. The town served as an important hub for French colonial dominance in that part of Indochina. In 1930, the French built a major road across Laos connecting Vietnam to Thailand. That road passed along the north edge of Tchepone. They constructed an airfield less than a mile northwest of the town in the 1950s. However, within a few years, chaos shook the land.[2]

After the end of French colonial rule in 1954, the area was torn by conflict between Royal Laotian Government forces and communist Pathet Lao insurgents supported by the North Vietnamese. The communists captured the town in 1958 and took the airfield in 1960. Tchepone became the most critical point on the ambitious transportation network North Vietnam constructed through Laos, the Ho Chi Minh Trail. It was the juncture of important roads and rivers. But at the same time, it presented a chokepoint constricted between ridgelines on either side of the valley, making it vulnerable to air attack.[3]

In 1959, North Vietnam's 559th Transportation Group directed the work to establish a logistics hub at Tchepone. They moved a substantial array of air defense weapons for protection. The 559th improved the road network, constructed revetted truck parks, built fuel and supply storage areas, and later oversaw petroleum pipelines and river transportation routes running through the area.[4]

After the United States escalated involvement in the Vietnam War in late 1964, US aircraft began pounding the area around Tchepone, attempting to interdict the flow of enemy men and materiel coming through Laos. The population fled. The town emptied. The airfield was destroyed. Nonetheless, the importance to the North Vietnamese war effort grew. Tchepone became the main logistics base for the entire Ho Chi Minh Trail network. It grew into the main collection and distribution point for men and materiel throughout Laos, Cambodia, and South Vietnam. The communists identified the place as Base Area 604, their largest logistics hub and communications center in the country. They protected it with one of the greatest concentrations of anti-aircraft guns in Laos.[5]

Lots of aircraft took hits over Tchepone, many shot down, including some of our own. After early losses, we placed Tchepone in a special category of caution. Gary Alton decreed that only the highest priority missions would be flown there, and then executed from higher altitudes with extreme care. No low-level reconnaissance. Indeed, all aircrews operating in Laos knew of Tchepone's notoriety, of the mortal danger that lurked there. The fighter pilots even had a song about the place. Highlights of a few of the verses give the gist:

I'm starting my pull
. . . when it all hits the fan,

A black puff in front
. . . and then two off the right,

Six or eight more,
. . . and I suck it up tight.

There's small arms and tracer
. . . and heavy Ack Ack.

It's scattered to broken,
. . . with all kinds of flack.

But I'll bet all my flight pay
. . . the jock ain't been born

Who can keep all his cool
. . . when he's over Tchepone.

Oh, don't go to Tchepone,
Dirty, deadly Tchepone.[6]

So fast-moving jet fighter pilots regarded Tchepone with trepidation. At our much slower speed and lower altitudes we certainly did as well. An understanding of Tchepone sets the context for what follows.

Ed Paquette approached me one day and asked, "How about doing some IR missions for us? They're a hoot. And I think you'd be perfect for them."

I knew about the infrared missions the 131st flew. They were risky: at night and low-level, between five hundred and a thousand feet above the ground, often in valleys or bowls surrounded by mountains, some rising thousands of feet. Karst formations randomly jutted several hundred feet to add to the dicey-ness.* I wasn't at all sure this was something I wanted to raise my hand for.

---

* Karst. Large protrusions of rock resulting from limestone erosion over millions of years. Towering formations thrust from the jungle floor in Laos and parts of Vietnam. Some are bigger than football fields rising vertically several hundred feet above the surrounding landscape. In some areas there are clusters of karst formations grouped together or running in long, impressive lines.

As I pondered, Ed continued. "You impressed me when I gave you your in-country checkout. You're doing good flying VR. I have no doubt you've got what it takes for IR."

I knew that Ed needed more IR pilots. His platoon consisted of him and Roger "Round Ranger" Thiel. Roger's nickname came from the fact that he'd completed the Army's rigorous ranger training and proudly wore the ranger tab at the top of the left sleeve on his uniform. He was also barrel-chested, giving him a somewhat stout appearance. He was an Army Ranger and he was a bit round; thus, he was a round ranger. Roger was a good guy, even if sometimes a bit cynical. His love of Spuds was obvious, as was his dedication to the mission. He and Ed alternated flying IR missions nearly every other night. After each tense mission, they'd come to the club late, usually after most everyone else had gone to bed. They'd sit at the bar, downing a string of whiskies, quiet in their own thoughts. On nights he didn't fly, Roger would demonstrate his more gregarious side, fully joining in whatever nonsense was transpiring in the club that evening. Everyone liked the Round Ranger.

"This has become a bit much for just Roger and me," Ed went on. "Plus, I've got a bunch of test flights I'm doing during the day."

Ed was also our assistant maintenance officer. I knew he was busy.

With a feeling in my heart that told me I should know better, I said, "Sure. Why not. When do I start?"

"How about tonight? Get some rest and dinner. I'll meet you in Ops at 8:00."

I went back to my hootch and slept a couple of hours. After our briefing, we headed to the airplane, an OV-1C, the model specially configured for the infrared system.

"Jump in the left seat. You're flying."

"On my very first mission?"

"Yeah."

Always the optimist, I said, "At least we've got a moon tonight. That'll help."

"Doesn't help. Sure, you can make out the mountains, but the bad guys can see us in the moonlight. We'll take some fire."

I took off and headed west climbing to altitude. I looked at Ed Paquette sitting in the right seat, tweaking the controls on the infrared panel. The system included a camera in the belly of the aircraft and a screen in the cockpit that could see what the camera saw. Camera film captured terrain and the heat signature of targets, such as cooking fires and vehicles. The technical observer in the cockpit could fix the location of the hot spots in real time, using doppler coordinates, always confirmed with map inspection.

Ed had no controls. He was at my mercy, totally trusting. We crossed the border and flew a hundred miles to our mission area. On finding a prominent road intersection, we determined the coordinates on the map, and updated our doppler navigation system before descending onto Route 23, one of the main avenues of the Ho Chi Minh Trail.

"Be careful of that doppler," Ed Paquette warned. "You'll see it goes into memory mode quite often. It still tries to show your course, but when you see that memory waring light come on, the system is relying on dead reckoning. It no longer has real-time doppler input. Don't trust it. It's a good tool when its working, but don't ever bet your life on it. Too many Mohawk pilots have died letting it fly them into a mountainside."

I took that warning to heart. I knew of scores of OV-1C losses in Mohawk units around the world, including Vietnam. I could only guess how many of those were due to doppler failures on high-risk, low-level IR missions at night. I'd take care.

The mission went well. We found areas that could have been enemy bivouac sites and truck parks. We passed those to Moonbeam for air-strikes. We took some fire, but each time it was behind us. It seemed that at five hundred feet, the gunners couldn't get rounds off until we were past. *Good thing for us*, I thought.

Before we headed home, Ed had me fly near the rising terrain to our east. He had me get close and then turned me into it, commanding, "Turn right."

I did, and then he immediately countered with a loud, "Turn left!"

It was no mistake. It demonstrated exactly what he wanted.

"See how the mountains loomed as we get too close?"

I did. The big dark shape of the mountain rose rapidly, like a vampire rising with his cape draping below his outstretched arms. I got the message. Looming.

"When you're flying IR and a mountain suddenly looms, turn away. Quickly. You're about to fly into it."

Another lesson from Ed Paquette that I'd never forget.

I flew several IR missions after that. I still mostly flew VR, though, which I loved dearly. It became a busy time, especially since I still had major responsibilities as the assistant operations officer.

One morning I saw that I was crewed with Warrant Officer Curt Degner for an IR flight that night. Curt was a pilot. He arrived in the 131st a little over a month after me. He'd been flying SLAR missions. He gained his nickname, "Astronaut," by going to twelve thousand feet on one mission to get over the top of some weather. His TO told the tale on their return. We never flew that high, even though the Mohawk could get up to somewhere above twenty-five thousand feet.

The "Astronaut" had moved over to the IR platoon shortly after I began taking some missions for them. He'd sometimes fly as a right seat system operator. Curt was an infrared expert. He'd worked for Texas Instruments on infrared development and production before enlisting in the Army and going to flight school. He knew the Mohawk IR system inside and out, better than any of our technical observers. Curt loved to operate the system on missions. He could tweak it to max performance and get better results than even our most experienced TOs. On this flight, he'd fly in my right seat. Early that afternoon he cornered me with a proposal.

"Hey, sir. Looks like we're flying together tonight."

"I saw that."

"You know how the intel guys are always bemoaning the fact that there's no good coverage of the Tchepone area? How they're having trouble figuring out what's going there? How they've been saying that MACV is in the same boat?"

"Yeah?"

"Well, I've come up with a mission plan for an area search of the whole section there. We'd cover every square foot. Get some good stuff for them."

"Sounds intriguing. But you know we're forbidden from getting anywhere near Tchepone unless it's assigned as a priority mission for some special purpose."

"Looks to me like the fact it's turned into an intelligence black hole justifies us getting some coverage. I've got the mission all laid out for a ten-mile by ten-mile box: flight paths, turns, doppler updates, everything. I can get us overlap on each run, so we'll have good coverage of the whole box. We can get our assigned IR mission finished and still have plenty of time left for this. I figure we can get it done in less than an hour. What do you say?"

I took a deep breath and let rationalization get in the way of sound logic. "It needs to be done. Let's do it."

That night, we headed into the Foxtrot area of Steel Tiger and finished our on-the-books mission. We got everything requested, passing reports to Moonbeam for possible airstrikes later that evening. We headed north. As we approached our hundred-square-mile search box around Tchepone, Curt had me descend to fifteen hundred feet above sea level.

He reassured me. "That will put us about eight hundred feet above the valley floor. It'll also clear us over the nearest surrounding hills."

"How about the taller ridges and peaks in the area? I know some are pretty close and go well over two thousand feet."

"I've got them all marked. I'll give you an altitude change or turn you. Don't worry, I'll keep us clear."

I still worried. Curt Degner was good. He'd planned an ambitious mission, but not insane. He'd incorporated navigational checks and double-checks. He'd track our exact location throughout the flight. If ever any doubt, we'd abort, climb to altitude, and go home. The only real unknown is what the enemy anti-aircraft crews might have in store for us.

I followed Curt's course, altitude, and turn commands. Some of the hilltops slid awfully close beneath us, but we were OK. We had a radar altimeter that showed exactly how high we were above the ground directly below us. But that only helped some. The instrument looked directly below, not to the front. The mountain we'd fly into lurked ahead, not below.

We completed several tracks before the guns started shooting. Most of the fire initially came from a rising hill just to the northwest of Tchepone. Other guns joined in, firing from positions all over the area. They seemed to be lobbing shells at our sound. Nothing came that close. Rounds exploded behind us and well off to our side. The gunners threw big stuff at us, 37 mm and 57 mm, possibly larger. Most went off well above us. *Thank God it's a pitch-black night.*

I felt smug as we headed home. We'd done something pretty extraordinary and hadn't even gotten a scratch. I don't think either of us truly realized how insanely lucky we had been until we heard a chilling call on the radio.

"Mayday, mayday, mayday. This is Covey 410. Yellowbird 52 has gone in. I say again, Yellowbird 52 has gone in. He's crashed. I cleared him on a pass, then saw explosion. Fire still burning. Just north of Route 922, about ten miles west of the border."

"Oh shit, Curt. Yellowbird. That's a B-57 call sign. Wonder if it was target fixation?"

"Could have been. Or triple-A. We saw a lot of big stuff shooting tonight."

"Yeah." I paused. "We did."

At our post-mission debrief we mentioned that we'd been able to get some film at Tchepone at the end of our flight. The intel guys' eyes lit up. We passed along updated anti-aircraft locations from where we'd taken fire. We headed to the club, expecting it to be mostly empty that time of night.

It wasn't. A bunch of guys were having an especially riotous time of it. As we stepped through the door, we found ourselves in the traffic pattern for night carrier landings. We angled to the left, slipping through the crowd to the bar.

A slurred voice announced, "Hey, the IR guys are here. Set 'em up."

Jac put two shot glasses on the bar and reached for the bottle of Drambuie. It was Blue Blazer time. A bunch of my VR brothers had been in the club for a while. Mitch Waldran tossed down one of the flaming drinks just as we showed up. The idea was to fill a shot glass with any whiskey or liqueur that would burn. Most did, but some better than others. The beverage of choice in the Spud Club was Drambuie.

With the flame burning bright, the imbiber was to hold the shot glass high while everyone coaxed him on. He'd put it to his lips, drink it quickly, and slam the glass down on the bar. If the contents were gone and a flame still burned around the rim, he got mission success and did not have to drink another for the rest of the night. If he did not finish it all, or if there was no flame around the rim, he had to do it again until he got it right.

I actually enjoyed Blue Blazers and rarely did any damage to myself or my surroundings. Drambuie tasted good, especially after a tense flight. That night I got away with only slightly singing one side of my scraggly mustache. I slammed the empty shot glass on the bar, smiled at the dying flame still fluttering around the rim, and wiped my mouth with my left forearm. That got a chorus of cheers.

Curt Degner's turn came next. It must have been his first time. Jac made the ceremonial pour. Mitch Waldran held his Zippo lighter against the top until the flame caught. Curt held the glass tentatively. Attention in the room turned his way, chants urging him on. "Go, go, go."

He raised the flaming glass only slightly and brought it swiftly toward his mouth. Then he made a fatal mistake. He hesitated at the worst moment. Blazing Drambuie gushed from the glass and splashed across his face. The sweet gooey liquid stuck to his skin, engulfing it in fire. Jac, our bartender, had the presence of mind to fetch a towel from behind the bar and throw it to Waldran who beat the flames out. Curt was red in the face, both from embarrassed bewilderment and something akin to first-degree burns. Someone put a hook next to the bar where forevermore hung a towel, immediately available for any future Blue Blazer incidents in the club.

The next morning, I didn't arrive at my desk in ops until 9:00 because of my IR flight the night before. As soon as I came through the door, the flight operations clerk said, "Intel wants to see you in the II shop* ASAP."

I went in. The analysts had our mission film spread out across their light table. It filled the entire surface. The analysts beamed. "This is the best coverage of Tchepone we've ever seen. Look at all this stuff you found." One analyst pointed to some of the key points of interest. "And you got the entire area. That's never been done—by anyone."

My flight operations clerk came through the door just as the analyst added, "We've already sent an intelligence summary to MACV. They're excited. The film is going to them on a special courier flight later today. Good job."

My clerk interrupted, "Captain Reeder, the CO wants to see you and Mister Degner, right now."

Oh shit, I thought. I headed to the company orderly room posthaste. "Astronaut" was already there, waiting for me by the first sergeant's desk. As soon as I walked in, the first sergeant said, "Go on in."

Curt and I knocked on the door jam and entered on Major Alton's bark. He was red-faced, obviously angry. Curt Degner looked sunburned from the incident at the club, but he paled in comparison to the crimson ire we witnessed on the face of our company commander. I'd never seen him like that before or ever again since.

Major Alton bit his lip and said in the most measured tone he could muster, "I just heard about your mission last night. I understand you did a complete area search around Tchepone and got complete coverage of the entire area, including tracks directly over the town. Is that right?"

Curt and I responded in unison, not knowing what was coming next. "Yes, sir."

Our commander fixed an angry glare right into each of our eyes, shifting from me to Curt and back to me.

"You are aware that I put Tchepone off limits, except for the highest priority missions, and then at higher altitudes and get right in and get out?"

---

* II shop. The Imagery Interpretation element of the company intelligence section.

Again, together, "Yes, sir."

His measured tone was gone. He yelled, "Well what the hell did you think you were doing? Flying a low-altitude area search; going back and forth and back and forth all over the heaviest concentration of anti-aircraft in Laos."

I started, "We thought . . . "

"You thought. You didn't think. That's the problem. You disobeyed my direct order. I should rip your wings off right here and put you both up on court-martial charges."

He glared. "But I won't. Get out of here and don't ever do such a stupid fucking thing again."

Once more, in unison, "Yes, sir."

I added awkwardly, "No sir, we won't."

As we turned to leave, I could see his emotion was more than anger. It was his fear that we could have been killed, the same as a father's fear for the safety of his children. Gary Alton's restrictions on our operations around Tchepone were driven by his desire to protect us—at least as much as he could in this raging war taking the lives of so many aircrews over Laos. Our unit had lost too many great guys. He didn't want us to be two more.

That night the Spud Club was much more subdued. I think many of the guys still nursed painful heads. I stood at the bar, slowly sipping a drink and sharing lies with the Lowdermilks when a familiar face strode through the door, Captain Charles Finch. Charles was a Catkiller, a pilot with the 220th Reconnaissance Airplane Company, right next door, just west of us on the airfield. They flew O-1 Bird Dogs, a small tandem-seat, single-engine airplane used for reconnaissance and directing artillery and airstrikes. They flew their missions inside South Vietnam, not out of country, across the border like us. But they risked their lives over some of the most treacherous real estate inside South Vietnam. The Catkillers flew in and around the treacherous Demilitarized Zone, or DMZ, fifty miles to our north, around Khe Sanh, and into the A Shau Valley, a festering nest of North Vietnamese activity—all high-risk missions, indeed.

What made Charles truly special, though, was the fact that he was another of our flight school classmates. It was good to see him and share even more lies. He invited us to the Catkiller Club the next night. I went with Mitch Waldran and the Lowdermilks. We found three more of our flight school classmates there, Mac Byrd, Roger Cerne, and Don Long. Besides us six Mohawkers in the 131st from the same flight school class, we had four others right next door in the 220th Catkillers. After that night, we shared visits regularly. We enjoyed reminiscing and telling tall tales.

I continued to take infrared missions when needed, but the bulk of my flying was always VR, my favorite. I loved flying armed Mohawks on daytime photo reconnaissance. Engaging targets with our rockets was a bonus at the end of most missions. Regardless of the day's mission, it was always good to get to the club and unwind.

True to form, I was in the club the evening of January 9, 1969. It was a day much like any other. I'd flown a VR mission, taken some good photos, found four enemy trucks hiding under trees waiting to continue their drive after darkness fell that night. Landing late in the afternoon, I scarfed down dinner at the mess hall before heading to the Spud Club. I finished a drink, and Jac poured my second. Before I took my first sip, Frank Griswold walked in the door. He'd just left ops. He came with bad news. "The Catkillers have a plane down. No comms, no good location. It's dark and he'd be out of gas a while ago."

"Who's the pilot?" I asked.

Frank looked at the piece of paper he held in his hand. "Captain Mac Byrd, pilot. Lieutenant Kevin O'Brien, artillery observer in the backseat."

Oh shit, not Mac Byrd. I looked at the Lowdermilks, standing nearby. My glance shifted to Mitch Waldran. We were all classmates; all went through nine months of flight school together. We'd drank with him at the Catkiller Club. Stunned shock numbed my expression and my heart. I saw the same expression as I looked into the eyes of my classmates. We four grabbed our drinks, moved close, and said nothing. We'd get word to Steve Ward and Billy Wood later.

There was hope, but not much. We all assumed the worst. It was dark; the weather was bad; Mac was out of gas. There weren't many places he could have made a survivable crash landing in the jungle. It would take every bit of his pilot skill to get through this. But we shuddered, all of us knowing Mac had struggled in flight school.

Major Alton added, "We'll launch our morning VR early tomorrow, SLAR missions too. Every mission, coming and going, take some time to help the Catkillers search. We'll hope they find 'em soon."

I flew the morning VR into northern Steel Tiger. We checked in with King, the C-130 airborne search and rescue coordinator, after takeoff. He gave us a rough last known position. There were already 220th Bird Dogs orbiting, searching. We checked the area, staying clear of them, but saw nothing. We broadened our search. Still nothing. We headed out into Laos for our mission. We searched again on our way home. Nothing.

Next day, I walked to the 220th area. I ran into my friend and class-mate, Charles Finch. He was exhausted after being up much of the night and flying search patterns most of the day. He filled me in on some of the details.

"Mac and I were scheduled to layover at Dong Ha last night. I landed at 6:30 not knowing that Mac was still airborne. It was getting really dark. I was shocked to learn where he'd been headed. He had been gone too long. I was worried. I climbed up into the control tower and called him on the radio. He told me he'd been working around Khe Sanh, identifying targets for the artillery. He diverted to help a recon team in contact to the south. He helped save their bacon, decided he didn't have enough gas to get to Dong Ha, so was going to try to make it to Phu Bai.

"He didn't know exactly where he was because of weather and dark-ness. I told him to climb and head east—that we were trying to pick him up on radar. He said he had to descend to get below the clouds and find his bearings. My last transmission to him was, 'Mac, you have to climb.' I never heard back. I knew he must be out of gas and had to ditch in the trees. I'm afraid we've lost a good friend."

I tried to keep hope alive and said, "We'll keep looking. All of us. You guys are up there all day long. We're making a search on every mission, both going and coming back. Search and rescue is activated. 'King' is using every available asset."

We spied Roger Cerne, another classmate in the 220th. Roger and I had been enlisted men together at Fort Sill, Oklahoma. We suffered the brutality of officer candidate school (OCS) together. And we went through flight school together. Now, we were neighbors at Phu Bai. Roger saw us and quickened his pace.

"I'm going up to look for Mac. Want to come along?"

"Absolutely. When?"

"Right now. Go get your gear and meet me on our flight line. I'll be ready to go."

I returned with my survival vest, pistol, helmet, and gloves and found Roger standing by his airplane. It was tiny compared to our Mohawks. I put on a parachute, climbed awkwardly into the cramped backseat and buckled in. We searched for hours and found nothing.

Mac Byrd left a lovely young wife and a beautiful baby girl. A gloom hung over the 220th and the 131st. We all searched and searched over the days ahead. We never found anything of the wreck or our friend.*

---

* Hugh McNeil Byrd's crash site was never found, his body never recovered. Today, he remains missing in action (MIA), status: "Unaccounted For."

CHAPTER 6

Sawadee

TIME FOR GRIEF IS SHORT IN WAR. HO CHI MINH'S QUEST FOR VICTORY in the South never slowed. Our missions didn't end. I flew nearly every day for the rest of the month. I flew mostly daytime visual/photo-recon. A third of the time, though, I flew infrared at low level, on dark nights, in rough terrain, my senses sharp.

I turned the cockpit lights so dim I could barely read the instruments. My head stayed on a swivel, scanning for looming mountains or killer Karst jutting suddenly from the jungle floor—all the while, fiddling with the doppler, trying to stay on course. My TO backed me up, staying oriented as best he could, by following the imagery on his scope. I enjoyed flying infrared for the challenge and the intensity, the regard one got from the other pilots for being one of the daring few IR guys. It was not unlike being a rodeo bull rider, looked at as being a bit over the edge.

Of course, daytime VR pilots earned respect of a different sort, hard as that might be to describe. On IR missions you took a lot of fire, but that wasn't the greatest threat. The rounds were generally off the mark in the dark. There, your end would more likely come from slamming into an unseen mountainside in bad weather on a moonless night.

On visual recon, in the daylight, you stood a far greater probability of being hit by anti-aircraft fire, of being blown from the sky. If you were able to eject, you'd likely be killed by the enemy once you hit the ground. Word was that not many prisoners were taken in Laos. Most Spud losses were on VR missions. Still, that was my favorite way to fly.

IR ranked second—though every time I climbed into the cockpit for an infrared mission, I felt like that bull rider taking a wrap of rope around his hand just before the chute opened for his ride. The biggest downside to IR was that you couldn't shoot back. No guns on the airplane.

I had learned much about my young self during those first months flying Mohawks in combat. It was not that I was unafraid. Quite the opposite. I was afraid almost every mission. But I was able to overcome it. Courage came from my ability to contain fear, push through it, and do what had to be done, even with angst swelling in the pit of my stomach.

On Fridays, our VR missions ended in Thailand. We landed at the Royal Thai Air Force Base in Ubon. We flew there each week, at the end of our photo-reconnaissance missions. We'd deliver intelligence products to the "Wolfpack," the 8th Tactical Fighter Wing intelligence section. We gave them copies of our weekly intelligence summaries and copies of significant SLAR and IR imagery as well as noteworthy photographs. The next morning, we'd answer questions they invariably had after looking over the material. Our stuff was often the talk of their shop—most especially the infrared imagery from the area search Curt Degner and I did over Tchepone. We'd gotten unbelievable coverage and invaluable intelligence information on that mission, in addition to our well-deserved ass-chewing.

Next stop —the 497th Tactical Fighter Squadron, the "Night Owls." By the time we finished with the 8th Wing, the 497th crews were just starting their day. They were night fighters. Like our SLAR and IR guys, Night Owl crews adjusted their sleep patterns so they could operate at night. And like us, they wore black flight suits. Theirs were because of their unique and dangerous nighttime role in the air campaign. That set them apart from the other Air Force fighter squadrons, much like our distinction among Army aviation units. Having so many things in common gave our two organizations a strong affinity for one another, contrary to the high-level squabbles among Army and Air Force generals over aviation roles and missions.

At the tactical level, among the warriors waging the war, we all got along well. Our night flights often worked together, either through a forward air controller, or sometimes directly in contact with each other. We'd report where we found moving vehicles along a roadway and talk them in for a strike.

The Night Owls flew one-, two-, or three-ship missions at night, looking for trucks to destroy. Sometimes they found their own targets. Often, they got assistance in locating or illuminating targets from the C-130 flare ship, "Blind Bat." They also had a working partnership with "Spectre" AC-130 gunships and, of course, our "Spud" OV-1 SLAR or IR birds.

The Night Owl F-4Ds usually carried both bombs and flares. Solo mission aircraft had the ability to drop flares to locate targets on one pass, then come around and drop bombs on the next. With multiple fighters in a flight, one would drop flares, maintaining near constant illumination, while a second F-4 attacked any trucks seen. When Blind Bat dropped flares, the F-4s had only to identify and strike, keeping well clear of the supporting flare ship. That was done either through vertical separation with the F-4s remaining below the C-130's altitude, or by clearly artic-ulated, well-understood lateral separation, each remaining in its own agreed block of airspace, away from the other.[1]

When working with Spectre, the Night Owls often took on the mis-sion of flak suppression for the AC-130 gunship. While Spectre worked his destructive magic, the 497th fighters orbited; ready to strike any anti-aircraft gun unwise enough to open fire. If the gunship finished its mission without the need for any flak suppression, the AC-130 become a FAC, leading the Night Owl F-4s onto any nearby targets appearing on its sensors.[2]

And then there was us. When Night Owls were in our area, they always appreciated the lucrative targets we passed their way. On occasion, Moonbeam, the nighttime airborne controller, would pair one of our SLAR or IR birds with a Blind Bat flare ship when he had a couple of Night Owl F-4s in tow. Our Mohawks found targets and called them to Blind Bat who illuminated the area with flares before working the 497th aircraft in on a strike. The results were often stunning.[3]

But those were all night missions, flown with side-looking radar or infrared. The VR photo-reconnaissance missions all took place in the daytime. They didn't work strikes with the 497th. Why, then, were the VR pilots the ones getting to enjoy an overnight in Thailand once a week? Two reasons: First, VR often did reconnaissance and took photos the morning after a 497th nighttime attack. Those pilots would be available, to meet face-to-face with the intel folks at Ubon, to go over images and answer questions based on what they'd seen with human eyes. Second, our daytime VR missions were, by far, the most dangerous flown in the 131st. They took more fire, received more hits, and had the most crew members killed and wounded. For those two reasons, the decision was made, long before, that the Friday VR flights would land at Ubon, deliver products, attend briefings as required, and spend the night, before flying the next day's missions en route back to Phu Bai.

On January 17, 1969, I flew as Major Kennedy's wingman. He was the VR platoon leader, the one who selected the crews for all our visual recon missions. He assigned us the mission into the northern part of Steel Tiger, into area Echo. Frank Griswold, company operations officer and my boss, led the other VR flight that day into the southern areas Foxtrot and Golf. Jon, "Sour" of the Sweet and Sour Lowdermilk twins, flew Frank's wing. That meant we'd all be together in Ubon at the end of the day. I looked forward to the adventure with my friend, Jon, and to be in the company of two seasoned and respected gun pilots.

Frank Griswold and Jon Lowdermilk launched in the morning. Major Kennedy and I took off in the early afternoon. We crossed the border and turned right. The northern part of the Laotian panhandle was magnificent in its breathtaking beauty. The rugged Annamite Mountains rose to more than six thousand feet, the tallest peak above seven thousand. Mighty Karst towers stood as stone guardians cloaked in foliage, posted in scattered formations, watching over verdant valleys, wandering streams, and small farmsteads below. The contrasts of colors and stark elevations filled me with awe. But the spell was broken by the pummeled roads of the Ho Chi Minh Trail spoiling the splendor of the view.

Bombardment scarred the land. Disfigured roadways stretched from Mu Gia and Ban Karai passes, winding southward toward Tchepone. American air strikes left the routes as shredded ribbons littered with the residue of destruction. The signs of tumult reminded us, too, that the enemy held these passes and roadways dear. They defended them well with large-caliber anti-aircraft guns. They'd shot down many planes where we operated that day.

Major Kennedy dove down to get a forward panoramic camera shot of Mu Gia Pass while I stayed at altitude to cover, should he run into trouble. We switched, and I did the same for the road coming out of Ban Karai Pass. After I got back to altitude, he took a vertical photo over Ban Laboy Ford. Large-caliber rounds exploded high, off his left wing.

"I've got the son-of-a-bitch," I called. I rolled in and let go two pairs of rockets. That stopped the gun long enough for him to escape.

We looked carefully along the roadways, performing visual reconnaissance as we headed south. We took a few target-of-opportunity photos of a new bridge and possible truck hiding areas along the way. We turned southwest to swing wide around Tchepone, and then it was done. End of mission. I listened to Major Kennedy call the sector radar controller as we headed toward the Thai border.

"Lion, this is Spud 3, flight of two, inbound to Ubon on the zero-three-zero at 70 nautical."

"Roger, Spud flight. Squawk thirty-two hundred."

We turned on our transponders, devices that transmitted distinct codes when queried by radar. We usually turned them off during missions, not wanting to give the enemy any advantage.

"Radar contact, Spud 3. Continue. Expect handoff to approach control in twenty miles."

We landed uneventfully at Ubon. We did our 360-degree overhead approach. It was no big deal there. Air Force fighter formations performed any number of impressive pitchout patterns when they returned from combat missions. We only drew notice because of our different-looking airplanes, and the fact that we were Army, coming off missions over Laos. That was definitely different. We were the only US Army airplanes flying missions in Laos.* We attracted attention when we landed at airbases in Thailand.

---

* A small number of Army helicopters flew select, classified missions into limited eastern portions of Laos in support of MACV-SOG special operations teams. The aircraft always returned to

We parked next to our other Mohawks. Frank and Jon had landed hours before. We secured our planes and walked toward the Wolfpack tactical operations center. We found the intel shop and dropped off packages of reports, photos, and imagery. We stopped by the 497th to see who was there.

"Hey, Spuds! How you doing?"

It was Lieutenant Colonel Stan Clark, the Night Owls operations officer. He was a good guy. We chatted with him for a bit. He said there might be a few pilots already at the club; more would come later in the evening, but the guys flying that night were getting ready for their missions and wouldn't show up until well after midnight. We headed to the officers' club.

It was early and only a few pilots hung around. I was surprised it wasn't livelier, even at that time of day. The place had a reputation among clubs in Southeast Asia. It ranked among the wildest. That notoriety came from the personality of one of our country's great combat aces, Robin Olds.*

Colonel Olds commanded the Wolfpack at Ubon two years earlier. He was a triple-ace with twelve confirmed kills in World War II and four in Vietnam for a career total of sixteen. He'd been awarded the Air Force Cross (America's next highest award for heroism after the Medal of Honor), four Silver Stars, and six Distinguished Flying Crosses. He was flamboyant, married to a Hollywood actress. He insisted on tough air-to-air dogfight training and thumbed his nose at Air Force leaders who didn't agree. A visible symbol of his defiance of restrictive rules was his out-of-regulation waxed handlebar mustache. Robin Olds was a hard fighter and heavy drinker. His pilots loved him and celebrated the camaraderie and esprit he instilled. That's what the Ubon club was all about. His guys trained hard, partied hard, and fought and died as the Air Force's best. His legend lived on in the Ubon Officers' Club.[4]

South Vietnam. See John Plaster, *SOG: The Secret Wars of America's Commandos in Vietnam* (New York: Simon & Schuster, 1997).

* Ace. A military aviator who shoots down five or more enemy aircraft in aerial combat. The kills must be confirmed by a witness, photo, or film.

Major Kennedy introduced me to Irene, everyone's favorite Thai bartender. She smiled and set us up with drinks. We joined a couple of F-4 guys and chatted for a while. Kennedy picked up on their interest in our airplanes. He focused on one who went by the nickname "Judge." His real name was Roy Bean. Judge Roy Bean had been a notorious nineteenth-century hanging justice of the peace in West Texas; thus, the nickname.

Kennedy cast out the tease. "Come to Phu Bai and I'll take you up on one of our Mohawk missions. You can fly my right seat, dual controls. It'll give you a whole new perspective on flying."

"Yeah, that sounds great. I've got some time off coming."

Then Kennedy planted the hook. "Perfect. Only thing I ask in return. A backseat ride in your F-4."

The Judge didn't pause. He jumped right into the net. "Can do, my friend. You've got a deal."

Major Kennedy grinned at his catch. "Great!"

We went to the base exchange, shopped for things we couldn't get at Phu Bai, and bought two cases of beer. The crew at Phu Bai liked Thai beer. The brand was Singha. It was good. We hauled the cases to his plane where we stowed them in the belly. We each grabbed our small gym bags and walked to the taxi stand for a ride into town.

We checked in to the Ubol Hotel, a bit of a dive, but comfortable, cheap, and centrally located. We cleaned up, changed clothes, and met up with Frank and Jon in the lobby. We all headed to a nice restaurant a short distance down the road.

Major Kennedy surprised me with his mastery of foreign languages when we entered the establishment. He offered the Thai greeting, "*Sawadee kraap.*" The well-dressed staff responded with smiles and slight bows, "*Sawadee.*" The maître d' hurried over, welcomed us in perfect English, and escorted us to our table. Waiters pulled out chairs and seated us. They laid cloth napkins across our laps. We ordered a round of Singha beers. We toasted. I wiped froth from my sorry mustache.

I noted an ashtray on the table so reached for my pack of Marlboros. Before I got a cigarette to my lips, a waiter held a gold lighter perfectly before me, ready to light my smoke. I took a puff, inhaled deeply, and savored my delight. *What a charming greeting, Sawadee. What a pleasant welcome to Thailand. How nice to be here, away from war, far from danger. No rockets, no mortars, no shooting.*

Thailand was a marvelous place. Less than two hundred miles from Vietnam and the war that raged there. A little over fifty miles from Laos, the bombing, death, and destruction; the guns always poised to kill us. I felt like we'd flown to some distant land on the other side of the globe, a lovely and civilized place where we could relax and enjoy ourselves.

The menu offered a wide selection. We all ordered Kobe steak. It was wonderfully tender and flavorful but had to be locally produced. It couldn't have been the fine beef imported from Japan. The price was too crazy cheap, less than two dollars in Thai currency. That included a vegetable and sweet desert. We switched to cognac after dinner and settled into conversation, recounting flying exploits and tales of life in Thailand.

Jon brought up, "I've heard stories of aircrews having a grand night on the town here, visiting an infamous Thai steam bath. I think the name is Sabai-Thong. They get a good cleaning and can take the lovely bathhouse girl out for dinner and dancing at one of the clubs in town. If they're lucky, they'll get her back to their hotel room for the night."

Major Kennedy nodded. "True. And some of the guys living here, stationed at the base, brag about steady girlfriends they call their *Thirak*. I think it means something like their 'own true love.'"

I couldn't help myself. "You sure do know some of the Thai language, sir."

He gave me a look before he said, "You don't need to 'sir' me when we're off duty, out drinking in Thailand. Back at Phu Bai, yes. Enjoying ourselves here, just Joe will do."

I never got comfortable with that.

He finished, "Most of those relationships are over by the end of tour. Though, I do hear of a few guys who marry their Thai girlfriends and take them back to the States."

We finished probably two cognacs too many and decided to call it a night, almost. Kennedy and Griswold headed back to the hotel. Jon and I still had errands to run.

I'd been given a wad of Thai money and a couple of order forms. A row of shops lined the street a little over a block away. All were still open, even at that late hour. We went to the first business, checked the name on the door and went inside. I delivered the orders for two party flight suits. The forms had a place for measurements and another to specify which patches were to be sewn on, and where. Next week's crews would pick up the finished products and bring them back to Phu Bai. I also got a bunch of loose patches our guys wanted. Those filled a small bag. The proprietor insisted he measure both of us for tailor-made suits. He'd have them ready within a week. They'd be real cheap. I declined. So did Jon. We did stop at the shoemaker next door, and I had my foot traced for a new pair of dress wingtips. Those would be ready in a couple weeks.

Back at the hotel, I crashed and was soon fast asleep. I woke with a start in the morning worrying I'd overslept. I hadn't. We got back to the airfield and spent time with the intel guys at the 8th Wing going over the stuff we'd given them the day before. They'd had time to look it over and were eager for us to help clarify a few points and offer some personal insights.

We met our observers at the airplanes. They all had big grins. I climbed into the cockpit with my head hurting from too much of too many kinds of drinks the night before. I held my oxygen mask to my face, set the control dial to 100 percent, and took several deep breaths. Pure oxygen did wonders in clearing away the morning cobwebs left from too much partying the night before. We didn't have to wear our masks below ten thousand feet, so I turned the oxygen system off and set the mask back in its place.

We cranked our aircraft and taxied out, one flight slightly behind the other. With its wide ten-thousand-foot runway, each flight was able to take off in formation, something we couldn't do on our shorter and much narrower runway at Phu Bai. It was great, Major Kennedy and I rolling down the runway together, breaking ground at the same instant, and departing toward the morning sun, already in tight formation.

All went well. We completed our Steel Tiger missions and headed home.

On the way, Kennedy asked, "Have you ever seen Khe Sanh?"

I answered, "No."

"Let me show you."

We flew right over the old Marine Corps base. It had suffered the worst siege of the Vietnam War. Major Kennedy noted, "It lasted several months. Over twelve thousand friendly casualties. Nearly a thousand Americans killed. Hell on earth. It all only ended a little over six months ago."

I unconsciously keyed my mic. "Oh, Christ."

My heart sunk. I'd never seen anything like it. The whole countryside looked like the moon. Craters everywhere, big, small, and everything in between. There was nothing but churned earth and debris, the shape of the runway barely discernible. All a dull ashen grey. Not a living thing. Complete annihilation. The worst devastation I'd seen on earth. An utter and horrible contrast from my delightful time in Ubon.[5]

We continued southeast and landed in the early afternoon. My first trip to Thailand had been an experience I'd never forget. It would not be my last.

The approach of the 1969 Tet lunar New Year had the attention of everyone at Phu Bai. A year earlier, the North Vietnamese Army and their Viet Cong guerrillas launched their big offensive across all South Vietnam during the agreed holiday ceasefire. It failed to achieve any lasting tactical success, but turned out to be a strategic victory, a turning point in American resolve. The Americans and their South Vietnamese allies defeated the communist uprising within a matter of hours and days everywhere across the land, with one exception. The exception had been the nearby city of Hue, only eight miles up the road. Fighting raged there for weeks with thousands killed and wounded on both sides; over five thousand civilians dead.

Phu Bai had been probed, but no major attack and no loss of aircraft. Still, our commander, Gary Alton, worried over the possibility of something as bad or even worse this year. He was not going to risk it. We began planning the evacuation of our aircraft to Thailand over the lunar holiday. All flyable Mohawks would go. Crews moved the broken ones into the hangar. The Beaver stayed behind as well. No one was keen on flying that single-engine relic across hostile Laos.

We sent all the SLAR and IR birds to Ubon. Our armed VR airplanes split between Ubon and Nakhon Phanom (NKP). I headed to NKP. It would be a very different experience from my last trip to Thailand. Ubon was much more cosmopolitan, but NKP was a life's experience unto itself that I'd not soon forget. The town sat right on the Mekong River, the border between Thailand and Laos. No one was ever certain of what evil lurked just across the water. So much of Laos changed hands so often. The airbase sat a few miles west of town. It was like something out of an exotic action-adventure movie.

The first time I landed, I was immediately impressed by the aircraft arrayed on the parking ramps. I looked around and saw big gutsy A-1 "Skyraider" and smaller T-28 "Nomad" close air support airplanes, as well as several A-26 "Invader" attack bombers, all veterans of the Korean War. I also spotted O-2 "Skymaster" and OV-10 "Bronco" forward air control aircraft, as well as several cargo planes and a variety of helicopters.

Once we checked in and got rooms assigned, we dropped our stuff and headed to the officers' club. We fit right in. Good bunch of guys flying all sorts of curious airplanes on secret and top-secret missions up and down the tapestry of Laos. Some units had lost several aircrews but were all dedicated to their missions. They also all knew how to party and raise hell in the club.

Clubs filled a special need for flight crews during America's Indochina War (Laos, Vietnam, and Cambodia). They existed as places to unwind after tense combat missions. Alcohol and absurd antics helped that process for many. The clubs also served as dens of camaraderie— brothers gathered together, sharing their exploits, their thrills, and their grief. And the clubs became halls of learning, places where experience and lessons passed from one to others. They helped us maintain our sanity in the midst of the insanity we faced every day.

That first night we got invited into the informal bar filled with drunken aviators recounting successes and close calls from that day, or the night before. They shared harrowing stories of extraordinary aerial exploits along the dark corridors of this very secret war. They told of

Laotian generals and kings, loyalists and insurgents, of Thai commandos, Chinese mercenaries, American Special Forces, CIA operatives, clandestine airlines, and on and on. As I listened, those strange tales formed a vision in my mind. I saw a richly textured, darkly tangled, intriguingly beautiful thing with the face of Medusa—its very beauty there to destroy any who lingered too long. This fascinating secret conflict, a hidden adjunct to the Vietnam War, was as deadly as it was alluring.

The story telling ended as one of the "Sandy" A-1 pilots finished his drink and threw his glass, shattering it against the wall. He shouted, "Shit hot!"* I sat, a bit flabbergasted, as others followed suit. They downed their drinks and hurled their glasses. I noticed a large bull's eye painted on the concrete wall, the intended target.

The guy next to me said, "Go ahead, Spud. Throw yours! Barkeep's got boxes of 'em. It'll cost you a dollar a glass."

I did, and it felt great. Flying insane missions, drinking heavily, sharing stories, and breaking glasses. *Does it get any better than that?* I thought.

No, but in war, things turn in an instant. Two days later, on February 15, I was with my observer, getting ready for our afternoon VR mission. I'd be flying as Frank Griswold's wingman.

Frank approached. "Just heard some bad news."

"What?"

"Stan Clark went down last night. The 497th ops officer. We saw him last month, in Ubon."

"Yeah, good guy."

"Yeah."

"Are they working a rescue?"

"They got his back-seater early this morning. They don't think Stan got out. No emergency beeper. Not much hope. Worse yet, the lead A-1 covering the rescue went down. Hit by 37 mm. No chute. No beeper. Aircraft exploded on impact. He was one of the Sandy's from here. Those are the guys we've been drinking with at the club."

My voice cracked. "Bummer."

---

* Shit hot. A common phrase among military aviators that means something along the lines of "absolutely fantastic."

We strapped into our Mohawks and took off. We listened for beepers on the emergency frequencies, made a few calls in the blind. Flew over the area, looking. Nothing. No luck. Two more guys gone.

A few nights later, we went to the Nail Hole, the small unit club for the pilots of the 23rd Tactical Air Support Squadron, call sign "Nail." They flew the O-2 and OV-10 forward air controller missions over Laos. We worked together a lot. Our SLAR and IR missions passed targets that they'd strike with fighter aircraft. We'd often call them toward the end of our VR flights to see if they had any lucrative targets for us to shoot before we went home. It was good to live among these compatriots and get to know those voices on the radio as faces who quickly became friends.

As we prepared to end our stay at Nakhon Phanom and return home to Phu Bai, our Nail friends gave us a memento, the Spud Gun. It was actually the Nail Gun, but our model would become the Spud Gun as soon as it got to our club. It was great fun. The apparatus involved a simple design, three beer cans, duct tape, a tennis ball, lighter fluid, and a Zippo lighter. It shot tennis balls at amazingly high rates of speed.

The Tet holiday passed. The communists had not attacked Phu Bai beyond their usual 122 mm rocket strikes and infrequent ground probes. All was well, so we bid farewell to our hosts at NKP and Ubon, started our engines, and flew back home with a whole new perspective on our business in Laos.

"Mohawk Mission"
OV-1A Mohawk in Southeast Asia
Captain Bill Reeder - 131st Aviation - October 1968-November 1969

Armed OV-1 Mohawk over southern Laos.
SOURCE: MARK KARVON ART STUDIOS, WWW.MARKKARVON.COM

Captain Bill Reeder Jr., the author, Phu Bai, Vietnam, 1969.
SOURCE: AUTHOR'S COLLECTION

Major Gary Alton, the commander, SPUD 6, "Mr. Clean."
SOURCE: ALTON FAMILY COLLECTION

Classmates: From flight school to Mohawk qualification course to Phu Bai—all together. Left to right: Jon "Sour" Lowdermilk, Joe "Sweet" Lowdermilk, Bill "Light-foot" Reeder Jr., Steve "Drop Tank" Ward, Billy "Sack Rat" Wood, Mitch "Mad Bomber" Waldran.
SOURCE: JON LOWDERMILK COLLECTION

The classmates in caricature.
SOURCE: STEVE WARD COLLECTION

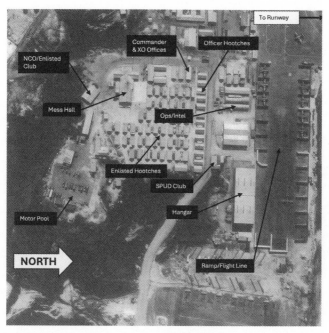

131st company area on Phu Bai Airfield, South Vietnam.
SOURCE: PUBLIC DOMAIN, US ARMY PHOTO, ANNOTATED BY AUTHOR

131st flight line and hangar.

OV-1 Mohawk with side-looking airborne radar (SLAR).

Our U-6 Beaver, SPUD 69.

Major Max Davison, OV-1 instructor pilot. My teacher, mentor, and friend. He taught me how to fly the Mohawk like no one else could. I survived Vietnam because of the flying skills he taught me and the insights he instilled.

Specialist 5 Steve Easley, technical observer.
SOURCE: STEVE EASLEY COLLECTION

Major Hank Brummett—Mohawk gun pilot extraordinaire.
SOURCE: HENRY BRUMMETT COLLECTION

Captains Burwin Reed and John Pfeiffer, Phu Bai, 1966.

The Old Gun Pilots. Left to right, back: Hank Brummett, Gary Alton, John Kelly, Harry Durgin. Front: Fox Hower, Neil Ostgaard, Mark Bellamy.

A few of the many aircraft that flew over Laos.

The Enemy Threat

North Vietnamese MIG-21 fighter.

SA-2 surface-to-air missile (SAM).

The Enemy Threat

23 mm anti-aircraft gun.

Captain John "Buick" Bingham.

Specialist 5 Bud Lacy.

The Xe Kong River, near Attapu in southern Laos—once my favorite low-level flying place. The Bolovens Plateau (and PS-38) is in the background.

Captain Frank Griswold—to whom I owe my life.

Mickey K., the CIA case officer at PS-38. Photo from two years earlier, on assignment in the Congo.

Tom N., Mickey K., General Vang Pao, and Burr S. at Long Tieng secret base in Laos.
SOURCE: MICKEY K. COLLECTION

Major Joe "Magnet Ass" Kennedy. Visual Recon Platoon Leader.

Specialist 5 Ed Shulda, intelligence analyst and aerial observer.
SOURCE: ED SHULDA COLLECTION

Big hole in Kennedy/Shulda airplane.

Joe Kennedy's big hole, April 9, 1969.
SOURCE: KENNEDY FAMILY COLLECTION

First Lieutenant Joe "Sweet" Lowdermilk surveys damage after a 37 mm hit on May 5, 1969, that wounded his aerial observer, Chief Warrant Officer Holland.
SOURCE: JOE LOWDERMILK COLLECTION

Warrant Officer 1 Curt "Astronaut" Degner. The company's infrared wizard.

Phu Bai Tower.
SOURCE: STEVE EASLEY COLLECTION

Captain Mitch "Mad Bomber" Waldran.
SOURCE: WALDRAN FAMILY COLLECTION

Last Flight Celebration. Major Fiely and Major Kennedy, carried by Lieutenant Seiden and Captain Ward.

Captain Larry "Fox" Hower.

Captain Hower's airplane after his first flight on his second tour of duty in the 131st. A 37 mm found him and took a big chunk of his tail.

CHAPTER 7

PS-38

MY TIME AT NAKHON PHANOM GAVE ME NEW PERSPECTIVES ON THE war in Laos. I better appreciated the different types of airplanes and what they did out there. I saw the risks everyone took, not just us Spuds. Sadly, we'd lost many crews. But others had, too. I still didn't know much about what was happening on the ground. More than anything, what I learned at NKP helped me discover how much more I didn't know. I'd gathered pieces of information about the CIA airlines operating in the region, but only speculative whispers about CIA ground operations. Pondering Laos brought to mind a quote by Winston Churchill. "It's a riddle wrapped in a mystery inside an enigma." What was going on there? What were all the players really doing? I wanted to know more.

That opportunity came unexpectedly on my next VR mission into the southern part of the Laotian panhandle. By that time, I had advanced to mission lead. I'd become the experienced pilot, the one who flies the lead Mohawk, analyzing, deciding, and directing every action; the guy responsible for mission success or failure; for bringing his flight team home intact. On that mission, I flew with Joe Lowdermilk on my wing. Our aerial observers joined us for the mission brief. The day's task was to photograph specified points along Routes 92 and 96 and perform visual reconnaissance along both routes and the Xe Kong River.

We strode to the aircraft, completed our preflight checks, and showed off our precision team skill with our synchronized startup and taxi out of the parking revetments. We stopped just short at the end of the runway. We positioned close to each other, two warbirds ready for whatever lay in store. I called the tower with a line I'd learned from Max. I put some swagger in my tone as I keyed the microphone. "Phu Bai tower. This is Spud 5, flight of two of the Army's finest, ready for takeoff."

"Roger, Spud flight. Cleared for takeoff."

I rolled down the runway and pulled smoothly into the sky. Joe, not far behind, quickly joined up. We flew in tight formation, Joe close under my right wing. We headed west through wispy clouds, climbing to five thousand feet, the morning sun at our backs. We passed just north of the A Shau Valley before hitting the Laotian border. My senses peaked every time I entered Laos. Yes, war raged in Vietnam, but Laos was an altogether different place. It was the lair of fire-breathing beasts, lying in wait—ready to shoot us out of the sky. I called to loosen our flight formation, and Joe fell back to trail several hundred feet behind.

I checked in with the Hillsboro airborne controller as we crested the Annamite Mountains. I avoided the highest peaks, clearing the ridgeline by a thousand feet. I took in the view to the west, beautiful in the early light, its apparent serenity deceiving. Thick green jungle rolled as a carpet over the hills and valleys as far as I could see. I began to descend to our working altitude, turning left toward our first assigned area.

I dropped to several hundred feet above Route 92, one of the major roads of the Ho Chi Minh Trail network. Joe stayed a couple thousand feet higher, ready to roll in and fire rockets, if needed. I flew down the route at a fair clip, but low enough and slow enough that I could make a good visual appraisal of the roadway and keep a lookout for trucks or supplies hidden under the jungle trees.

Route 92 wound southward, cutting through the jungle, beneath the high Annamite Mountain peaks just to the east. Bomb craters pockmarked the route as it moved down a long, relatively flat stretch of land. Key points stood out, grossly disfigured from repeated heavy strikes.

I alerted my right-seater as we approached the first photo target. He sat ready, his finger by the camera control. I lined up, turned my head, and looked down through the bug-eyed side canopy window. I could see directly below the airplane. When we were just about over the photo target, I keyed the intercom and said, "Start." The observer activated the camera, taking a series of overlapping vertical shots. "Nowww . . . stop." We had our first photos of the day.

I flew on down the road, making two more photo runs, one with forward shots from our panoramic nose camera. In those forward-looking pan shots, I had to capture both sides of the road just as it dropped into a small valley, running toward the abandoned village of Ban Bak, on a prominent bend of the upper Xe Kong River. Intel suspected a communist logistic base in the area. They hoped we'd get it on film.

The instant I finished the shots, I turned hard left and pulled the stick back into my gut, screaming for altitude. We'd taken both 23 mm and 37 mm fire from Ban Bak on past missions. I didn't want to get any closer than I had to for the photos.

Across the river, I spotted Route 96. I dropped down and followed it as it climbed out of the river valley and wound its way through the hills, southward toward Attapu.* We had two more photo targets to get. My observer made notes about the condition of the road, focusing on chokepoints and stream crossings, noting the extent of damage from recent airstrikes and the state of repair. In most instances, communist work crews fixed the worst of the damage quickly, so that trucks could again pass. They built bypasses around the most devastated spots. It was tough to close a road. Anything short of a B-52 arc-light strike had a hard time completely shutting down a route for more than a few hours.** Even then, traffic could be flowing again after only eighteen to twenty-four hours.[1] If things got too bad, the enemy shifted their trucks to another part of the trail network, sometimes miles away.

I called to my wingman. "You want the next two?"

"Roger that."

"OK, go on down. I'll climb and keep you covered."

---

* Today it is more commonly spelled Attapeu and pronounced At-ah-poe. In 1969, it was always Attapu.

** A B-52 strike, called an "Arc Light" during the Vietnam War, normally consisted of three heavy B-52 bombers, flying in formation at high altitude, each with a mixed load of up to 108 500- and 750-pound bombs. Each Arc Light strike could demolish more than three hundred football fields of ground, a rectangle 1.2 miles long by .6 miles wide, destroying and killing nearly everything on it. The NVA suffered debilitating losses due to these strikes. John T. Correll, "Arc Light," *Air Force Magazine,* January 2009.

Joe made the final two photo runs. On his last, muzzle flashes erupted.

I called, "You're taking fire. Taking fire. Get out of there."

The rounds came up behind him. Not worth expending any rockets. We might need them later if anything serious happened. He was past those meatheads by the time they started shooting. He was OK. My observer dutifully noted the position on his map and gave me the coordinates. I called the gun site to Hillsboro. A FAC could put in a flight of fighters if he didn't have anything better.

We continued our recon of Route 96 to just shy of the Cambodian border. That's where the end of the Ho Chi Minh Trail joined the upper branches of the Sihanouk Trail, funneling men and materiel northward from the communist-controlled Cambodian port of Sihanoukville on the Gulf of Thailand.

I made a sharp right turn to avoid entering forbidden Cambodian airspace. We flew west, weaving through the steeply rising mountains to get over to the Xe Kong River again, this time right where it flowed across the border into Cambodia.

We'd never taken any fire in this area, so I dropped down on the water. I loved to do that along this stretch of river, banking sharply, trying to follow the river's course as closely as I could, staying below the trees that grew along the banks whenever possible, and getting right down on the water when I could. Stupidity personified, but it was great fun.*

"You are too low, Wild Bill! Your props are making wakes in the water."

I double clicked my mic button. Two rapid clicks meant either yes or that I heard and understood the last transmission. I hugged the water, continuing to make wakes a bit longer, then pulled back hard on the stick, ballooning up and climbing for some altitude.

We flew northeast, right over the town of Attapu. The town seemed untouched by the war. I didn't see any obvious damage to the huts that formed the town. I noticed a few folks walking about, undisturbed at the

---

* I wouldn't learn until years later that was exactly where we'd lost one of our crews in 1966 (Captain Robert Nopp and PFC Marshall Kipina, both missing in action until their remains were finally recovered in 2018).

sight of an airplane. The town's main street served as the airstrip used by the clandestine CIA airlines, Air America and Continental Air Services.[2] It looked in good shape.

We'd considered Attapu as a possible landing site if ever we had an aircraft emergency in the area. Problem was, we were never quite sure who controlled the town, friendlies or Pathet Lao communist forces who'd kill us in an instant. Most of the inhabitants of Attapu were ethnic Lao. Their commitment was to the pro-western Royal Lao Government. However, a few had split loyalties, happy to support the Pathet Lao when advantageous. The tribal minorities in the surrounding countryside were a mixed bag, some pro, some con, some neutral.[3]

Attapu was a market town. It sat at an elevation of only 330 feet at a key point in the Xe Kong River basin. High terrain surrounded the broad fertile valley. Mountains rose to the east and south. The mighty Bolovens Plateau towered to more than three thousand feet, only five miles west. Many of the highland ethnic minorities on the plateau were staunchly anti-communist and aligned with the Royal Lao Government. This was the case of the Nha Heun ethnic group, living atop the eastern portion. Just below them, however, at the base of the high Boloven bluffs, lived the Oy, a tribal minority that mainly sided with the communists. All around Attapu was a perilous region of clan politics and shifting associations of convenience.[4]

I'd learned that less than 10 percent of the area population lived in the town Attapu. The majority, over 90 percent, lived in small community clusters or individual family farms. Seventy percent of the population of the region were lowlanders, mostly ethnic Lao, farming on the river basin. The remaining 30 percent, principally ethnic minorities, dwelled in the surrounding mountains. They held animist religious beliefs, feeling that animals, plants, rocks, and rivers all possessed a spiritual essence. In farming, they practiced upland agriculture, eternally rotating fields, cutting and burning ever new swaths of jungle vegetation to create fresh farm plots; a practice known as swidden farming. They hunted to supplement their harvests.[5]

From Attapu, we flew north, continuing to climb. I looked down at the seemingly peaceful settlements scattered along the west side of the river, wondering who might live there, what they did, and whose side they were on. I answered myself, *Most likely, they just want to be left alone with their farms and families.*

On previous flights, I'd seen a small airstrip atop the impressive Bolovens Plateau, now towering to our left above the river. I decided to check it out.

"Close it up. We're going to make a low pass over that strip on the plateau. Tuck in tight."

We climbed to five thousand feet, turned left, and didn't roll out until we were heading almost due south toward the strip. I started a gradual descent, gaining speed along the way. Joe's right wing was only slightly behind and below my left wing. We were close, lookin' good. We crossed the end of the airstrip, just above the treetops, at something over three hundred knots, around 350 miles per hour. It went by quickly, but I could see buildings and uniformed Laotians of some ilk. At the far end of the strip, I pitched up, turned right, and dropped back down on the treetops. I had Joe fall back a few hundred yards so that he flew a comfortable loose trail behind me. I was pretty sure everything on the Bolovens Plateau was friendly, so no worries.

A call came over the emergency radio frequency that all aircrews monitored. "Aircraft buzzing PS-38, this is Statehouse zero one."

Oh shit! I worried I'd screwed up but replied confidently. "Statehouse zero one, this is Spud 5. Hope you enjoyed the show."

"Roger that, Spud. Come by any time. You can give me a call on 121.5."

"Roger, Statehouse. See you again."

I transmitted to Joe. "Sounds like an American."

"Yeah, I'm sure he is."

The airstrip showed on our map as Ban Konghang. I asked my observer to mark it as PS-38. I suspected it was some sort of a clandestine base and that I'd spoken to the CIA agent running the operation. During our stay at Nakhon Phanom, I'd heard stories of CIA involvement in the civil war raging in Laos.

Our own work for MACV was all classified, and our missions into Laos secret. We knew of American Special Forces teams inserted into

Laos by MACV-SOG.* We saw and spoke with Air America pilots flying the skies over Laos, rumored to be the CIA's airline. And there was that strange assortment of airplanes and helicopters parked on the ramp at NKP, each involved in its own secret missions all over the country of Laos. I'd seen aircraft fly in there with US markings, Laotian markings, Thai markings, or no markings at all.

I wondered what all the secrecy was for. North Vietnam knew what we were doing. Their communist Pathet Lao cronies knew as well. We were bombing the hell out of them. Royal Lao forces were fighting them with tons of American equipment and supplies, delivered by American airplanes, albeit "civilian" Air America and Continental Air Services aircraft. So, what was the secret? I suspected just to keep all this from the American people and possibly even from a more specific audience, Congress.

I'd only learn much later that it was also to maintain the charade of the 1962 International Agreement on the Neutrality of Laos in which all parties recognized the neutrality of Laos and agreed to withdraw foreign forces from the country.[6]

Laos's problems began with the French colonization of Indochina in the late nineteenth century. Even before then, Laos endured pressure from its powerful neighbors, seeing its boundaries wax and wane over the centuries. Laos had reached its peak of territory, power, and prestige in the mid-1600s as the Kingdom of Lan Xang. The kingdom splintered after the monarch, Souligna Vongsathe, died without an heir. Over the two centuries that followed, Thai, Vietnamese, Burmese, and Chinese armies invaded and ransacked the land, taking slaves and expanding their own boundaries.[7]

France came to the rescue in 1893, reuniting much of the former kingdom and reinstating the monarchy, placing the land under its

---

* MACV-SOG. Military Assistance Command Vietnam—Studies and Observations Group. An innocuous name for a highly classified group of special operations personnel. One mission was to insert small teams into Laos to perform surveillance along the Ho Chi Minh Trail, and to conduct raids and prisoner snatches. A SOG recon team (RT) normally consisted of three American Special Forces and eight to ten indigenous tribal fighters.

protection as a part of French Indochina.* That only doomed Laotians to France's colonial exploitation of resources and labor while enduring a massive French program to populate Laos with Vietnamese immigrants. Ethnic Vietnamese soon became the majority population of every Laotian city, save the royal seat of Luang Prabang.

After World War II, an independence organization formed, the Lao People's Revolutionary Army, popularly known as the Pathet Lao, or Lao Nation. The Pathet Lao was a communist political movement allied with Vietnam's similar, but more powerful, Viet Minh. Together, they fought the French, seeking independence for both countries as communist states. They won. With mounting setbacks in Vietnam, France granted nominal independence to Laos in 1953, and the Royal Lao Government took control of the country. However, the Pathet Lao controlled large segments of territory, principally in the thinly populated east. Nonetheless, it carried much broader sway by piggybacking on the communist Viet Minh's influence over Laos's large urban Vietnamese populations. They worked together through the Indochinese Communist Party.

The Viet Minh defeated the French soundly in Vietnam the following year. Negotiations in Geneva led to agreements ending the war with France. The 1954 Geneva Conference dismantled French Indochina and formally granted independence to Laos, Vietnam, and Cambodia. But turmoil would long embroil all three.

The Geneva Agreement divided Vietnam at the 17th parallel with a three-mile-wide demilitarized zone on either side. A communist government, under Ho Chi Minh, controlled the North. A flawed democratic government ruled the South. Free popular elections were to be held in 1956 to unify the temporarily partitioned country. Ho Chi Minh's government violated the treaty terms on several counts. The government in the South announced it would therefore not participate in the 1956 elections. They claimed the elections would be far from free, ensuring a communist victory. Conflict ensued.

------

* French Indochina. Established in 1887 as an expanding federation of French colonial entities in mainland Southeast Asia. It included Vietnam (as three territories: Tonkin, Annam, and Cochinchina), Cambodia, and after 1893, Laos.

The United States saw danger in allowing the region to fall to communism. Americans felt a threat to their very existence based on post–World War II communist successes in China and North Korea on top of the Soviet Union's chokehold on Eastern Europe and the appearance of "subversive" communist parties in the West. America believed communism posed a monolithic threat, orchestrated from Moscow, bent on a global domination through revolution. And the Soviets had the atomic bomb since 1949. American leaders believed in a domino theory threatening to topple governments across Southeast Asia and beyond if the peril wasn't stopped in Vietnam and kept out of Laos. President Eisenhower sent money, weapons, and advisors as battles erupted across South Vietnam. The president also aided the Royal Lao Government with money and, later, American Special Forces advisors.

As South Vietnam strengthened its defenses below the demilitarized zone, North Vietnam sought alternative routes to supply and reinforce its military efforts. It looked west to Laos where it already had a significant military presence in the eastern regions. Partnering with its Pathet Lao allies, it began construction of the Ho Chi Minh Trail network.

In 1959, North Vietnam invaded Laos with more than thirty thousand troops. The Pathet Lao, refusing efforts to incorporate them into the Royal Lao Army, joined with the North Vietnamese Army in attacks against Laotian government forces all along the Lao–North Vietnamese border. They had successes against the Royal Lao Army, staying to occupy their gains. The United States increased aid. North Vietnam sent more troops and boosted work on building and defending their Ho Chi Minh Trail network. Thus began the Laotian civil war.

The conflict escalated. The Soviet Union got directly involved, supplying heavy weapons. North Vietnam increased its troop levels. Communist advances accelerated. The United States began delivering arms, including T-6 attack aircraft to the Royal Lao Air Force. The new Kennedy administration ramped up support. The American government initiated a covert air campaign with American pilots flying B-26 bombers from Thailand to support the Royal Lao Army and Hmong tribal guerrilla forces. Air America set up shop at Udorn Royal Thai Airbase to support Special Forces activities in Laos, as well as resupply Royal Lao forces.

Thailand became a pipeline for the delivery of helicopters and quantities of artillery, along with providing training teams and commando units for sensitive special operations. The CIA became more active in conducting supportive covert activities.

All soon came to a head. In 1960, communist forces had overrun the capital city, Vientiane. Royalist forces launched a counterattack from the south. The Soviet Union conducted a massive airlift into Vientiane, their largest since World War II. Thai commandos launched operations into Laos. The United States deployed bombers from Taiwan to Thailand, alerted a carrier task group, and put an airborne brigade on alert. The Royal Lao Army pushed the insurgents from the capital, driving them onto the Plain of Jars, more than a hundred miles north, and then pushed them still farther north. In response, North Vietnam escalated the deployment of combat units across their border.

The opening days of 1961 began with the North Vietnamese Army attacking far to the west, running the Royal Lao Army off the Plain of Jars. The Soviet Union expanded its delivery of heavy weapons. The US and Thai weapons deliveries also increased, including more attack airplanes and helicopters. Air America received additional aircraft and upgraded its facilities at Udorn. The United States established a formal Military Assistance Advisory Group (MAAG) in Laos, staffed by uniformed military personnel. American Special Forces advisors put on their uniforms.

Then the Bay of Pigs happened in April. Cuban dictator Fidel Castro soundly defeated the invasion of his island by a CIA-trained force of fourteen hundred Cuban refugees. The disaster caused the administration to rethink its strategy in Laos. The United States sought a ceasefire to be followed by an international agreement creating a neutral and independent Laos. Negotiations dragged on into 1962 before finally achieving success. All the while, the CIA expanded its role, forming thousands of Hmong tribesmen into a clandestine army under the leadership of a young, impressive, and brilliantly ambitious Hmong major, soon to rise to the rank of general, Vang Pao. The CIA also succeeded in developing additional tribal guerrilla forces in other parts of the country, including the lower Laotian panhandle.

On July 23, 1962, fourteen nations signed the Declaration on the Neutrality of Laos. Six of the most significant were the Soviet Union, China, North Vietnam, South Vietnam, Thailand, and the United States. The international agreement formed a three-part coalition government with pro-American, pro-communist, and neutral factions. The agreement required the withdrawal of all foreign troops, both regular and irregular, as well as foreign paramilitary formations. Thus ended the Laotian civil war—but only on paper.

The United States complied with the treaty. The communists did not. The Laotian civil war continued with barely a pause. The North Vietnamese Army stayed in place, expanding their forces, not withdrawing any, building the Ho Chi Minh Trail logistics network, defending it with combat forces and growing numbers of anti-aircraft weapons; pushing manpower, munitions, and supplies to their army in South Vietnam; and actively supporting the Pathet Lao's fight against the neutralist government.

The United States, wanting to appear in compliance with the 1962 agreement, answered with a covert CIA-run military campaign orchestrated from the US embassy in Vientiane, Laos. It was run by CIA case officers deployed in the field across the country. Air America and Continental Air Services supported their fighters. A variety of American and Thai aircrews, as well as brave and aggressive Royal Laotian Air Force pilots, provided aerial bombardment and close air support. The effort focused on supplying, training, and advising Royal Laotian forces along with the Hmong Clandestine Army and other indigenous guerrillas fighting against communist adversaries. At the same time, America publicly denied any military involvement in the country. We knew the North Vietnamese stayed in Laos in violation of the Geneva agreement, that they had the backing and logistical support of the Soviet Union and China. North Vietnam, the Soviet Union, and China knew Americans were on the ground in Laos and that American war planes dropped tons of bombs in support of Royal Lao operations and to interdict the Ho Chi Minh Trail. But the charade went on—and our secret missions were part of it.

We stayed low, skimming across the treetops. I detected a shallow valley leading north. We dropped into it. The valley became a gorge, the sides steepening as we continued down the streambed. The gorge ran perpendicular into a good-sized canyon. I was looking straight ahead at a granite wall with one of the most magnificent waterfalls I'd ever seen. *God, that's gorgeous.* With little time to react, I slammed the stick hard against my knee, rocking up on my right wing. My Mohawk's belly faced the falls as I made the sharp turn down the canyon. I counted myself lucky that I hadn't splattered us onto the rock cliff standing solidly behind the stunning waterfall. My observer only grinned in delight. My wingman stayed well back and a bit higher, watching the insanity unfold before him. After making his own turn into the canyon, he brought his Mohawk down, falling in behind me. We all took in the majesty of so many spectacular falls cascading down the cliff faces beside us. We popped out of the bottom of the canyon, right back on the Xe Kong River, about fifty miles above where we'd started at the Cambodian border.

We climbed for altitude and pointed toward home. On the way, we checked in with a forward air controller and expended our rockets on something he'd seen along a hillside. The place had already been obliterated by bombs. Only a small cluster of trees remained in a slight hollow. He marked the target with one white phosphorous rocket.* Joe and I made three quick rocket runs, taking a good bit of fire on the first, then none. The FAC gave us credit for a dozen enemy soldiers killed and two trucks and a gun destroyed. We flew on back to Phu Bai, content with the day.

---

* A projectile making a large, bright incendiary flash on impact, scattering white-hot fiery material, and leaving a big puff of smoke. Historically used for marking targets and setting smoke screens. White phosphorus causes severe penetrating burns on human skin. It keeps burning as long as exposed to oxygen and is therefore difficult to extinguish. Because of this, US military policy restricted its use against targets where civilians might be affected. It was not formally banned by international treaty, however.

CHAPTER 8

Thank God and Martin-Baker

I RETURNED TO PS-38 OFTEN. EVERY TIME I FOUND MYSELF IN THE neighborhood, I got in the habit of flying low along the Xe Kong River then climbing to gain altitude above the rim of the Bolovens Plateau. Once high enough, I'd make a U-turn and dive down to buzz the strip. I always ended with a steep right turn on the treetops, departing west. I picked up the shallow valley I'd discovered, followed it north to the canyon. I admired the magnificent waterfall as I cranked my Mohawk hard to the right, dropped down into the canyon, and spit out back over the Xe Kong. I'd then climb and go back about my business.

We talked to the American, call sign "Statehouse 01," anytime he was on the site. On learning our capabilities, he asked if we could get some photos of a couple of areas for him. We obliged, got the film developed, and dropped the prints to him the next day. We rolled them into a long, cylindrical film canister. We delivered it via a drop-chute in the cockpit floor as we flew low over the airstrip. I saw the American looking on. He was thrilled.

Toward the end of February, I was at it again. My flight school classmate, Mitch Waldran, flew my wing. Our mission assignment took us to Area Foxtrot, quite near where the boundaries of Laos, South Vietnam, and Cambodia came together. Thus, its name, the Tri-Border.

It was a pleasant day, clear weather with unlimited visibility. We'd not taken enemy fire either, at least none we knew of. On completing our photo and reconnaissance assignments, I gave Mitch a call.

"Hey, how 'bout a run up the Xe Kong and a pass by PS-38?"

Waldran responded enthusiastically. He was game for anything. "Roger. Let's go."

We came upon the river slightly north of the Cambodian border. I settled right down on the water, happily churning wakes with my prop wash.

Mitch shouted on the radio. "Shit, Wild Bill! Did you see that?"

"See what?"

"That cable you just flew under."

"No way. You shittin' me?"

"No, sir. You just flew under one big fucking cable strung across the river."

I was so low I flew right under it and didn't see it. Must have been strung between high trees. I figured the bad guys had seen my screw-off river runs and decided to snag themselves a dumb pilot and his airplane. I knew I was lucky to be alive. Stupidity personified. And my poor observer. He trusted me and enjoyed my antics. Childish games that could have gotten us both killed. I never flew low along a river again. I think I grew up a lot that day.

Young men facing death mock it. They taunt it, feeling invulnerable. I was not far past adolescence when I got to Vietnam, only twenty-two. I'd been given an agile flying machine with rockets to shoot and loads of excitement to be had. Things happened, sure. People got killed, yeah. But not me. Death stalked the other guy. Nothing would happen to me.

That all changed that day on the Xe Kong River. I was shocked into manhood at the ripe old age of twenty-three. I was not invincible. I was nearly killed. But for the grace of God, that cable could have sliced right through the cockpit. It should have. I was damn lucky. I knew it. I would always remain an aggressive young pilot, doing what needed to be done in war. But I'd never be so stupidly juvenile again. I felt I'd changed when I landed back at Phu Bai.

The flight schedule board hung on the wall in operations. The board listed the next day's missions. The operations officer, Frank Griswold, got the crew assignments from the platoon leaders, and he or I hung the name tags next to the scheduled mission taskings on the board. One of us would sort out any conflicts between SLAR, IR, and VR require-ments when they arose. Steve Ward, the maintenance officer, posted the airplanes he selected for each mission. His task was to manage the hours flown, so each airplane went into the hangar for its required servicing on a schedule that kept enough flyable aircraft available each day to meet mission requirements. When we brought one back shot full of holes, that torpedoed his plan and made him most disagreeable.

I worked near the entrance to ops, not far from the flight schedule board. The front of my desk butted up to the front of the flight operations specialist's desk. We faced each other. He maintained all crew member flight records, completed reports for signature, and did whatever typing needed to be done. A large safe and several file cabinets lined the wall behind him. The operations sergeant had a desk in the back right corner of the office, opposite the operations officer's larger workspace in the left rear. There was a door between the two. It was one of two entrances to the intelligence section. The other was outside, on the other side of our small ops-intel complex. A sandbagged wall topped with barbed wire surrounded the buildings and a connected van. Our missions were, after all, highly classified.

Griswold's phone rang. I glanced over to see him take the call and smile. He hung up the phone, walked to the schedule board, and picked up some name tags to post.

He grinned. "Just talked to Major Kennedy. You're flying with me on tomorrow's VR."

I barely looked up, deep into a crash writing project. "That's great. Thanks."

"Tomorrow's Friday," he reminded me.

"Oh, Friday!" I perked up. I'd forgotten what day it was. "Overnight in Ubon. Shit hot."

"Thought you'd like that. Buick and 'Sour' Lowdermilk have the other VR, so they'll be there with us."

He reached up to hang the nametags. "Oh, and your observer is a crew chief, Specialist Armstrong. He's been working his ass off, putting in lots of long hours. Steve Ward wants to reward him with a trip to

Thailand. You can go over the camera procedures and ejection seat stuff with him this afternoon."

"Will do."

We took off at nine in the morning on February 28. Since I had an inexperienced observer, we took the southern mission, leaving the more intense anti-aircraft threats around Tchepone and the mountain passes to the other team. I flew lead this first day. We'd swap for the return home tomorrow. We had a good mission. The sun shone brightly in the blue sky. All went well. We completed all assigned tasks. We didn't see or hear any enemy fire. We landed at Ubon and went through the standard post-mission drill. We released our two aerial observers to make their way to town and enjoy their evening. They'd meet us back at the aircraft at eight o'clock the next morning.

As we walked from the flight line, I noted the big AC-130 "Spectre" gunships on the ramp. They called Ubon home. Each one looked menacing; big aerial battleships painted a ghostly black with deadly guns sticking out their sides.

We strode past a parked B-57. Not a common site at Ubon. They were based at Phan Rang Airbase in South Vietnam, their unit affectionately known as the Doom Pussy Squadron. They used the call sign "Yellow Bird." The airplanes were sleek twin-engine jet bombers, sitting low to the ground. They did airstrikes over Laos with some of the aircraft specially equipped to fly and find targets at night. This one had limped to Ubon for an emergency landing after taking a 37 mm hit in the tail. It left a large hole in the horizontal stabilizer. *How did this thing keep flying? Lucky crew.* My shoulders shuddered as I walked by. I shook my head.

We met our observers at base operations the next morning to go over the day's tasks. I reviewed everything with Armstrong in detail. He'd done well the day before, but I wanted to be sure things were fresh in his mind, especially after the night on the town I was sure our guys had. Once again, Buick and Jon Lowdermilk would take the northern section of Steel Tiger while Frank and I had the south. They took off first. We followed a few minutes later, me flying Frank's wing.

On the way to take our first photos, we flew over the decimated town of Ban Thateng just off the northern edge of the Bolovens. There, Routes 16 and 23 intersected. The town was a key to controlling access onto the plateau. I recalled an earlier mission to the place when I was summoned for close air support. In mid-January, Hillsboro called our flight, asking if we could respond to a request from a Raven forward air controller* for emergency air support.[1] We were the closest armed aircraft. We agreed. I flew as Frank Griswold's wingman on that mission, as well.

Once we got the call on that January mission, we turned southwest and pushed up the speed. Frank checked in with the FAC. He apprised us of the situation. A Royal Laotian unit secured the town, but communist Pathet Lao, reinforced by regular North Vietnamese, attacked from the east. Enemy mortars rained down and probing attacks had begun.

We arrived to see mortar explosions and burning huts. Wafts of smoke met, joining as a single grey column rising in the sky. The Raven fired rockets, marking the places we were to hit. We made several passes at different targets. We expended our last rockets and turned toward home just as two T-28s showed up with bombs. I heard later that our strike slowed the initial attack, buying time until the T-28s got there. The friendlies held and the attack ended—at least for the moment.[2]

Ownership of Ban Thateng seesawed after that. I wasn't at all sure who controlled the ground as we flew over on March 1. Looking down, I saw only blackened ruins of a once thriving community. We pressed on.

Our reconnaissance began at the southern end of Route 96 where the Ho Chi Minh Trail and Sihanouk Trail merge. That was about forty miles east of Attapu. We worked north from there, completing photo runs and noting the road conditions. Specialist Armstrong did well operating the cameras. Though he had not a clue where we were on the map. He also kept his stomach under control, which was sometimes difficult for right-seaters on VR missions. The rapid climbs and descents and

---

* Ravens were volunteer US Air Force fighter pilots serving as forward air controllers for covert operations in Laos. They flew small single-engine propeller airplanes, the same type O-1 Bird Dog aircraft flown by the Army Catkillers, next door to us at Phu Bai. The Raven planes were unmarked. The pilots wore civilian clothes and carried identification issued by innocuous civilian agencies. They worked under the direction of the US embassy in Vientiane, not the United States Air Force.

abrupt turns to line up photos or jink away from anti-aircraft fire got to a lot of guys. Armstrong hung in there.

We'd been asked to look for improvements along a road running east from Chavane. We found lots of fresh roadwork. The communists obviously intended this to be a major throughway from the Route 96 north-south spine of the Ho Chi Minh Trail, to funnel supplies to the North Vietnamese Army and Viet Cong guerrillas inside South Vietnam.

Frank dropped down for a closer look and to get some low-level photos. I stayed high, keeping him in sight, ready to pounce if he drew fire. As he pulled up, he announced, "There's a bunch of fuel drums stacked under the trees on the south side of the road. Got good photos. I'm going to put some rockets on 'em and see what we get. Cover me. Then, come in behind and hit 'em. I'll cover you."

"Roger."

Frank rolled in, fired a pair, then another before pulling up. His rockets hit and exploded, detonating bigger explosions. Flames erupted and roared through the trees. I followed.

I keyed my radio. "Nice stuff, lead! I'm in."

"Hit about a hundred yards short of mine. To the west. I saw more stuff there."

"Roger."

I did a slow wingover, letting the nose of my Mohawk fall steeply toward earth before leveling my wings, lined up on the target. I fired two pairs of rockets. The tree line burst into flame.

"That's enough, Wild Bill. Let's save our rockets. We've still got the rest of the mission to fly."

"Roger. Looks like we did plenty of damage here."

I fell into loose trail, a few hundred feet behind Frank as we climbed, heading north. I relaxed, congratulating myself—*Nice strike. We did good.*

WHAM! An explosion rocked the aircraft. I saw a bright flash to my right, heard the boom, felt the concussion—all in the same instant. The airplane snapped onto its left side then rolled violently back to the right. Fragments tore into the cockpit, ripping superficially into our flesh. Debris whirled about. Flames blazed outside. Smoke billowed inside, foul in my nostrils with the smell of burning fuel and hydraulic fluid. Chaos engulfed my consciousness. My senses overwhelmed. Reality became so unreal.

I arm-wrestled the stick in the fight of my life. I pulled the power back on the right engine and then the lever that feathered the propeller. I struggled to get the thing flying. Caution lights flashed. Instruments tumbled. The number two fire light glowed red. I glanced right, past Armstrong. He stared straight ahead, terrified. *Poor guy.* Flames engulfed the wing. I pushed my foot hard against the rudder pedal, slipping the airplane away from the flames. I pulled the fire handle, stopping fuel flow to the right engine. I hit the fire bottle switch, activating both extinguishers. The flames stopped.

I looked at remnants of what had been my right engine. The propeller was gone, the engine cover blown away; only a few smoking parts remained. The wing was a mess of holes. We needed to get the hell out of there, away from bad guy territory, and we needed to land soon. I turned southwest and headed for PS-38, the nearest safe haven.

I called Frank. I spoke as calmly as I could so I'd be clearly understood.

"5, this is 6. We took a hit. I think 37 mm. Barely flyable. Turning southwest, trying to get to PS-38."

"Roger. Coming around to find you." A few seconds later. "Got you. I'll come give you a close look. Can you hold steady?"

"Not able to maintain altitude. Single engine. Damage to right wing. Every time I try to level off, the plane starts to roll onto its back. Have to stay in a descent to keep up airspeed."

"Roger. I'm making mayday calls to get things moving. We'll get a rescue package cranking just in case."

I quickly saw that I couldn't make it to PS-38. I wouldn't have enough altitude. I'd be below the elevation of the Bolovens Plateau before I got there. I set my hopes on an alternate, almost the same distance but over two thousand feet lower.

"I'm not going to make PS-38. I'll be too low. Turning toward Saravane."

"Roger, I'm on you. Doesn't look good. You've got holes all over your right side. I don't see an engine. Just a gaping space. Your entire right wing leading edge is shredded."

"Roger."

I flew northwest, steadily losing altitude. I crossed the Xe Kong River, seeking the lowest ground, following a valley that seemed to be leading toward the Saravane. Frank confirmed my course in between making emergency radio calls. He worked to get a rescue package going. That would normally be a Jolly Green search and rescue helicopter covered by a flight of A-1 Skyraider attack planes. Still, I planned to land on the airstrip at Saravane. I prayed that it remained in friendly hands. Frank would hopefully be able to confirm that before I got there.

When I made my next call, that concern was no longer an issue. "We're not going to make it to Saravane. Losing altitude too fast. I'll get as far west as I can before we punch out."

"Roger. I've got you in sight."

I talked to Armstrong. "We're not going to be able to land anywhere. We'll have to eject. Get ready. Remember to grab the upper handle with both hands and pull down hard toward your knees when I give you the command. Don't worry about the canopy. We'll go through it."

The Mohawk did not have command ejection. In other words, I could not eject both of us. We'd each have to fire our own seat. Armstrong reached up and held the upper firing handle with both hands, waiting. The jungle rose quickly. A few hundred feet above the ground, I keyed the mic and said, "Eject, eject, eject." Armstrong sat there.

We always told our observers that if we ever had to eject, we'd give the command three times, then they'd be sitting there by themselves, starring at an empty space where their pilot used to be because we'd be gone. Easier said than done.

I don't know why Armstrong didn't go. I thought he'd just frozen. But if I'd pushed the mic switch to radio instead of intercom, perhaps he didn't hear me. Regardless, he sat there.

I held the stick in my left hand, turned toward him and pounded his shoulder with my right. As we approached the trees, I pulled back on the stick. The Mohawk slowed and began to roll right, settling into the treetops. With branches slapping across the windshield in front of him, Armstrong finally pulled his handle and left the airplane. In one motion, I let go of the stick, reached up with both hands, and pulled my handle.

Problem was, my head was still cocked to the right, my neck bent slightly when I went out.

The ejection seat trainer gave quite a jolt when we'd used it in the qualification course in Alabama. The instructor, Mr. Meadows, told us that was nothing, though. The trainer used only a small charge that gave us about 7 Gs. He told us an actual ejection would fire us out at 18 Gs. That's eighteen times the force of gravity.

The ejection seat in the Mohawk was a Martin-Baker Mk5, first produced for the Navy in 1957. It employed an ejection gun. Bang, and you shot out at eighty feet per second. Later seats would employ rocket technology, delivering less jarring acceleration. The Mk5 was a cannon. It was a good seat with an excellent safety record. It had limits, though. The parameters for a zero-altitude ejection called for a level attitude and ninety knots airspeed. By the time I got out, we were coming through the trees, falling below eighty knots, and in about a sixty-degree right bank.[3]

When I pulled my upper ejection handle, it brought a fabric screen down over my head. I remember the blast and the punch of eighteen instantaneous Gs, of momentarily blacking out, seeing green foliage, feeling the jerk of the parachute, and hitting the ground with a thud. There was not time for full chute deployment or even a single swing under the canopy. But I was alive.

It worked. Thank God. And thank you, Martin-Baker.

I got out of the parachute and surveyed my situation. How strange for a pilot to sit in a cockpit one instant, as messed up as that was, then suddenly be on the ground in such a strange, foreboding place. It was the most unreal sensation I'd ever had.

RATA-TAT-TAT, RATA-TAT-TAT. Machine gun fire! I heard voices in the distance, shouting, screaming. I pulled my .38-caliber revolver from the holster on my hip. I held it, looked at it. *Six shots. Then fumble to load six more bullets, one at a time. No way! This will not be another Custer's Last Stand.* I stuck the pistol back in its holster and pulled the radio from my survival vest. I extended the antenna and transmitted.

"Spud 5, this is 6 on guard."

"Six, this is 5. I have you loud and clear. Are you OK?"

Phew. Got comms. I sighed in relief. "Yeah, I'm OK."

"Listen to me. I'm going to fly over you. I want you to move in that direction as quickly as you can."

"Will do."

Frank made a low pass over me. That was the direction I needed to go. I heard more gunfire. Voices closer. I called him again. "I've got bad guys down here. They're shooting at me. Sounds like they're shooting at you, too."

"Roger. There's a village in the opposite direction from where I'm sending you. I saw people coming out with weapons. Keep going."

I moved as fast as I could. I was a bit busted up, but confident I could get through the jungle faster than the small guys chasing me. I broke into a run, crashing through the undergrowth.

Frank turned sharply, just above the trees. I heard his rockets fire. Felt them impact a short distance behind me. He made two more runs before climbing to a safer altitude. That slowed the enemy and bought me time.

It seemed like forever, but it was less than an hour before Frank had good news. "I've got a helicopter inbound. Should only be a few minutes out. See if you can find a break in the trees and move to it."

"Roger. I'm looking. How's my right seat?"

"No comms yet. We've been trying. We've got a good fix on his chute though."

A moment later, he called again. "Chopper is close. He'll call you on this freq."

Soon, I heard, "Spud 6, this is Pony Express. We see your crash site and parachute. We are looking in the direction your wingman said you are moving. Can you pop smoke?"

"Roger. Popping smoke now."

I took a smoke marker from my survival vest, removed the cap and pulled the pin. It spewed smoke.

"This is Pony Express. I've got orange smoke."

"That's me. I confirm orange smoke."

"Roger, Spud. We are dropping a penetrator through the trees. Just lower the seat and grab hold. We'll pull you up."

I'd never seen anything like it before. The Army did not have survival training on par with the Navy and Air Force. I had no idea what to expect. A metal cylinder came through the trees at the end of a steel cable. It hit the ground. I went to it, pried down a hinged flat arm and stood by. I called on my survival radio, "Ready."

As the penetrator lifted, I sat on the arm, hugging the cylinder. I grabbed hold of the cable with my right hand. It continued to rise. I held on tight. I got close to the helicopter. It was a Huey, not a Jolly Green. A crew member leaned out the open door and screamed, "Let go of the cable! You'll smash your fingers. Hold around the penetrator."

I did and watched as the part of the cable I'd clung to, just above the top of the cylinder, rolled up into a pulley. That would have been nasty.

The one who'd been yelling, a big burley guy, grabbed hold of me and pulled me inside. The seats had been removed from the backend; just open space remained. I collapsed on the bare floor, thankful to be alive.

The crew member shouted, "We see your other pilot. We're coming around to get him."

He kicked me with his foot to get my attention and handed me an M-16 rifle. "Here, take this and shoot out the left side. We're taking fire." I complied.

Small arms and machine guns sent tracers zipping by. Frank gave close air support with rockets as the helicopter crew called enemy positions to him. The pilot held steady as he flew the helicopter toward Armstrong.

Apparently, my crewmate had not moved far from his parachute. He had problems with the radio and could not figure out the smoke marker. Luckily, he'd come down beside a small clearing and moved to it. When he saw the helicopter, he stepped into the open and waved his arms. The crew saw him on their final approach to get me. There'd be room to land.

After they'd hauled me on board, they circled back. They picked him up in a jiffy, pulled in power and headed west. A second helicopter, which had remained high, fell into trail and followed. I stopped shooting and sat with my back against the rear bulkhead, breathing deeply and smiling at young Armstrong, so thankful he'd been saved, so grateful we were both alive.

The Huey flew to the military hospital on Ubon Airbase, a little over an hour distant. Along the way, my savior gave me his helmet so I could speak with the cockpit. I thanked the pilots about eight times. I so appreciated them risking their lives to save ours. The pilot told me his unit was the US Air Force 20th Special Operations Squadron. They were stationed at Udorn Royal Thai Airbase, 170 miles northwest of Ubon. They flew both H-3 and UH-1 helicopters on covert special operations into Laos. Their aircraft bore no US markings. Their uniforms had no insignia to identify their rank or nationality. This crew happened to be working on a communications site in the Laotian panhandle. They heard Frank's mayday calls and responded. Good thing because the formal rescue package was still some distance away. I knew I owed my life to the Pony Express.[4]

Medics met us on the hospital pad at Ubon. They put us on stretchers and wheeled us in. After X-rays and exams, the doctor sent me to a ward with orders to stay in bed. The diagnosis: cervical compression with a cervical sprain, along with a bunch of cuts and bruises and bad hair. A medical technician put a neck collar on me and took me to the ward. On arrival, two nursing assistants cleaned my wounds, gave me a sponge bath, and transferred me onto a nice clean hospital bed. I lay there numb. *Hell of a day. Hope Armstrong's going to be OK. Where's Frank?*

Frank Griswold had stayed on station too long. He covered me with rocket fire and slowed the bad guys so I could get away. He wouldn't leave the scene until Armstrong and I had been rescued. He provided close air support to the rescue helicopter throughout. By then, he was about out of gas. He didn't have enough to get back to Vietnam or to Thailand. He headed to PS-38. As he approached, he called on the radio. An American voice assured him that the strip was in friendly hands and told him the wind direction and speed. He also warned of the rough undulating runway surface. Frank landed at the small airstrip on fumes. He noticed fifty-five-gallon drums on pallets by the side of the runway. He taxied there and parked.

Groups of Laotians in military uniforms gathered round. Frank hoped they were, indeed, friendly. He breathed easier when he saw a tall westerner emerge to greet him as he climbed out of the airplane. His observer stayed nervously in the cockpit.

"Hi, I'm Mickey, how can we help you?"

Frank put out his hand. "I'm Frank, Frank Griswold, Captain United States Army."

They shook hands. Frank said, "My wingman got shot down. Hope he's OK. Was just rescued. But I'm outa' gas. Can you help?"

"Can do. We'll have to hand pump it out of the drums though. You parked in the right spot."

Frank climbed onto the Mohawk and opened the fuel port. A Laotian soldier held up a fuel nozzle at the end of a barely long enough hose. Frank stepped onto the wing, reached down, and took it. He got back on top of the airplane and held the nozzle in place while the young soldier worked away on the hand pump stuck into the top of a barrel. It took a while, but they pumped enough fuel to get him home.

Done refueling, Mickey and Frank talked a few minutes.

"Can I offer you a beer?"

"No thanks. I don't dare. I'm flying."

"How about a Coke?"

"A Coke, yeah. Thanks. And one for my observer?"

"Sure. Comin' up."

Mickey nodded to the guerrilla soldier by his side. "Two Cokes."

The young Laotian responded, "Can do to do!"

He disappeared and soon scampered back with two cold cans. He handed one to the observer, who by that time had climbed out of the airplane to pee. He gave the other to Frank, who shook his head in disbelief.

Frank downed the soft drink while he and Mickey chatted. He learned that Mickey was the CIA case officer for a group of Laotian fighters based at PS-38. He'd only just arrived, so he wasn't the American we'd been working with at the site over the past weeks. His responsibilities included a Laotian Special Guerrilla Unit based there. Local Nha Heun tribesmen filled the ranks of the SGU. They looked like tough warriors. That's about all the information Frank gleaned, but he was impressed by the tall American and his dedication to his task, there at the end of the world on the edge of the Bolovens Plateau. Frank handed Mickey the empty can with a big "thank you." He took off and made it back to Phu Bai.

Two old friends came to my ward the next afternoon, Buick and Frank. Major Alton had them fly a Mohawk from Phu Bai to check on me to be sure I was OK. They walked to my hospital bed with Irene, the lovely young bartender from the officers' club. The club was only a short distance away. They carried a bottle of champagne and four glasses. The ward nurse turned her head, pretending not to see. Frank popped the cork, filled the glasses, and made a toast. "Here's to you, Lightfoot." We all four drank and Irene gave me a big kiss.

"Wait. Lightfoot? What's that about?"

"That is about you outrunning the bad guys through the jungle for almost an hour. No more Wild Bill. You are now, and forevermore, Lightfoot of the Spuds."

CHAPTER 9

Rest and Recuperation

THE DOCTOR RELEASED SPECIALIST ARMSTRONG FROM THE HOSPITAL the next day. He kept me a while longer because of my injuries. The day I finally got discharged, Gary Alton sent Mitch Waldran in a Mohawk to pick me up. We flew back to Phu Bai at altitude. Mitch asked how I felt being back in the airplane. I had no qualms.

"I'm fine. Ready to get back on missions."

And I was. It felt good to be in a Mohawk cockpit again. I wanted to return to flight duties as soon as I could. I wanted back in A-model gunships. I had a few rockets I needed to shoot on top of an enemy 37 mm gun pit near Chavane.

We landed at Phu Bai and taxied off the runway. Major Alton had formed the entire unit on the ramp. He stood at the front with a soldier holding the company guidon. As we came abreast, he snapped everyone to attention and brought them to a smart salute. I opened my canopy and saluted back. Their eyes stayed on me. Their care touched my heart. Overwhelmed, emotion rose inside me. My eyes filled with tears. I'd come home.

I climbed out. Champagne flowed. Handshakes and greetings followed. The guys from the seat shop came up. They were the ones who maintained our ejection seats, inspected the explosive charges, and packed the parachutes. Their sergeant proudly handed me an upper ejection seat handle with its attached face curtain, just like the one I'd pulled to punch out of my airplane. Each of the guys had signed the inside of the curtain. A memento I'd cherish forever.

Next stop, the Spud Club. But I was hurting. I wore a brace on my neck. I was still on meds. So, I enjoyed a Coke, chatted for a short while, and headed to my hootch.

First thing the next day, I trotted off to the flight surgeon to get my "up slip," my permission to return to flight duties. "Not so fast," he said. "I'm sending you to the hospital to see an orthopedic surgeon. When he clears you, I'll give you an up slip."

Real fucking fine, I thought.

I saw the orthopod at the 22nd Surgical Hospital, there on the base. He told me that even though nothing was broken, he had concern about my injuries and how well I might recover. He told me to stay in the neck brace, continue meds, do nothing, and come back in two weeks. I showed up a week later, told him I felt fine, and asked for release from any restrictions. He had me move my head around and tested the strength of my neck by pushing mildly in different directions. I clenched my teeth and complied, trying my best to mask my pain.

"You're an obstinate son-of-a-bitch, Captain Reeder. Here you go."

He handed me a piece of paper with something scribbled on it that I couldn't read. I took it right to the flight surgeon. It was good enough for him. He gave me my up slip. I got scheduled for a flight the next day—a VR mission into southern Steel Tiger.

I flew VR into Laos for the next three days, then three nights of IR missions, then either VR or IR every single day for the rest of the month. I didn't take a day off. Of course, that meant three more Friday overnights to Ubon in March. *Break my heart!*

Those first three IR missions after my shootdown were interesting. I flew with a brand-new guy to the unit, Specialist 5 Bud Lacy. We briefed and strapped into the cockpit. I could tell he was anxious.

"First mission in Vietnam," I asked.

"Yes, sir!"

I tried to calm him. "Relax. It'll be fine. We're a team in the cockpit. We work together. Don't worry about the sirs. Just be honest and frank with me. Don't hold back. Tell me what you see and what you think. The good and the bad. Don't be afraid to tell me what you want me to do.

Either for a better IR run or to keep from running into a mountain or avoiding triple-A.* We're both doing this mission together. I rely on you. OK?"

"Yes, sir." He swallowed. "Yes."

"Don't hesitate to ask me any questions you have."

"OK."

We took off and headed west. Not far into Laos, the "Fuel Pressure High" light came on for the right-side engine.

"Shit, sir. We got a light."

"I see it, Bud. There is no immediate danger, but the emergency procedure calls for us to return to base. What do you think?"

"I think we should return to base."

"That's right. And that's what we'll do. Good thinking."

"Thank you, sir."

We turned around and flew home without incident. The next night we tried again. I could tell my novice TO was a bit shaky.

I reassured him. "Not to worry. We got our problems out of the way last night. Should be fine tonight."

"Right, sir."

We headed into Laos for another try. The Engine Chip Detector light came on for the left engine. I turned around once more and landed. Another mission aborted. The very next night we tried again.

"Third time's a charm, Lacy."

"Hope so, sir. The guys are saying I'm a jinx."

"You are not a jinx. We've just had some airplane problems. It happens. Get your head into your system and have it ready to go when we get across the border."

"Yes, sir."

"And don't overdo the sirs."

"Yes, sir."

The airplane worked fine. Specialist Lacy's infrared equipment functioned well. I helped him a bit with his navigation skills, cautioning him about how flakey the Marconi Doppler could be. He had his system up

---

* Triple-A. A commonly used reference to Anti-Aircraft Artillery, or AAA, the 23 mm, 37 mm, and bigger guns trying to shoot us down.

and running and he was getting some stuff. We passed several targets to Moonbeam. He seemed to finally relax and get into his element as an IR TO. He probably couldn't see my smile.

Suddenly, he began shouting. "Break left, break left!"

As I pushed the stick hard left, I saw a stream of 23 mm tracers arching over us. A bit too close.

Lacy proudly announced, "I pressed the store button on the doppler. I got the grid coordinates close to the gun."

"Good job. Call it to Moonbeam."

I talked the rattled young man through his radio call to the airborne command and control aircraft. He was nervous but did well. We settled back into our mission, overflying another area filled with target heat signatures on his system. As he settled down, I asked, "How'd it feel to get shot at?"

He replied, "It pissed me off that we couldn't shoot back."

"Well, you might be a natural for VR observer. Keep that in mind for the future."

"I will."

We continued flying for a bit and then got hosed again. I felt the young man had seen plenty for his first mission.

"Enough of this," I said. "It's a little too hot out here tonight. We've got what they sent out for. Let's go home."

"Roger that."

Out of harm's way, I gave him some encouragement. "You did well tonight, Bud. Congratulations. You flew your first combat mission, you got shot at—twice—and all the while you worked your system well, operated the doppler, kept track of where we were, and passed targets on the radio. That's a lot to be proud of."

"Thanks a lot, sir. So, I'm not a jinx?"

"No. You are not a jinx. Just the opposite. You proved yourself a good TO. Tonight, you earned your black flight suit."

The pace continued into April, although I did take two days off. I also spent time getting checked out in our U-6 Beaver. I flew with Major Fiely, an instructor pilot as well as our company executive officer. He signed me off. I was then qualified in yet another airplane, as archaic a beast as it was. Actually, it was quite fun to fly. I enjoyed showing off its slow-motion prowess in short field takeoffs and landings. I could do both in less than a thousand feet. Still, I flew mostly visual recon. I loved the mission. And keeping active on the VR schedule earned me more trips to Thailand.

The risks were still there, certainly. Flying daytime photo-recon was a dangerous business. I'd been shot up several times and shot down once. Other Mohawks took damaging hits as well; 23 mm and 37 mm anti-aircraft guns too often found their mark.

One perilous mission took place in southern Steel Tiger on April 9. Frank Griswold flew lead that day with Major Kennedy on his wing. Those two flew together frequently. Much of the time, they took the most dangerous missions, often encountering heavy anti-aircraft fire around Mu Gia and Ban Karai passes and Ban Loboy Ford. They made a good team that brought back extraordinary film. However, in the process, they found plenty of trouble. Joe Kennedy took hits on many occasions. He brought back planes with more holes shot in them than any of the other pilots. That led to his nickname, "Magnet Ass." He'd soon live up to that in a big way. At the same time, Frank Griswold earned a new nickname for himself.

The two took off from Phu Bai with the call signs Spud 5 and 6 on a mission into southern Steel Tiger. Specialist 5 Ed Shulda was Kennedy's observer/camera operator. Ed, an analyst in the company intelligence shop, was a tried and trustworthy aerial observer. He was also a soldier. Before he trained in intelligence, he served on long-range patrol teams in Europe. He wore a Ranger tab on his uniform sleeve. That meant he was a tough guy. He proved his worth on many VR missions. He was near the end of his tour of duty but enjoyed flying VR too much to pass up the opportunity to fly that day.

Griswold and Kennedy conducted a visual recon down Route 96 to the southern end of Steel Tiger. They completed their assigned photo runs along the way. Afterward, they flew by Attapu and made a low pass at PS-38, delivering photos through their drop chutes. They headed east, doing reconnaissance almost to the juncture of the Cambodia and

Vietnam borders. They next planned to work their way back to the Xe Kong River and check it north to its end, then go home.

As Griswold turned the flight west, he saw something. The team orbited at altitude.

Frank called Joe. "Do you see that?"

Kennedy clicked his mic twice in the affirmative, and said, "Looks like a truck."

Griswold wanted to see if there was more than just one truck. "I'm going down to take a look."

He dove low and pulled back up. "Yeah, it's a truck. And there's a bunch more stuff in the trees. Maybe more vehicles. We'll hit the one we see and put a few rockets in the tree line, as well. I'll call a Covey FAC and see if he wants to bring in a strike here after us."

"Roger."

"You go first. I'm in position to cover you."

"Roger. I'm in hot."

Major Kennedy rolled onto his wing and raced downward to the target.

WHAM! WHAM! His Mohawk shuddered from two hits in rapid succession. Kennedy fought the stick to keep control and get the Mohawk into a climb. The cockpit filled with smoke. The airplane shuddered.

Shulda looked out his side. "Sir, the entire engine cowling is gone. I am looking right at the engine. Can't believe it's still running."

Kennedy notified Griswold. "We've been hit. Maybe twice. Something big."

Frank flew close. After checking Kennedy out from all sides, he reported, "You've got damage along your right side and wing. Cowl is gone. Engine is just sitting in the breeze."

He paused a moment before delivering the clincher. "You've got a big hole in your back end. Just aft of the speed boards on the right side. It's big enough for someone to stand in."

"Roger. Stick is shaking bad. The whole airplane is shuddering. The engine's still running, though. I've got good power on both, and the instruments are fine. Headed to Ubon."

"I've got you. Your tail looks like it's got a bit of a wobble. You might lose it. Once we get over Thailand, you guys can punch out. Be ready before that, if it comes off. You'll only have an instant to eject."

"Not going to do that. We'll get this thing on the ground."

"You better be ready, just in case. It doesn't look good."

Griswold made the mayday calls. A Jolly Green rescue team launched with A-1 attack airplanes. A flight of F-4s arrived in minutes. They flew off to one side. Kennedy and Shulda had a fighter escort all the way to the Mekong River. If they went down in bad guy country, they'd have immediate close air support.

Frank Griswold kept cautioning his friend about the tail falling off. Kennedy kept resisting, insisting it would stay on long enough for him to land the airplane at Ubon. Despite such bravado on the radio, he and Ed Shulda remained ready to immediately pull their ejection handles should the worst happen.

Joe Kennedy descended on final approach. The tail wobbled visibly as he slowed for landing. Crash trucks lined the runway. An ambulance stood by. Scores of people moved outside to watch. Frank Griswold flew just behind him, holding his breath as he looked on.

Kennedy squeaked the airplane onto the runway in a perfect landing. He taxied to parking and shut down. He turned to young Ed Shulda. "You did well, young man. Held it together nicely. Good job."

Ed breathed a big sigh of relief. He'd survived a near-death experience. He looked at his pilot, to whom he'd entrusted his life. "Thanks, sir. On the outside, I was calm. On the inside, I was terrified. You got us down safe. Thank you."

They both smiled, but Shulda had the weaker grin. Neither was ready for what they saw when they climbed out of the cockpit. They pushed through people gathered round the back of the Mohawk gawking. They saw it. Couldn't believe it. The hole was huge. Griswold had been right. It was big enough for someone to stand in.

With that mission, Major Joe Kennedy confirmed his nickname, "Magnet Ass." Frank Griswold had been teamed with Kennedy on many of the missions where he took hits. He'd also been my lead the day I was shot down. Now, Kennedy had a hole the size of a wheelbarrow in his airplane. Frank Griswold earned his new nickname, "Jinx."

In May, I was due my R&R, my rest and recuperation break. The Army authorized every soldier in Vietnam a week's leave around midway through their tour of duty. The approved locations included Bangkok, Thailand; Hong Kong; Kuala Lampur or Penang, Malaysia; Manila, Philippines; Taipei, Taiwan; and Tokyo, Japan, all for a five-day stay. Soldiers could choose Sydney, Australia, or Honolulu, Hawaii, for seven days. Most married guys went to Hawaii. That's what I did.

Once approved, I sent my leave dates to my wife, Amy. She got airline tickets for the same dates. The military flew me at no cost. She had to pay her way. That's why Hawaii worked so well for married guys; it had the most reasonable air fares from the mainland.

Days before my departure for Hawaii, I flew a VR mission in southern Steel Tiger. Lousy weather, getting worse. Dark clouds billowed and boiled, their bottoms settling ever lower, their tops churning higher and higher. This day, Joe Lowdermilk flew lead with me on his wing. We did what we could getting photos; some proved simply impossible because of the clouds.

We approached the southern end of Route 96 where the mountains fold into foothills before dropping onto the broad Xe Kong River valley. We were about twenty miles northeast of Attapu.

Joe began a wingover and called. "I see something down there. I'm going to take a look, maybe get a photo."

"Roger. Got ya. Whaddya see?"

"Not sure. I'll let you know."

Joe's right wing suddenly snapped up, the airplane wobbled, then rolled level and climbed.

"I'm hit. Big flash. Loud. Observer reports damage to the right engine. Lots of holes. Engine's still running, tough. Gauges OK. Not going to shut it down for now."

I put a pair of rockets where I thought the gun might be. Neither of us saw anything before the hit.

"I've got you."

"Thanks. I'm heading to Ubon. Not sure about getting over the mountains to Phu Bai. I'd be screwed if I lose that engine."

"Roger. Hold steady and I'll come take a look."

I flew close and moved my position all around his Mohawk. "You definitely took a hit. I see holes in the wing, also in the engine cowling and along the right side of the plane. Nothing on the belly or left side. I'll make your calls. You just fly the airplane."

"Will do. We got some fragments in the cockpit. Observer took a piece of it. He's hit. Hoping not too bad. He looks OK, but worried."

Joe's observer that day was one of our intelligence officers, Chief Warrant Officer Holland. He was not a pilot or a school-trained observer. He was one of our imagery analysts, an intel guy. The folks in the intel shop regularly came on missions. They were as gutsy as anyone. They wanted to see firsthand what we reported back to them—to come to a better understanding that would inform their analyses. A dedicated group of people.

Joe flew west. I positioned myself behind him and a bit high on his right side, just to keep an eye on things, especially for fire from that engine.

"How's it going?" I asked.

"OK, so far. Engine's running, still got oil. Observer's hurting, though. He says his side burns like hell."

Joe commented a little later, "Right seat is hanging in there. He is smoking a cigarette. Says he'd never make a good cowboy. Getting shot hurts too much."

We made a straight-in approach to Ubon, a very gradual descent in a nice formation with me staying a little above and behind. Thank God his engine kept running. I didn't touch down when Joe did. I flew low, just above the runway, then pitched up to the left, climbed, then made a steep spiral turn to landing. I taxied over and parked by Joe's Mohawk.

Air Force medics helped Holland from the airplane and into a waiting ambulance. There was a good bit of blood on the back of the seat. Joe and I went into the operations center for a debrief. We answered lots of questions. We then hiked over to the hospital to check on Holland. He was fine other than a hole in his back just below his right shoulder blade.

They'd keep him a day, then he could go back to Phu Bai to recover. Getting the airplane home would be more of a challenge. The maintenance team counted fifty-seven holes; a good-sized one in a propeller blade. Amazing it didn't come apart.

The swelling dark clouds grew into a solid line of thunderstorms. Joe thought we'd spend the night in Ubon. I had obligations back at Phu Bai. I'd promised the group of Donut Dollies* a tour of our ramp and a visit to one of our parked Mohawks. I'd committed through a friend I'd made in the group, Rosemary Thunder. They'd be waiting after work. The weather at Phu Bai was OK. The thunderstorms erupted only over Laos and eastern Thailand. I'd made a promise to some lovely young ladies. We needed to go. Joe was not at all happy.[1]

We climbed into the cockpit in pouring rain. I left my aerial observer to check in on Holland and enjoy the night in Ubon. Joe occupied the right seat. He'd be my copilot. We took off, headed east, and climbed to nine thousand feet. There was no one else in the air. The Air Force cancelled all its flights for weather. We pressed on.

Thunder clapped and lightning flashed around us. As we buffeted all over the sky, Joe sat beside me, scowling. "If you get me killed, I'll really be pissed off."

I smiled. "We'll be fine."

We hit horrendous updrafts and downdrafts, slamming us about. Finally, we came out of the turbulence on crossing the Annamite ridgeline. No problem with the weather at Phu Bai. We made it back in one piece. Three days later, Steve Ward took me to Danang in our Beaver to catch my flight to Hawaii for R&R.

It felt strange to be on a commercial airliner high above the Pacific Ocean. We landed at Hickam Air Force Base, just outside Honolulu, and boarded busses for the drive to Fort DeRussy on Waikiki Beach.** In the same day, I'd gone from the midst of war to the tranquil beaches

---

* Donut Dollies. Young women who volunteered for service in the American Red Cross Supplemental Recreation Overseas Program. They brought morale-boosting games and refreshments (sometimes donuts) to troops in the field, providing a touch of home.
** This is now the location of the military hotel, the Hale Koa, with the finest beach on Waikiki. A part of the old fort is also maintained as a historic museum.

of Hawaii. The world seemed strange. Bright colorful life swirled around me, yet I didn't feel a part of it. It was as if I watched but wasn't there. An odd sensation.

Then the bus stopped, and reality returned. A group of women waited nearby. I got off and found my wife, Amy. We hugged, then she stepped back, looked at me, pointed to my chest, and asked, "What's that?"

I managed a guilty smile. "It's a Purple Heart." I had two ribbons on my khaki uniform, one that everyone got, simply for being in the military at the time, and the other for the injuries I'd gotten when I was shot down. Amy's dad had two Purple Hearts from World War II hanging on his wall. She knew what the ribbon looked like.

"And how'd you get that?"

"I got shot down. Nothing major. I'm fine."

She frowned. "And you didn't tell me?"

"Didn't want to worry you. Sorry."

Already, the tensions that had strained our marriage for some time began to surface there in paradise. Still, we enjoyed our time in Hawaii.

We stayed at the Kahala Hilton, a bit out of the way on the far side of Diamond Head. However, it was a marvelous, first-class hotel that offered rooms at a fantastically discounted R&R rate. It was beautiful. Palm trees, gardens, grass, and pools with swimming dolphins. I got a tropical drink from the bar and found a chair under an umbrella on the beach. I leaned back, breathed deeply and relaxed. Looking across the waves, the war in Vietnam seemed so very far away.

I'd gone to a year of high school in Hawaii. It was a treat to revisit my old stomping grounds. I found my best friend from Roosevelt High, Alan Kajikawa. He'd only recently returned from Vietnam himself. He'd served as a Navy corpsman with the US Marines. The Marine Corps does not have their own medics. They use Navy medical corpsmen who wear the same uniform and go into battle by their side, treating their wounded. Alan had been in the 2nd Battalion, 4th Marine Regiment at Dong Ha. I remembered landing there, months ago with my gastric emergency. Neither of us knew how close we had been. We had dinner with Alan and his wife Carol that evening. We went to the Pagoda Floating Restaurant, a lovely place not far from Waikiki.

The next day, I rented a small four-seat Cessna at the Honolulu Airport. I wanted to take in the view from the air. Before I could fly the plane on my own, an instructor pilot had to confirm my skill. He concluded the checkout by saying that I should be the one instructing him. Guess I'd become a pretty good pilot, flying combat missions for over six months. I took Amy up for an aerial tour of Oahu, along Alan and Carol. I'm afraid I flew the Cessna as if it were a Mohawk. Alan got out wide-eyed, saying it was a flight he'd never forget.

My seven-day sojourn in Hawaii ended. I returned to Vietnam, curiously comfortable back among my fellow Spuds, even amid the hazards of war. I was ready to get back to work.

I'd returned to a bloody page in American history. A big battle raged in the A Shau Valley, just thirty miles west. On May 10, 1969, the 101st Airborne Division launched the attack to clear the valley of North Vietnamese Army regulars along with Viet Cong insurgents. The 101st lived at Camp Eagle, only a few miles down the road from us. The US 9th Marine Regiment and two South Vietnamese infantry battalions and a cavalry squadron joined the 101st's 3rd Brigade in the fight. Major General Melvin Zais commanded the 101st Airborne Division. The 3rd Brigade commander, Colonel Joseph Conmy, led the force in the field.[2]

One mountaintop proved the costliest prize in the battle. The plan called for a helicopter assault to push the enemy from the valley floor. Other forces would block their retreat and destroy them before they escaped into Laos. Like Custer and his 7th Cavalry at the Little Bighorn, Colonel Conmy and the 101st expected their foe to run. Instead, in both cases, the enemy stood and fought—and they brawled with tenacity.[3]

On May 13, as part of the effort to cut off retreat, Conmy ordered attacks to secure the prominent terrain on the west side of the A Shau Valley. That included two of the tallest hills, 916 and 937.* The helicopter assault on Hill 916 went well, securing the hilltop quickly. A ground attack on Hill 937 did not go well at all. Soldiers struggled up the steep hillside through dense jungle, bamboo thickets, and tall elephant grass.

---

* Hilltops in Vietnam were named for their elevation, in meters. Hill 937 was 937 meters high, 3,074 feet.

Unknown to friendly forces, the North Vietnamese 29th Regiment held Hill 937 with a large force in well-prepared positions with a powerful array of anti-aircraft.[4]

We'd take off on missions, watching medical evacuation helicopters circling overhead, waiting their turn to land on the helipad at the 85th Evacuation Hospital, right next to the western end of the runway. The enemy downed and damaged several helicopters, and the American attackers lost scores of soldiers, dead and wounded, every day. They finally took the hilltop on May 20. Seventy-two American soldiers died, 374 wounded, and seven missing in action. The American press called Hill 937, "Hamburger Hill."[5]

As the battle for Hamburger Hill raged, another disaster struck, this time in the air. On May 18, I led a flight of two Mohawks, returning from a mission over Laos. When we checked in with Waterboy, he announced the landing direction at Phu Bai to the west. That meant we had to go out over the ocean to set up our approach. As we neared the coast, I saw a huge fireball ahead, over the water. Tense mayday calls filled the airwaves. Then we got a call.

"Spud 5, this is Waterboy. How's your fuel? We just had a Marine Corps KC-130 go down. Need you to check the area for survivors if you are able."

"Roger, Waterboy. We're good for another hour. I saw the explosion. We're on our way."

We arrived to see nothing but debris floating in the water. No sign of survivors. We searched until our fuel ran low, and we turned toward Phu Bai to land. We learned later that all the aircraft belonged to the Marines. The KC-130 was actively refueling a flight of F-4s when another Marine F-4, separate from that mission, collided with the tanker plane. It exploded in the air. The crash killed all six crewmen aboard the KC-130 and the two pilots in the F-4 that hit it. The crews of the two F-4s being refueled survived. One airplane lost control and the crew ejected. They got picked up by a nearby helicopter. The other airplane, though damaged, flew back to its base and landed safely.

Then on the night of May 24, an anti-aircraft gun nailed one of our AC-130 Spectre friends with two explosive 37 mm rounds. The gunship was on a truck-killing mission over the Ho Chi Minh Trail in Laos. The hydraulic system failed. The pilots fought the controls. They jockeyed the power levers of different engines to hold a course toward Ubon. The pilots ordered the crew to bail out once safely over Thailand. They attempted to land the battered airplane but skidded off the runway. A wing struck and tore off. The mighty ship exploded in flames. The eleven crew members who bailed out survived. The two pilots attempting to land the battered gunship died.[6]

May 1969 was a tough month in Southeast Asia. The war raged, awful as it had ever been. I'd gotten away for R&R leave right in the middle of the chaos. Turmoil flamed before I left. It blazed after I came back. I'd enjoyed my rest and recuperation, but I now had months more of war ahead, along with responsibilities for a new unit mission getting underway in Thailand.

CHAPTER 10

Plain of Jars

EARLIER IN MAY, MAJOR ALTON BROUGHT TWO VISITORS TO OPERA-
tions. They looked out of place. They wore dark suits with white shirts
and ties. They had fancy black wingtip shoes, like the ones I'd had made
in Thailand. Mine were already quite dusty, just sitting in my locker.
Theirs looked clean and freshly shined, an amazing sight in Vietnam. I'd
never seen anything like it. Both walked with purpose, exhibiting an air
of importance. *Who are these guys?*

Major Alton introduced them. "Colonel Duskin, Mr. Smith, this is
Captain Bill Reeder, our operations officer."

I'd only just become the new operations officer. Frank Griswold had
taken over company executive officer duties a few days before. Major
Alton's tour of duty was ending in June. Major Fiely already busied himself preparing to take his place. It made sense for Frank to go ahead and
step in as XO. That made me the new ops officer, a huge responsibility
for a junior captain.

I shook hands with the visitors. Major Alton added, "Colonel Duskin
is the Army attaché at the US embassy in Vientiane, Laos. Mr. Smith is
on the embassy staff as well."

Humph, I thought. *A colonel in civilian clothes. Interesting job.* "Nice
to meet you."

"They're here to talk about putting some of our 131st Mohawks at
Udorn Airbase in Thailand. They will be there to fly special missions
into northern Laos. Highly classified and very sensitive. It's all approved.
We'll be working directly for the embassy."

I learned that Ambassador Sullivan had pressed MACV headquarters on the issue for months. He wanted some 131st SLAR and IR Mohawks for his use. MACV finally approved the mission, and these two embassy representatives had come to coordinate the details.

The situation in northern Laos was different than the ongoing fight in Steel Tiger in the south. In the south, the 7th Air Force ran the interdiction campaign against the trail. That headquarters was based at Tan Son Nhut Airbase in Saigon, not far from MACV headquarters. We followed their protocols, including integration into their air tasking order, the daily plan for missions into Steel Tiger. Even though MACV J2 controlled our operations and received our intelligence products, 7th Air Force incorporated our missions into their master schedule. In addition to sending our reports and imagery straight to MACV, copies went to 7th Air Force Intelligence as well.

That was the drill in the southern panhandle. Operation Steel Tiger and associated campaigns sought to disrupt the logistical flow along the Ho Chi Minh Trail. The 131st played a small but critical role in that effort. All echelons placed premium value on the intelligence we collected, as well as our ability to develop real-time targets for immediate strikes by attack aircraft.

In the north, the war was a different beast. At the same time North Vietnam pushed men and materiel south, down the Ho Chi Minh Trail, they waged a wider conflict in the north. There they aimed to directly confront the Laotian government and turn the country into a communist state. A communist Laos would be an ally on North Vietnam's western flank. It would serve as a buffer between them and their historic rival, Thailand.[1]

North Vietnam prioritized its campaign in the south, along the Ho Chi Minh Trail network. They placed most of their effort there to keep logistics lines open, feeding their war machine in the south. However, at the same time, they also supported the ongoing civil war in Laos's north. The North Vietnamese Army with their Pathet Lao allies occupied and controlled large swaths of territory in the north and east of the country. The internationally recognized government ruled the western regions, fighting to contain communist advances and preserve their sovereignty.

Government authority rested with the prime minister, Prince Souvanna Phouma, in the Laotian capital, Vientiane. King Sisavang Vatthana, the country's nominal monarch, sat atop the throne in the royal capital, Luang Prabang, 140 miles north. The lines between the battling government and communist forces wavered back and forth as a seesaw with much of the fighting taking place in and around the Plain of Jars.[2]

The Plain of Jars was an archaeological treasure. Ancient peoples chiseled stone cylinders of various sizes. Thousands lay across the huge five-hundred-square-mile plain. The vessels played an important role in the burial customs of an Iron Age civilization that disappeared nearly two thousand years ago. During the nineteenth century, French colonial rulers named the place the *Plain des Jarres*. This led many to refer to it as the PDJ.

The broad open plain occupied a crossroads of two early cultures, one spreading from the Mekong River basin to the west, the other from the shores of the Tonkin Gulf to the east. As centuries passed, the region became a cross-cultural mixing pot. Contact between groups enriched some, but it also ignited conflict between competing factions. These historic patterns still played out in the ongoing civil war.[3]

As wet and dry season conditions mandated over passing years, communist and Royal Lao government advances ebbed and flowed one way, then the other. One indigenous group found itself caught in the middle, the Hmong. They drew their identity, their sense of being from their homeland, the hills and valleys around the Plain of Jars. They were animists, believing that animals, plants, and places have an interconnected spiritual essence. They loved their families, their farms and hunting grounds, the way they lived each day. Broader political views were split, some favoring communist causes while others leaned toward the Royal Lao Government. That changed when North Vietnam invaded Laos in 1959.

The invasion swept into some Hmong villages. It threatened their way of life. The United States recruited and equipped Hmong soldiers to fight the invaders and their communist Laotian allies, the Pathet Lao. The Hmong proved to be capable, hard-fighting warriors. From their ranks emerged a most competent and ambitious leader, Vang Pao, who rose quickly to the rank of general. He led the Hmong as a powerful fighting force to counter the tide of the communist advance. The Hmong became and remained staunchly aligned with the western cause, a potent part of the Royal Laotian force, the CIA's Secret Army.[4]

The United States trained and supported the Hmong as well as the rest of the Royal Laotian Army and Air Force. It also used American bombers and attack aircraft to strike North Vietnamese and Pathet Lao targets around the Plain of Jars and farther east all the way to Laos's border with North Vietnam.[5]

It was into that environment that I, as company operations officer, was to establish a 131st presence at the Udorn Royal Thai Air Force Base, to work for the US ambassador in Vientiane, Laos. Things were about to get very interesting.

I flew a C-model to Udorn for initial coordination with the staff at 7/13th Air Force Headquarters there. The 7/13th had complex command responsibilities. The headquarters directly controlled US Air Force (USAF) fighter, reconnaissance, and search and rescue squadrons stationed at the base. It also supported some of the other air elements directly involved in the ambassador's air campaign in northern Laos. That now included us. The 7/13th took care of the necessary infrastructure, administration, logistics, and ops/intel support activities on the base, but the embassy ran the show for folks like us. Other more secretive elements at Udorn, such as Air America, operated on their own with no recognizable ties to 7/13th.

Embassy officials told us to bring an airplane with no US markings. That sounded odd and not quite right. I had no idea of the legality of operating US Army aircraft from Phu Bai without markings. Moreover, if this was to be the rule for all our planes operating from Udorn, we'd be continually covering and repainting markings as we rotated airplanes for maintenance and repair. I suggested an alternative. We'd be allowed to cover the offending letters with three-hundred-mile-an-hour tape as required (olive drab duct tape). It could then be easily removed. Recommendation accepted.

I brought Captain Tom Bratcher with me. Major Alton decided Tom would initially head up the effort at Udorn. On landing, I saw rows of F-4s parked in revetments. They belonged to the USAF fighter and reconnaissance squadrons assigned to the base. I also noted the Air America compound, its several buildings and hangars with a mishmash of different aircraft parked on their ramp, both helicopters and airplanes. The airplanes ranged in size from large C-130 and C-123 transports, to smaller Beechcraft planes and Pilatus Porter short takeoff and landing utility aircraft. A slew of Hueys and a few H-34 Choctaw helicopters sat parked there as well. There could have been some Continental Air Services airplanes mixed in. Hard to tell. Most everyone believed that the CIA ran both Air America and Continental. Further down the ramp, I saw several unmarked T-28s lined up, side by side.

Tom and I exchanged greetings with a small group of the Air Force players we'd be working with at the base. We set up coordination meetings for the next day. At the meetings, we concluded arrangements for parking, fuel, and operations and intelligence support for pre-mission threat briefings and our post-mission debriefs, as well as imagery processing. The 7/13th Air Force would feed all our information to the embassy by secure means. We maintained open channels direct to the embassy, ourselves, as well.

The following day we taped over the markings on our Mohawk and flew to a clandestine airstrip deep in Laos at the village of Long Tieng. They called it LS-20A. That day, I learned the difference between PS and LS. PS, as in PS-38, meant Pakse Site. That terminology applied to those sites supporting operations run by officials out of the southern Laotian town of Pakse. LS simply meant landing site in other parts of Laos.

We found Long Tieng a most exotic place. It made the austere base at Nakhon Phanom look cosmopolitan by comparison. Long Tieng was strikingly more primitive. The site was eighty miles north of the Laotian capital, Vientiane; seventy miles southeast of the royal capital, Luang Prabang; and only twenty miles southwest of the Plain of Jars. It was in middle-of-nowhere Laos, yet occupied a strategic place as the principal operating base for the secret war in the north.

The compound nestled in a bowl surrounded by mountains on three sides with a karst ridge rising high just off the end of the airstrip. The runway inclined upward toward the karst. That meant, regardless of wind direction, we had to land to the northwest, toward the karst ridge, and take off to the southeast, away from it. The strip was only 2,200 feet long, less than half the length of Phu Bai.

Folks paid a lot of attention to our different-looking airplane when we landed. Indigenous militiamen gathered round. A guy herding livestock across the runway gave us a long stare. A couple of Air America pilots came by to say hi. They looked like they'd stepped off a jungle adventure movie set, unshaved, with wrinkled white shirts and crumpled airline pilot hats.

A familiar face approached. Colonel Duskin came to greet us. He looked like a senior official should, but wore casual clothing, appropriate for the jungle.

He shook our hands and said, "Welcome, guys." He turned and waved us on. "This way."

We passed a large cage with an Asiatic black bear inside. "That's Floyd. He drinks beer. They're just careful not to let him have too much."

We went into a building and found ourselves in a big room with a large table, chairs, and maps on the walls. A few other Americans joined us along with some Royal Lao Air Force pilots and a group of indigenous Hmong officers. I didn't believe General Vang Pao was among them because he was not introduced.

I found that we'd been summoned to Long Tieng for an orientation. A briefer laid out the ambassador's war campaign in the north and our place in it. He started with a historical overview, then a summary of the enemy and friendly situations, recent events, and future estimates and plans. He told us the Hmong were the centerpiece of ground operations in the north, that the Plain of Jars was the prize, and that the goal was to push the North Vietnamese Army and Pathet Lao off the plain and keep them off. He emphasized that, at all costs, the enemy had to be blocked from advancing on the royal capital of Luang Prabang or the national capital, Vientiane.

Colonel Duskin took over and gave us our mission.

"We want you flying SLAR and infrared missions at night over and around the PDJ.* You are to identify enemy targets for strike aircraft and gunships. The intelligence you gather will increase our situational awareness and better inform our decision-making."

He let that settle a moment then added, "You'll have one special IR mission from time to time. We want you to run the Mekong River all the way to the Chinese border. We think they're floating stuff down the river and possibly running trucks along remote roadways, using them as supply routes from China. That's over three hundred miles each way, a good deal farther following the river and roads. You'll have to watch your fuel carefully."

He looked at Tom then shifted to me. "Remember, you work for the ambassador. This was his plan. Day to day, the CIA station chief and I will oversee your operations. We'll stay on top of your performance and make any adjustments the ambassador might direct. I will be your principal point of contact at the embassy. The 7/13th Air Force will provide your routine mission support on Udorn."

The point was perfectly clear. We were to fly secret CIA missions in northern Laos under the control of the US embassy in Vientiane.

After the briefing, Tom and I stayed and talked with some of the folks. We found two quite interesting. They were both CIA guys. They shared, in general terms, what was going on in Laos from their end. That helped fill in some of the knowledge gaps I had about the operational environment we'd be operating in.

We found out that the CIA had been involved in Laos for quite a while. After the 1962 neutrality agreement, the United States ended its uniformed presence in Laos. However, as America watched the communists violate the accords, senior officials knew they had to act, but settled on a covert response. Not wanting to publicly violate the agreement, the United States charged the CIA with the task. The agency took on the mission of recruiting, training, equipping, and advising Royal Laotian forces, including formations of indigenous fighters. The effort was to be clandestine, a secret war.[6]

* PDJ. An abbreviation from the French for the Plain of Jars, *Plain des Jarres*. Commonly used by everyone at Udorn and Long Tieng.

We'd had a glimpse of that at PS-38. The main US effort in the panhandle was the massive air interdiction of the Ho Chi Minh Trail, including such supporting activity as MACV-SOG operations not too far across the Laotian border. There was, however, another war in southern Laos. It involved ongoing battles between government forces and the communist North Vietnamese and Pathet Lao. The government fought those battles with regular Royal Lao military forces as well as indigenous Special Guerrilla Units (SGUs) recruited from local tribal communities—all equipped, trained, and advised by the CIA, and supplied and transported by Air America and Continental Air Services. That covert fight was for the ownership of towns and villages and the control of roadways and key pieces of terrain. Some of those operations benefited the main American effort in Steel Tiger, but most took place as a separate war, its existence kept most secret from the rest of the world.[7]

Major Alton dispatched two Mohawks to Udorn on May 20, 1969, to kick things off, one IR bird and one SLAR. We sent over two crew chiefs and a couple of maintenance guys. Soon, we increased the numbers to four airplanes and twenty-one personnel. The 131st Udorn detachment was in place.

Those additional missions, flown from a faraway base, impacted our capabilities at Phu Bai. Still, we tried to keep everything running full speed. Steve Ward worked hard to maintain our aircraft availability as high as possible. MACV helped by increasing our aircraft authorization from eighteen Mohawks to twenty and assigning additional personnel in critical specialties.

Our Udorn team stepped up to the task. The aircrews flew hazardous missions, facing daunting anti-aircraft fire while negotiating treacherous terrain with mountaintops higher than nine thousand feet. Maintenance crews put in long hours keeping the birds flying and the systems operating. Everyone worked hard. Off duty, they played hard. The base put the crews up in town because of the special nature of the missions.

Udorn was much like Ubon, only better—nicer hotels, great restaurants, and a heck of a night life. The base contracted a downtown hotel for the 131st. What a deal. The Spuds flying out of Udorn got credit for a Vietnam tour of duty while living it up in Udorn, Thailand. The guys in

Phu Bai, Vietnam, lived in shabby hootches along a muddy street, eating crumby mess hall food, and contending with hootch maids washing their clothes on a concrete slab, beside them, as they showered. Not to mention enduring rocket and mortar attacks and the town off-limits. While the Phu Bai Spuds suffered life in the combat zone, the guys in Udorn, Thailand, were living in a hotel in a town with paved streets and sidewalks, eating in delightful restaurants, and sleeping in nice hotels with laundry service. There were risks flying the northern Laotian Barrell Roll, sure, so the guys earned it; but they did live the good life in Udorn.

Our missions got underway. The results were impressive. The embassy was pleased.

I'd fly to Udorn once every couple of weeks. As operations officer, I had the responsibility to ensure all was going well, especially with such a critical, high-visibility operation that had been put in place personally by the US ambassador in Laos. We routinely rotated airplanes from Phu Bai to Udorn to ensure they always had reliable aircraft with peak performing systems. So each time I'd go, I'd take a fully mission ready replacement Mohawk.

Since I only went to Udorn once every two or three weeks, I did not fly as a mission pilot there. I would, however, jump in a right seat on occasion and fly as TO, trying not to muck it up. I grabbed my first operational flight with Tom Bratcher, an IR mission into the PDJ. All our missions from Udorn were night missions. That day, we took off a little early so Tom could show me the Plain of Jars at dusk, to give me an appreciation for that part of our mission area.

We crossed high mountain ridges, slipping between impressive towering peaks. Much higher and we'd need to use our oxygen masks. I recognized Long Tieng as we flew over. Tom began a descent. I saw the vista of the Plain of Jars open before us. The expanse of the place impressed me. Daylight faded, but I could make out the shape of jars, some quite huge, laying everywhere across the plain. The scene was beautiful, even amid the deep scars of war. No wonder the Hmong loved this land, their ancestral ties, and their way of living. They hated the communists who sought to take it all away from them. They swore to fight the North Vietnamese and Pathet Lao to their dying breath. They nearly did.

Night fell. We dropped down low and began our infrared runs in earnest. I did my best to record each significant target.

SNAP! *What the hell was that?* I looked over at Tom. His head was down. He raised back up and said, "I can't see. Must have taken a round. Stuff in my eyes. I can't see. I can't fly."

Sure enough, a bullet tore through the windshield. It made a big hole that splintered the glass, spraying tiny shards of glass into Tom's face and leaving hundreds of spiderweb cracks across the windscreen. I wasn't sure how long it would be before the whole thing crumbled to pieces.

My thought, sitting in the right seat of a C-Model IR bird: *What! I've got no controls.* But Mohawks had an auto pilot. I went to work.

"Got it, Tom." I immediately engaged the autopilot and used the control knob to steer us away from the threat and climb to a secure altitude. I set a course for Udorn, knowing we could punch out once across the Mekong River, ejecting over friendly territory. There was no way I was going to try to land a Mohawk with the autopilot control.

Tom sat there, rubbing and blinking his eyes as I fiddled with the autopilot control. He squinted several times.

"I think I can see good enough to fly."

"OK. Well just sit there for a while. Hopefully, you'll be able to take over and land when we get to Udorn. Can you see out that cracked windshield?"

"I think so."

Great.

I made the radio calls. Tom resumed flying the machine once we got close. I sat tense during the approach. He landed fine. We parked and got Tom to the base hospital. Doctors irrigated his eyes, cleaned his lacerations, and released him to recover in his hotel room. Tom Bratcher returned to flight duties two days later. Quite a guy.

We had filled the detachment at Udorn with some of our finest pilots. That meant sending Tom Bratcher the likes of Curt Degner, our infrared guru; Warrant Officer Lysle "Lizard" Barthlome, his understudy; and Captain "Slick Rick" Coleman, a University of Nebraska linebacker who played in four bowl games, the Sugar Bowl, Cotton Bowl, and two Orange Bowls. Rick excelled as an Army Mohawk pilot. He later replaced Bratcher as detachment commander. We finished the team with more of our best—and as it turned out, some of our craziest guys.

Not infrequently, the hotel became a wild place, a romping room of Spud shenanigans. It was not at all uncommon for some to bring girls back to their rooms. Often late-night drinking parties ensued in the bar or by the pool. On a particularly crazy evening, one of the pilots jumped off the roof, or at least from a third- or fourth-story balcony, into the pool. The buffoonery got loud applause and cheers, but the stunt could easily have ended in tragedy. The foolish things young men, feeling invincible, will do.

I remember someone cautioning me about smoking too much. I was a one- to two-pack a day guy. My response as I inhaled deeply, "We don't know if we'll live to see tomorrow. I should worry that I might get lung cancer in my old age and die at forty? Give me a break."

It was strange. We all had this sense of invincibility, an "it happens to the other guy" mentality. At the same time, we saw the specter of death looking us right in the eye. We must have figured, "When our time comes, it comes. No sense in worrying about it." We all embraced the credo, "Eat, drink, and make merry; for tomorrow we may die."

Our aircrews at Udorn made a name for themselves, both in raising hell and boldly flying some of the most harrowing missions in Southeast Asia. They flew night after night, dodging anti-aircraft fire and weaving through valleys and high mountain peaks. They funneled information to airborne command and control centers. They passed targets along to strike planes and gunships. They did what the ambassador had hoped in support of the CIA's secret Hmong army. Some of those missions were terrifying; others, not so much.

One flight worth recalling involved my classmate Billy Wood, the Sack Rat. One day, he ferried a replacement airplane from Phu Bai to Udorn. He flew solo, all alone. On that flight, Billy also carried the mail for the Spuds living in Udorn. He climbed the Mohawk to a relatively safe ten thousand feet and headed west. Somewhere over the middle of Laos, he was overcome with gastric distress. He had to shit, and he had to go badly. It wouldn't wait.

With no place to land, Billy reacted brilliantly. He put the airplane on autopilot, which held heading and altitude. He grabbed the silken postal service mail bag, opened it, and dumped the letters on the floor in front of the empty co-pilot's right seat. He then unfastened his seatbelt and disconnected from his ejection seat couplings and leg restraints. As he scooted up out of his seat, he unzipped his flight suit and pulled it down below his waist along with his underwear. Billy somehow placed one foot where he'd been sitting and, with much difficulty, got the other over onto the right side of the cockpit, straddling the center instrument console. The back of his head pressed against the overhead panel. He positioned the empty mail bag beneath his butt and let go his bowels.

Problem was, a lot missed the bag. His runny shit splattered all over the place. He fastened himself back in his seat and landed. Billy Wood, the Sack Rat, never lived down the mess he'd made in the cockpit nor the foul, stained letters he delivered.

Another memorable mission occurred a couple of weeks later.

I flew a SLAR bird to Udorn. I'd arranged a flight aboard Moonbeam, the nighttime C-130 airborne command and control center (ABCCC). The mission consumed twelve hours. I'd spend that next night and get some sleep before flying back to Phu Bai with another Mohawk. One of our intelligence analysts, Chief Warrant Officer Vaughn Hillgren, came with me. He looked forward to being onboard the ABCCC and he wanted to check out the intel operation on that end as well.

We arrived in Udorn. All went according to plan. The flight in the C-130 was quite an adventure. We enjoyed seeing how it all worked. We got to spend hours with the people we talked to while flying our missions over Laos. They told us that because of the weight of the ABCCC command-and-control module and the full load of fuel they needed for the all-night mission, we would not reach safe three-engine airspeed until thirty minutes after takeoff. That meant if we lost one of the four engines before then, we'd be in serious trouble. I didn't know if that was true or just a poke at us from the Air Force, but it added to the excitement of the experience.

I spent a good deal of time with the controllers in the belly of the airplane. I was impressed, watching them work one of our Spud Steel Tiger flights, passing targets to a FAC for an airstrike. The flight crew invited me up to the cockpit. I sat up there for a good while, enjoying the view.

Dawn broke as we landed. I was ready to head to bed for sleep. Instead, a message waited with instructions to fly on to Bangkok and spend the night there. We would return to the 131st early the following morning. It turned out our Chinook helicopter friends on the other side of the Phu Bai runway had a special order in Bangkok ready for pick up. They ordered wood-carved elephants from a certain store in Bangkok. The elephants served as the unit's farewell gift to departing aviators. The unit used the call sign Pachyderm, thus the elephants. Because we made periodic trips to Thailand, we'd routinely pick up the elephants for them. Their latest order was ready. Two Pachyderm pilots were leaving within days. It made sense for us to get their farewell mementos, even tired as we were. No problem. Only an hour and twenty-minute flight, and we'd get to spend the night in Bangkok. *All right!*

We landed at the Bangkok Airport and taxied to the parking ramp for the JUSMAG* flight detachment. When we checked in, a soldier handed me a message:

> As soon as you have packages in hand, return to Phu Bai immediately. Your airplane needed for flight tonight. Mission critical.

Oh great! There goes our night in Bangkok.

We caught a cab into town through the craziest traffic I'd ever seen. *Dear God. Survive combat and die in a car wreck in Bangkok. Real fine.*

We found the store, got the elephants, and jumped in another taxi for the ride back to the airport. The fuel handler had just finished filling our tanks. We stowed the cargo, started the engines, and headed back to Phu Bai.

I climbed to nine thousand feet, set the course, and turned on the autopilot. I announced to Mr. Hillgren, "I'm pooped. I'm going to close my eyes for a few minutes. Just keep tabs on the instruments. Let me

---

* JUSMAG/JUSMAGTHAI. Joint US Military Advisory Group, Thailand. They maintained a small fleet of aircraft at the Bangkok Airport for travel around Southeast Asia and to receive and support official visitors.

know if you see any airplanes coming close, if anything goes haywire with the instruments, or if you see anybody shooting at us."

"Roger, sir. Will do."

I woke with a start. We were in the clouds. I had no idea how long I'd slept or where we were. I looked at Vaughn. He was sound asleep. I shook his arm.

"I thought you were going to stay awake for me."

"I tried. I was exhausted. I don't remember nodding off."

My thoughts turned to the World War II tragedy of the *Lady Be Good*, a B-24 bomber returning to its North African base after a mission in Italy. In the clouds, the crew overflew the airfield, continuing far into the Libyan desert, crashing over four hundred miles past their base. The crew perished after days of walking aimlessly across the hot sand. I worried we might have flown well out over the South China Sea without enough fuel to get back to the coast. We'd end up floating in the ocean.[8]

I tuned our instruments and got a fix on our location. I sighed and told Vaughn, "We're good to go. Phu Bai is dead ahead. I'll call Waterboy and set us up for an approach."

I lived through another one.

CHAPTER 11

War Rages On

In June 1969, our much-loved commander, Major Gary Alton, ended his one-year tour of duty in Vietnam. Spud 6, "Mr. Clean," headed home. He turned over command of the 131st to Major Linus Fiely, "Blanket." Major Fiely formed an effective command team, paired with his strong, respected executive officer, Captain Frank Griswold. Major Alton would be missed, though. He had been like a father. He looked after all of us as family. Though, too often, we Spud pilots behaved like spoiled teenagers, seeing what we could get away with, pushing boundaries until Major Alton sternly, but caringly, reined us back in. I'd never worked for a better man than Gary Alton. Nor would I ever again. He was the best.

Our missions along the coast of North Vietnam and into Laos, now all of Laos, continued. The war raged on through summer and into fall. Being operations officer kept me busy, but I still managed to fly most days. As always, I split my time between IR and VR with an occasional nighttime SLAR over Steel Tiger simply to keep up with what was going on throughout the company. Most days, though, it was still VR, always and forever my favorite.

Our VR crew had gotten smaller. Buick Bingham went home in April, taking a huge chunk of Spud humor and esprit with him. Round Ranger Thiel departed not long after. Major Alton, who always stepped up to take his share of the most hazardous missions, had now departed as well. That left Major Kennedy, Frank Griswold (busy with XO duties), the Lowdermilk twins, Mitch Waldran, and me (also busy as company operations officer). The two daily photo-recon missions required four pilots. With only six of us available, that made it tight for getting away for any training, R&R, or sick days, let alone just taking a day off. We flew a lot.

It was remarkable that out of the six 131st VR pilots, four of us were flight school and Mohawk course classmates. I always marveled that all six of us selected for the Mohawk qualification course from our flight school class went through that course together and all six ended up in the 131st in Vietnam. And now, four of those six made up two-thirds of the VR platoon. What were the odds?

Most often Major Kennedy and Frank Griswold flew together. Company policy did not allow Joe and Jon Lowdermilk to be on the same mission because they were brothers. No one wanted to lose two siblings at the same time, especially twins.

I had many an adventure with Joe or Jon on my wing, or me on theirs. We'd switch up who flew lead, mission to mission. Sometimes we'd split a mission in the middle, with one pilot taking lead for the first half and the other having it for the second. We all had similar experience at that point and competent decision-making skills. It was always important, though, to know who was flying lead, who had those responsibilities. Even so, we did not hesitate to share observations and suggestions. Whatever pairing, the VR Platoon always formed powerful teams.

I enjoyed flying with Mitch as well. He was always an aggressive, forward-leaning aviator. When together, we tackled our missions with gusto. I never flew with a better gun pilot than Mitch Waldran.

We'd always end our day shooting rockets. We worked closely with the Nail FACs out of Nakhon Phanom and sometimes Coveys out of Danang. Early in my tour, we'd ask ABCCC what FACs they had working an area. Before long, ABCCC was calling us saying that FAC so-and-so wanted us to check in with him before we went home. He had targets for us.

On one mission, Mitch and I found a lucrative target on our own in an area just west of the Demilitarized Zone. It was a poorly camouflaged bulldozer surrounded by piles of construction material. The bulldozer hid along a crudely cut roadway, under construction. It appeared to be a new branch off the Ho Chi Minh Trail reaching eastward. The roadway ran along a deep narrow valley at the bottom of a steep mountainside just above a small river. Karst towers clawed upward randomly there to rip off the wings of an inattentive crew.

To engage the bulldozer, we had to use steep dive angles. Otherwise, in that terrain, we'd lose sight of it in seconds. There'd be no time to fire. Between the terrain and the anti-aircraft guns, it was a dicey situation. But it was a good target. If we could take out that bulldozer, it would be a major setback for the enemy, at least for a time along that particular road.

I flew lead that day. I rolled in. My rockets hit close. They blew up a stack of material and got a big fire going. Mitch rolled in next. I stayed in position to cover him. He took fire, steadied his run-in, and let go two pairs. Good shot. One of his rockets hit the bulldozer. Nice explosion.

He'd held his run-in a bit long. By the end, I was yelling at him on the radio. "Pull up, Mitch. Pull up!"

The nose of his Mohawk finally cocked upward, but its downward slide continued for an agonizing instant before the airplane found its climbing legs and arched toward the sky. It barely cleared the ridgeline.

I heard Mitch's voice on the radio, filled with relief. "Got a little low. Never had target fixation before. Think I got it there. Couldn't take my eyes off the dozer. Pulled so many Gs coming up, my vision went black. Completely black. Couldn't see a thing for a few seconds. Time to go home?"

"Yeah. Time to go home you crazy son-of-a-bitch. You're one lucky guy."

"Yeah. Lucky."

In the days ahead, we returned to that same area. We fired on sampans loaded with supplies and large bundles floating down the river. We followed vehicle tracks leading off the roadway. They led to substantial caves, probably jungle warehouses.

One of our missions took us down Route 96 in the lower panhandle. We completed our photo runs and checked in with a Covey FAC. He had two stalled trucks on a bombed-out hillside between Attapu and Chavane. Mitch rolled in. I didn't see any rockets go. Instead, as he pulled up, clouds of dust puffed up well short of the truck. I rolled in and let go a few pairs of rockets. It looked like I'd done some damage.

"What's up, lead? All I saw was dust."

"Shit. I'll tell you when we get home. I'm out of ordnance."

After we landed, I walked to his airplane. The wings were bare. No rocket pods. No external fuel tanks.

I asked, "What happened?"

"I tried to fire rockets, and the wing stores* cleared. Just dumped everything. It all left the airplane at once. Just plummeted to the ground in a cloud of dust. Weirdest thing I've ever seen."

Mitch's Mohawk became the center of attention. As word spread, more guys kept coming by to see for themselves. The affair became the topic of discussion at the Spud Club that night.

Snide comments ensued. "So, tell us again what happened?"

"I pressed the rocket button. Instead, the wing stores jettisoned. Everything went at once, rocket pods, and fuel tanks."

One doubter chimed in. "OK, right, Mitch. Sounds like you set your armament panel switch to bombs instead of rockets."

Another exclaimed, "That's it. We'll call you the 'Mad Bomber.' That's who you are. Hello, Mad Bomber."

The name stuck. That became who Mitch Waldran was, the "Mad Bomber."

The thing was, Mitch did nothing wrong. He set the switches correctly. On careful inspection, our maintenance guys determined the cause to be an armament system short circuit. With the switches set to rockets, as they were, on pushing the firing button, the circuit shorted to bombs. Instead of firing rockets, the short circuit caused the wing shackles to open. That's how bombs were dropped. In this case, there were no bombs, only rocket pods and external fuel tanks. The system released it all, everything attached to the wings. Poor Mitch. Even so, he proudly bore his new nickname from then on, forevermore. Mitch and I grew close during

---

* Wing stores. Those things attached to the bottom of the wings. On our Mohawks, those included rocket pods and external fuel tanks (and .50 machine pods, early on). The airplane could also drop bombs from those same attaching points. No Mohawk ever did that in combat.

our time together in the 131st. We'd been acquaintances before. As VR pilots in the 131st, we became good close friends.

Mitch wasn't the only one anointed with a nickname around that time. A new pilot, Lieutenant Bill Seiden, arrived fresh from flight school and the Mohawk qualification course. He was eager to fly missions and move from FNG* to a proven Spud. Like everyone else, he began his time in the unit flying SLAR missions off the North Vietnam coast. On his third mission, the weather was horrible on returning to Phu Bai, as it often was. It rained hard. The runway was slick.

Bill landed and immediately pulled both power levers hard back, into full reverse. Normally, the system instantly changed the pitch of both propellers to produce reverse thrust. The engines quickly wound up to full power. The airplane stopped on a dime. Everyone did it. It enabled us to expedite clearing the runway. It was also fun to let everyone see how our Mohawks could stop in a very short distance.

The pilot just had to take care. Sometimes the circuitry screwed up and one propeller reversed and the other didn't. If the power levers were back full stop, one engine pushed backward at full power while the other pulled forward, again, at full power. The emergency procedure called for pushing the power levers forward to "ground idle." That brought both engines to minimum power and both propellers out of reverse. The pilot used brakes and rudder pedals to maintain directional control. Even when done immediately, it was a tough situation.

So Bill Seiden landed in a heavy rainstorm on a slippery runway as a brand-new pilot in the unit. He put the power levers in full reverse. The system failed. One propeller reversed and the other didn't. He got the power levers out of reverse but not before the Mohawk slid off the narrow runway and caught a ditch, breaking the landing gear and bending both propellers. That earned him the nickname "Slidin' Seiden."

Another nickname had been awarded a few months earlier. Steve Ward taxied into position for takeoff on a maintenance test flight at Phu Bai some months earlier. He pushed the power forward and pulled into the air. The tower called. "Hey, Spud. You missing something?"

---

* FNG. Fucking New Guy. A common term used among American service members throughout Southeast Asia and elsewhere to refer to new arrivals.

"What's that?"

"Check your wings. You left your drop tanks on the runway."

Steve looked out to see his wings slicing bare through the air. He never figured exactly what happened. Some glitch. Nonetheless, he'd earned his nickname, "Drop Tank."

Of course, I'd earned my nickname, "Lightfoot," for running from the bad guys when I'd been shot down. When that happened, I had no survival training. Now, months later, I got orders to go to survival school in the Philippines. Most of our pilots got to go because of our risky out-of-country missions. They'd attend either the Air Force or Navy program, some en route to Vietnam, others at some point during their tour of duty. It was too bad I'd not had the experience before I was shot down, rather than now. But, if nothing else, it was a nice week-long break out of the war zone—a chance to relax, throw down some San Miguel beers, and learn something.

I reported to the Navy school at Subic Bay. The program placed us with a group of indigenous Filipinos known as Negritos, forest dwellers who rank among the earliest inhabitants of the Philippine Islands. For three days we lived entirely off the land, using only the knives and waterproof matches we would have with us in our survival kits. We made shelters, collected water in tubes of bamboo, hunted animals and caught fish. The prize that gave our instructors the most excitement was a large jungle lizard that we cooked and ate.

When I'd been shot down, I had all confidence that I could easily outrun whatever short-statured local forces pursued me. In that regard, I was thankful I had not been to this survival school at that point. Our Negrito instructors all stood less than five feet tall, yet they moved through the jungle with such speed and agility that we couldn't keep up. They frequently had to stop and wait as we came panting and sweating through the brush behind them. If Frank Griswold had not fired rockets, as he had, to slow my pursuers, I had no doubt I'd be dead.

After survival school in the Philippines, I had a new perspective on the dangers waiting in the jungles below, a new respect for the enemy we faced. A book circulated in the company that gave insights into what those dangers held. When it came my turn, I read it straight through. The book, *Reported to Be Alive* by Grant Wolfkill, gave the author's account of his experience being held as a prisoner by the Pathet Lao for over a year.[1] Wolfkill had been an NBC news producer flying aboard a helicopter when it was shot down over Laos, near the edge of the Plain of Jars. His was a harrowing tale that none of us wanted to repeat. Several in the unit talked about saving one bullet for themselves rather than get captured and endure anything like that. After my experience, I just didn't know. Life was too precious not to fight for it, even through whatever horror came my way. My two-year-old son, Spencer, meant too much to me. I'd do everything to come home.

I returned from the Philippines to find I'd been given yet another opportunity. One of our pilots, Jeff Hillis, flew a highly classified mission, codenamed Homing Pigeon. It was more restricted than anything else we did because it involved signals intelligence, the interception of enemy communications over Laos. Homing Pigeon used a specially configured Mohawk, aircraft number 24. Jeff Hillis was the only pilot cleared for the program. For him to go on R&R, another pilot had to cover the flights in his absence.

The mission required a top-secret security clearance. That involved a special, in-depth, background investigation. The Army expedited processing, the clearance arrived, and I got cleared onto the special access program. Jeff left, and I flew each day until he came back. I found it quite boring compared to everything else we did, but it allowed me to smirk as I walked around the company area with an air that everyone should shrink with envy because I was doing such super-secret spy stuff. I even got a Homing Pigeon patch sewn on my party flight suit just like the one Jeff wore on his. After he returned from leave, we'd walk past each other and give a knowing wink. We were the guys.

When my Homing Pigeon week ended, I happily got back to my bread-and-butter IR and VR, most especially VR. Being a Spud gunship pilot gave me a sense of who I was, a mark of what I'd become. I'd journeyed far from a troubled youth and academic failure. After dropping out of college on academic suspension, I knew I needed to do something different. I found satisfaction in hard physical work and took pride in doing that work well. I took jobs on cattle ranches, fought fires with the

US Forest Service, and climbed poles as an apprentice electrical lineman with Southern California Edison before enlisting in the Army in August 1965.

I'd already learned the value of hard work before I joined the service, but the Army opened new doors for me, big doors. Starting as a private, the lowest enlisted rank, I grabbed hold of every opportunity that came. The Vietnam War helped. It had only got going in earnest a short time before I went to the recruiter in Santa Monica, California.* The Army needed officers. That meant space for me in OCS, officer candidate school. The Army needed pilots. That gave me the opportunity to go to flight school. Excelling there, I became one of a handful selected for Mohawks. Officer promotions came quickly. I went to Vietnam as a captain, only twenty-two years old. I succeeded in the Army as I never had before. I liked that.

Our VR missions faced growing concentrations of anti-aircraft. Larger-caliber guns increasingly joined the fray. Spud Mohawks took more and more hits. We brought home the bacon, though. Our photos delivered some of the best images available of activity along the Ho Chi Minh Trail. We spotted truck parking areas and logistical stockpiles no one else was seeing. MACV felt it was worth the risks we took. They continued to support and resource us as the war raged on.

---

* The Vietnam War had actually gone on for decades, beginning with opposition to French colonial conquest before World War II, resistance against Japanese occupation during the war, and the post-war fight against France's colonial rule, ultimately leading to their defeat, withdrawal, and division of the country into communist North and independent South. The United States picked up the anti-communist mantle in 1954 and began providing advisors and assistance to the Republic of Vietnam (South Vietnam). It wasn't until 1964, however, after the North attacked two US Navy destroyers in the Gulf of Tonkin, that the United States began a vigorous bombing campaign. The escalating ground war started with the landing of US Marines at Danang on March 8, 1965. I enlisted that August.

Chapter 12

All Good Things Must End

Time passed. Days, weeks, and months. The intensity of combat remained; our missions always exciting, often scary. Yet, there was a sense of belonging, of purpose. We were close in the 131st. We fought for each other and for those who depended on us. We did a job that we felt, in our hearts, needed to be done.

The war had lost its luster at home. Protesters filled America's streets. But there at Phu Bai, we lived as a brotherhood. We were doing something important, something bigger than self. We were in it together. We faced risks and we raised hell. Somehow, this crazy place had become a world we loved. We were addicted to war, to the fear, the fright—the exhilaration. Adrenaline rushed in our veins. We lived in the moment. Our senses tingled with the intensity of the chaos that spun around us. War was the most intimate life experience any of us had ever had. Such a strange pull. We all wanted to go home to be with our wives and girl-friends, to see our children again, and to pick up from where we had left off. We dreamed of it. We sang songs about it. At the same time, we knew we'd miss the fight, the camaraderie—the insanity. But few opted to stay. We only hoped we'd adapt OK when we got back in the real world.

Steve Ward, my classmate and our company maintenance officer, walked into operations on a late summer day.

"What are you up to? If you've got time, I need you. Got a Mohawk to go to Red Beach. Needs a good pilot to get in there. I'll bring you back in the Beaver. Whaddya say?"

155

Red Beach was a logistics base, next to Danang. They helped with maintenance support on occasion. Their airstrip was short, only 1,800 feet. That was tight for a Mohawk. We went in and out with a minimum fuel load, and most often, single pilot. Interestingly, Red Beach was where the US Marines had landed in Vietnam in 1965, kicking off the whole ground war.

"Sure. I'll take it. I'm ready for a break."

Ward went ahead in the Beaver. I did my preflight check of the Mohawk and followed. I landed to find Steve on the ground, waving me into a parking spot. We finished the necessary paperwork, climbed into the Beaver, and headed home.

On the way, Steve said, "Hey, I've seen a place on the coast, northeast of Hue, that I've wanted to check out. You game?"

It would add only a few minutes flying time to the trip, and I was interested to take a look at what he had seen. I answered matter-of-factly, using his nickname, "Sounds good, Drop Tank."

We flew up the coast past our normal turn point for landing to the west at Phu Bai. We dropped down to a few hundred feet over Eagle Beach, the 101st Division's recreation site where the off-duty "Screaming Eagle" soldiers went for a little relax time in the sand and surf. A couple miles beyond that, Steve banked steeply left and pointed down. "There it is. See?"

I didn't, so he rolled into a right bank and orbited. That put it on my side. "See it now?"

I looked at a small base with a nice airstrip that looked to be more than two thousand feet long. It sat right on a sandy beach at the northwest tip of the long strand of land that formed the coastline.

"Yeah. Looks nice. We gonna land?"

With that suggestion from the company operations officer, he said, "Why not?" and down we went. We pulled off the runway onto a small parking ramp and shut down. As we got out to survey the situation, a young US Navy officer approached at a brisk walk.

He confronted us. "What's your business here?"

I answered. "We don't have any business. Just wanted to stop in and check it out."

His brow furrowed and he said sternly, "You can't land here. This is a Navy facility. It's only for official traffic. You've got to go."

He looked over our airplane as we climbed back in. He peered into the back, seeing the space and the seats. He came around to Steve's side of the cockpit. He still had his door open. The guy's face appeared much softer.

"You ever fly to Danang?"

"All the time. We're just coming back from there now, headed to Phu Bai."

"You wouldn't be going there on Friday, next week, would you?"

"We could."

"Any chance of a ride? My R&R flight leaves then."

"Absolutely. No sweat. We'll just tie it in with a parts run."

With that exchange, we gained carte blanche landing privileges at the beach. We came back that Sunday with swimsuits and towels. We brought a couple of other pilots along with a crew chief and two maintenance guys. We returned a few more times in the weeks ahead. I don't think I ever informed the commander, Major Fiely, of our beach outings. No sense in spoiling a good deal.

So, we did have some fun in the midst of war.

One day, our flight surgeon, Doc Miller, asked if I'd like to go with him to Hue, the old imperial capital of Vietnam, only eight miles up the road.

"It's off limits," I said.

"Not for official business. I've got doctor stuff to do there. There's a requirement for two people in the jeep. You can ride shotgun, literally. At least M-16 gun in hand."

"Yeah, OK. I'd love to go then."

We drove to Hue. I watched the scenes pass by, storing impressions in my mental scrap book. I'd never been off base in Vietnam, save the short bus ride in the dark of night from Bien Hoa to Long Binh Post the day I arrived in country. I'd never seen poverty like that in my life; people living in hovels or sitting and lying on the side of the road; packs of dogs shitting and fornicating in the street.

WE DARED TO FLY

Meager enterprises struggled beneath tarps or sheets of metal roofing propped atop crumbling cinder block walls. Some peddled produce; others had foul-looking carcasses hung in open stalls, matted with feasting flies. Fish of all sorts lay in shallow trays. Every assortment of roots, bark, branches, and leaves filled boxes. They must have been destined to season some precious pot of food. A few stands peddled shirts and shoes, pants and sandals, and sunglasses and lighters. Much, I suspected, from the black market.

So, this was Phu Bai, the town outside our gate. There were no young men to be seen. All had gone to war, soldiers in the South Vietnamese Army. Phu Bai was a place of old people, women, and children. Our hootch maids came from here, as did our barbers, cooks, and laborers. This was their world. How blessed, by the luck of birth, it was not mine. I thanked God.

We pulled into the MACV compound in Hue. It was an impressive-looking structure, still scarred from the ugly battles of Tet, 1968, when Hue suffered the worst of the country's fighting. I waited in the jeep while Doc Miller went about his business. He was back in less than five minutes.

"Want to see the Citadel, the emperor's old palace inside a walled city?"

"If we can, yeah."

Doc drove a few blocks, crossed the Perfume River, and pulled into a gravel lot by its side. With the river to our backs, I gazed across a wide moat. Stones lined its sides, and it was filled with water. Across the moat, I viewed an extraordinary sight. The moat ran along the front of a thirty-foot-high brick wall that must have been a mile long. Strategically placed defensive bastions jutted toward the river. The largest guarded the center, a powerful symbol of the strength of what lay within.

We walked across the moat on a bridge. We proceeded into an entry portal through the wall, which must have been twenty feet thick. Midway, I scampered up a short flight of stairs on my left to take a picture of the South Vietnamese flag flying from a tall tower atop the massive center bastion. Once through the outer wall, we encountered a second moat and another inner wall. We faced three bridges crossing the moat. We took the middle one. We walked toward a huge golden-roofed structure atop a massive stone-block fortification. It had five passageways leading to the heart of the imperial city. We entered through the center one and beheld the old royal palace a hundred yards ahead. I felt humbled to be there.

As we retraced our steps back to the jeep, I noted damage done to the Citadel by the savage fighting that took place during the 1968 Tet battle for Hue. It reminded me how these people had suffered. They had endured war for so long. The end of my yearlong combat tour was in sight. I'd go home. South Vietnamese soldiers fought for decades. They'd still be fighting long after I'd gone.

Sad that the communists chose to take their fight to Hue in 1968 to make their stand in that historic citadel, so beautiful and culturally rich. I was pleased to see restoration efforts in progress, even now as the flames of war still blazed not so far away. We got to the jeep to see groups of children filing off buses, dressed smartly in their school uniforms. They were there to tour the royal grounds. Hue Citadel clearly held a special place in the hearts and history of the people of Vietnam. I knew I'd just had a most special experience.

The beginning of the end came with my exile to Saigon. The 131st kept a liaison officer with Headquarters, 7th Air Force at Tan Son Nhut Airbase, there. I don't know if Major Fiely thought he was doing me a favor, or if that was my punishment when he found I'd authorized flights to the beach without his commander approval. Regardless, over my strong protests, I left on a C-130 to serve my penance, sitting behind a desk. Captain Burwin Reed, recently assigned on his second tour of duty with the 131st, took my place as operations officer.

The 131st belonged to MACV J2 (intelligence). However, 7th Air Force integrated our missions into their daily air tasking order. Sometimes we'd help them by taking some of their priority photo-targets. To prevent any snags in the system, we had one of our pilots always working in their "Out of Country Reconnaissance Office" ensuring all went smoothly. Some guys enjoyed the time in Saigon. It had its perks. Nice room in an air-conditioned Air Force facility, regular hours, and the freedom to go off base. Unlike Hue and Phu Bai, Saigon was not off-limits. It was only "Be careful and don't do anything stupid."

I couldn't wait to leave that place. I was anxious to get back to Phu Bai and flying. They must have tired of my repeated messages arguing why it made more sense for me to return to flying than it did to stay at Tan Son Nhut. I finally got permission. I packed my bag and headed to the Air Force terminal to get a flight to Phu Bai, or at least as far as Danang.

The airman at the desk told me, "Can't get you out today, sir. There is a C-130 scheduled for Danang day after tomorrow."

"Thanks." *For nothing*, I thought.

"You might check with the crew of that airplane out there." He pointed out the window at a C-46 with no markings. He added, "Not sure who they are. Guys in civilian clothes. They came and asked for a fuel truck. Think they might be headed north."

I went out onto the flight line and made my way over to the plane, a big silver thing. The airman was right; it had a set of numbers on the tail and that was it. No military branch, no national markings, nothing. Two pilots stood a short distance away smoking cigarettes, while a fuel truck finished pumping gas.

"You guys headed north?" I asked.

"Might be. Where you headed?"

"I'm trying to get back to my unit at Phu Bai. The 131st. Call sign Spud."

"Spud. You're a Spud?"

"Yeah."

"We're on our way to NKP. Happy to swing wide and drop you off on the way. Climb in."

Probably Air America or Continental Air Services. I couldn't tell. They wore plain shirts with no logo. They were flying a hell of a distance out of their way to give me a ride, probably adding over an hour to their flight. Much appreciated.

I stuck my head in the cockpit after we took off. We'd leveled off at thirteen thousand feet. We chatted for a while.

The pilot commented, "You guys fly low, don't you? Get right down there and mix it up on the treetops."

"During the day, yeah. At night, depends. Our radar missions stay pretty high, about 5,500 AGL.* Infrared, lower. Maybe one to two thousand, depending on terrain."

"I know you guys have lost some birds."

"Yeah. We have." I let it go at that.

I asked, "You guys Air America?"

"Something like that."

They landed at Phu Bai and taxied to the south side of the terminal, not far from our ramp. I got out with the engines still running, gave a wave and headed to my hootch. I'd escaped from purgatory. Thank goodness.

Shortly after I returned to flying, I learned that one of the pilots in our Mohawk qualification course was lost. He'd gone down on October 3, flying infrared with the 225th Mohawk Company based at Phu Hep, about halfway down the coast to Saigon. Lieutenant Paul Graffe and his observer, Sergeant Ken Cunningham, never came back from a mission in the mountains of central South Vietnam. Officially, reports said they were MIA (missing in action). Most felt they were dead. Their bodies were never recovered.

Two weeks later, tragedy struck the 131st. Shortly after midnight, early on Friday, October 17, I was awakened in the night and told that Captain Larry Booth had not returned from a night SLAR mission out of Udorn. There wasn't much hope. He'd been operating over the Plain of Jars. He'd called at the end of his mission, en route to Udorn at 10:15. That was his last transmission. High mountains stood between him and safety. If he'd lost an engine, they'd be tough to cross. The area had few friendly airstrips. Those were treacherous even by day and impossible in the dark of night. The region was remote. If he'd been shot down or crashed, few would have seen.

An extensive search got underway at first light on October 17, both Air Force search and rescue and our own Spuds out there looking. No

---

* AGL. Above ground level. The altitude measured above the terrain, not above sea level, which is the altitude shown on the aircraft's altimeter.

trace. I got permission to fly to Udorn at the end of my VR mission later that day. We never found a thing. We mourned, we drank, we sang our crazy songs, and we got on with flying missions.

A few days later, our new commander, Lieutenant Colonel Frank Newman, called me to his office with an assignment.

"Reeder, we've got a mission I want you to take. You will fly an infrared bird to Tan Son Nhut for a special task. Highly classified. We chose you because you have the needed top-secret clearance, and you are one of our most experienced IR pilots. You're the right guy. I want you to take one of the Super C, SEAMORE,* airplanes. We're sending our best for this mission."

I questioned the logic. "That's the 73rd's area. They're right there at Vung Tau. Why don't they have the mission? Why us?"

"Because we are the special mission Mohawk unit. We do all the out-of-country stuff. We are MACV's personal asset. This is a MACV mission. Very sensitive. We've got it."

"Roger, sir. Sounds intriguing. When do I go?"

"Tomorrow."

The IR Platoon picked their very best to be my technical observer. He had a secret security clearance. That's all he needed. Only the pilot had to have top-secret clearance. We took off the next morning, climbed to altitude, and headed south along the coast. It was a great day to fly, smooth air, blue skies, and lush jungle, spreading like a huge green quilt, draped from the mountains, and running onto the long white strands of sandy beach that were being stroked by rolling surf off the endless Pacific sea.

I was taken with the view and commented, "Beautiful, isn't it?"

"Roger that."

"I mean this place could be a resort filled with tourists if there wasn't a war going on. It is absolutely gorgeous. I've never seen beaches like these anywhere. And I grew up on nice ones in California and Hawaii."

* SEAMORE. Derived from Southeast Asia Mohawk Requirement. The Army assigned two of these special OV-1C airplanes to the 131st for trials. We called them Super Cs because of their advanced infrared detection system. The equipment was heavy, making those two birds a challenge for any pilot experiencing an engine failure after takeoff.

"Right, sir. Maybe you should invest in some real estate before it's too late."

"Yeah, right."

We laughed.

We caught a ride to MACV headquarters after we landed. A colonel waited for us in the J2 offices. A major stayed with my TO, while the colonel escorted me through a vault door into a large, enclosed room. He shut the door behind us. The space felt tightly sealed.

"I'm going to bring you on to a specially compartmented classified program. This is above top secret. Very close hold.[1] Your right-seat is being briefed on the sensitivities involved. He will not be briefed on specific mission details. We'll keep his understanding as general as possible. He is only to operate the infrared equipment, and never talk to anyone about what you did here. Understood?"

"Yes, sir."

"You'll be going into Cambodia. Cambodia is not the same as Laos. Laos is a secret war, yes. But the Laotian government wants us there. They're fighting for their freedom. We're helping their cause. We give them military aid, along with CIA advisors and air support. And we're battering the Ho Chi Minh Trail in the process. Cambodia is entirely different. It is an independent sovereign country. Prince Sihanouk, Cambodia's ruler, allows the North Vietnamese to operate freely in his country, openly using Cambodia's principal port to move supplies into Vietnam. He opposes any American operations on his soil, or flights in his skies. That's why this mission is so much more sensitive than anything going on in Laos. No one can know you are there."[2]

He went on. "After the briefing, you'll both be asked to sign documents, agreeing to the mission and its risks. You don't have to sign. You don't have to take this mission. It is not an order. You volunteered for this. I hope your decision won't change once you know what we're asking you to do."

The colonel explained that we'd fly the next night. We'd head north from Saigon to our mission area, a hundred-mile sweep of terrain— across the border, in Cambodia. That first night we'd search a select target area within that swath. The intent was for us to cover several different target areas each night for five nights.

"As you near the border, call air traffic control and just say, 'This is Army,' give your tail number, 'going on French Leave.' That's all you need to say. 'Going on French Leave' lets them know to disregard your activities. They'll know you are cleared by the highest authority to do what you are about to do. Don't use your Spud call sign, just plain old Army so-and-so. That's it."[3]

"Got it, sir."

"Great. And know that you're on your own over there. No one can come get you if you get in trouble."

"Understood, sir. So long as my observer is fine with that, we're good to go."

We took off right after sunset that next night. The terrain was different from what we'd been used to. It was flat. Everything from Saigon, en route, and across the border varied no more than a few hundred feet in elevation. We'd have no problem holding a consistent five hundred to one thousand feet above the ground on all our search patterns.

We expected to bring back some good stuff. MACV was interested in identifying troop locations, truck parks, logistics storage areas, and other infrastructure—any enemy presence that we found on infrared.

I expected easy flying, so long as the weather held. There were some low hills, but they would be well off to the east of us. Everywhere we'd fly would be flat—with only one exception. One piece of terrain stood alone, higher than anything for many miles around. That was Nui Ba Den, what Americans called Black Virgin Mountain. It was on the northeast edge of Tay Ninh city. It thrust more than three thousand feet above the surrounding plain. That could kill you.

As we flew over Loc Ninh and turned northeast, I called. "Paris, this is Army 12718, French Leave."

"Roger, 718. We'll see you later."

We were on our own. I flew another three minutes to Bu Dop, passing over old French rubber plantations. From there, I tracked a road to the Cambodian border. A strange sensation settled on me as we crossed. I felt isolated from the world. We were so near, yet that place we'd left suddenly seemed so far away. We were alone, all alone in the Cambodian sky. I had no idea of the anti-aircraft threat, or what enemy soldiers might hold us in their sights. I hoped we were too low for the big guns, but I knew that put us in the range of anti-aircraft machine guns. *What would it be like if we got shot down? Could we evade and get back across the border? What would we say if caught? How would our captors react?* A few miles in, I turned left, and we made our first run.

All went well that first night. And the next. And the two after that. The weather remained clear and calm. No one shot at us. Did we catch them by surprise, or did they simply not want to give their positions away? I couldn't be sure, but I gave thanks for our good fortune.

Things changed on our last night. All started fine except for dark billowing clouds that had formed in the afternoon and rumbled into the night. As we finished our assigned search areas, the torrent began. I turned back across the border, climbed to altitude, and called air traffic control. "Paris, this is Army 12718 back off French Leave, requesting vectors to Tan Son Nhut."

"Roger 718. Turn to heading zero-nine-zero."

The fury of the storm hit, slamming us about. Lightning flashes burst across the sky. *This is the shits.*

"718, radar contact. Turn right to heading one-four-zero."

Headed home. Hallelujah.

The turbulence decreased then stopped. A peculiar air settled around us. We were still in the storm, but all was eerily calm. The lightning changed. It was surreal, almost supernatural. It danced around us in dazzling blue and purple hues. Glowing raindrops peppered the windshield. Blazing blue arcs spun round the props. So eerie to behold. We both sat in awe as we flew through the spectacle.* And then it was done. We landed at Tan Son Nhut, unloaded our film, debriefed, and went to bed. Next day, we flew back to Phu Bai.**

---

* Most likely Saint Elmo's Fire, a rare weather phenomenon involving the ionization of air particles within a high-voltage electronic field produced by a storm.
** The classified French Leave reconnaissance effort helped identify targets for covert B-52 strikes and provided intelligence for the April 1970 US/South Vietnamese Cambodia campaign.

I returned days before the Lowdermilks departed. They flew their last flight together on the same mission, the only time they'd been allowed on the same mission together their entire time in the unit. They made an impressive pass over our ramp, so low I worried they'd clip the top of a parking revetment. They received all the pomp and ceremony given to pilots on their last flight, including a hell of a celebration at the Spud Club. The next day, they were gone. Billy Wood had already departed. That left Steve Ward and me and Mitch Waldran out of our group of classmates. Since he'd arrived long after us, Steve Ward would be around for a good while longer. Mitch and I neared the end.

Over my remaining days, I flew missions into Steel Tiger and generally enjoyed nights in the club as an old timer. Early on, Mitch Waldran and I extended our tour length by two weeks so we could remain in the 131st. Our headquarters wanted to reduce the number of Spud pilots all leaving around the same time. Their solution? Transfer some out early to other units. With our extension, Mitch and I wouldn't go home until the second week in November. That left us with a few more days remaining.

Over that time, neither of us had any responsibilities beyond flying. We enjoyed the wind down as we got ready to go home. We flew, we sat in the club, and we shared words of wisdom with the new guys. We had become the seasoned old timers as our time now approached its end.

Mitch and I flew our last mission together, a photo-recon over Laos. On landing, throngs of Spuds met us on the ramp with cheers and popping corks as they doused us with champagne. We turned in our gear and spent the evening in the Spud Club. There we nailed our brass plaques to the board, bid our friends farewell, and stumbled late to bed. We rose early in the morning, shouldered our duffle bags, and climbed aboard the trusty Beaver for a ride to Danang. There, we boarded a C-130 to Cam Ranh Bay where we'd catch the freedom bird home.

We checked in at the passenger terminal to find we'd not depart for two days. That meant two days of waiting. It was an impatient time, a somewhat anxious time. We ate and we drank, and we waited. The night before we left, we both hung our khaki uniforms up in our room. Each had been carefully folded and rolled, but the duffle bags took their toll. We hoped the wrinkles might fall out with hanging overnight. I looked at them there, side by side. Both had Army aviator wings pinned above the left breast pocket. Each had a Distinguished Flying Cross ribbon just below the wings for some heroic deed. Mine also had the Purple Heart. I laid on my bed, the back of my head cradled in my hands on my pillow. I took it all in, and I beamed with pride.

We reported early for manifest call, checked our duffle bags, and waited. I looked at the big, beautiful civilian airliner, there to take us home. A soldier called my name.

"Sir, you're designated the senior officer, the ranking person. You'll be responsible for the passengers on the flight."

"Wait," I countered, pointing to a major standing nearby. "What about him? He outranks me."

"He's a doctor, sir. The designated senior officer must be a line officer. No doctors or lawyers." He made an entry by my name on his clipboard. *Real fine.*

They boarded me first. I picked a seat a little way back, by a window. The rest of the loading followed. Mitch found a seat by the window on the other side of the plane, across the aisle from mine. The plane filled quickly. A young nurse took the seat beside me. Mitch leaned forward and looked over. I grinned.

We took off. It was dawn. The pilot made a steep climbing turn out to sea and pointed east toward the rising sun. I was homeward bound. I thought of what I was leaving, of friends still there and those who'd never return, of all that I had done. I'd grown over the past year. I wasn't a boy anymore. The war made me a man. I looked at the world differently, more jaundiced to be sure. But in the intense cauldron of war, I found a joy that dwelt in every moment lived. Whatever lay ahead, I'd grab hold of that joy, bring it close, and hold it dear. I'd learned that life is precious and often far too short. No part of it should ever be taken for granted. I'd love my friends and live my life to the hilt.

Morning light shined through the window. The young nurse next to me, exhausted, fell asleep. Her head rested on my shoulder. I leaned against the window, closed my eyes, and dreamed of family, my young son Spencer, and all in life that was yet to come.

Epilogue

THE BRAVE PILOTS OF THE 131ST SURVEILLANCE AIRPLANE COMPANY
dared to fly daunting secret missions for three more years after I left. They
continued to take hits, they continued to lose airplanes, and they continued to risk their lives. Nine more Spuds perished in that time.

Shortly after I left, MACV finally caved to Air Force wailings and
directed the 131st to remove the weapons from our Mohawks. The Air
Force felt we encroached on their mission. They cited a 1967 Army–Air
Force agreement they claimed forbade what we were doing.[1] Despite
that agreement, MACV had authorized our weapons for self-defense in
an extremely hostile environment. I wouldn't be alive today if we did not
have armed Mohawks the day I was shot down. I suppose we pushed
the limit by engaging worthy targets at the end of our missions. What
a waste to bring unused rockets home when they could do much good
for the fight. The United States Air Force had enough. The rocket pods
came off.

Over those years, several of the old guys came back to serve in the
unit again. Larry "Fox" Hower and "Big John" Kelly were two of the first.
They returned in March 1971. John "Buick" Bingham and Roger "Round
Ranger" Thiel soon joined them. Fox had gotten his nickname on his
first Spud tour of duty. His bright red hair reminded some of a fox. The
name stuck.

The enemy did not have a warm greeting for Fox Hower when he
came back to Southeast Asia. Instead, his welcome was hot. Enemy gunners seemed to be waiting for his return. On his very first mission, only
days after reporting to Phu Bai, they unleashed a barrage of 37 mm shells

shortly after he crossed the border into Laos. He sat in the right-seat of the lead aircraft on a photo reconnaissance mission. A less experienced pilot flew from the left seat. The Mohawk had dual controls, either pilot could fly the airplane. Their mission supported Operation Lam Son 719, the large-scale South Vietnamese Army advance into Laos that attempted to cut the Ho Chi Minh Trail. The operation turned to disaster as the North Vietnamese blunted, then routed their foe. Fox found himself in the midst of the chaos.[2]

Fox later described his reception.

"The first round went by the cockpit, and it reminded me of a flaming soccer ball. I couldn't imagine how it could have gotten that close and missed! I shouted, 'Break left!' Nothing. Two more rounds went by, and I said, 'I've got it,' and just as I grabbed the stick, I felt the impact. The OV-1 Mohawk shuddered and pitched nose up. *Way* nose up! I pushed forward on the stick and nothing happened. The controls were jammed. I looked in the banana mirror over the panel and saw only two tails left on the bird! The aircraft shuddered as it stalled, I kicked a hard left rudder, and we started down. Nose first, straight down! The airspeed started to build, and at about one thousand feet we started up again. No elevator control. I remember saying something like, 'We better get out!' when something broke loose back there and I had control again."

The sky filled with flak. Fox took the Mohawk down to the deck to get out of it. All enemy fire stopped as he skimmed across the treetops. He headed to Danang because of the long runway and the crash-rescue assets there. He landed safely without a third of his tail.

Fox kept flying missions through February 1972 when he departed Vietnam for the last time. Before he left, the Army decided the Mohawks should be a military intelligence, or MI, asset. They redesignated the 131st Surveillance Airplane Company as the 131st Military Intelligence Company. The Army's MI leadership started building its own pool of OV-1 pilots, a new breed of MI aviators. A mix of old and new still flew the coast of North Vietnam and missions over Laos until fall 1972.

On September 1, 1972, the 131st moved from its longtime home at Phu Bai to Marble Mountain Airfield near Danang. They moved into the space vacated by the 245th Mohawk Company that had left Vietnam.

The next month, the unit relocated again, this time to Danang Airbase, three miles west. Captain Dan Fordiani flew the last Spud operational mission of the war on October 18, a SLAR mission along the coast of North Vietnam.

On February 4, 1973, the Army chief of staff, General Creighton Abrams, approved the Valorous Unit Award for the 131st Surveillance Airplane Company for the period from June 1, 1966, to December 31, 1968.[3] The award is given to a unit for "extraordinary heroism in action against an armed enemy of the United States."[4]

The 131st found its new home at Fort Hood, Texas, sixty miles north of Austin, the state capital. The company came under the 13th Aviation Battalion of the 6th Cavalry Brigade. Personnel turnover, property accountability, and maintenance challenges plagued the unit.

In March 1973, Major Burwin Reed took command of the company. He was the perfect choice. Burwin had been an instructor pilot in the OV-1 qualification course; he had two combat tours with the 131st at Phu Bai. He'd taken my place as company operations officer on his second tour. He was well respected. In short order, Major Reed had the 131st back on a track of excellence.

The Mohawk made its move fully into the military intelligence community on April 24, 1978. The 131st left the 13th Aviation Battalion to become B Company of the 15th Military Intelligence Battalion under the 504th MI Brigade, still at Fort Hood. Though the 131st lost its proud designation, B Company, 15th MI maintained its tie to the heroic lineage and traditions of the 131st, retaining the call sign "Spud" and displaying the brass plaque board of names from Phu Bai on its wall. Its designation changed once again on September 16, 1983, to A Company, 15th MI.[5]

The unit's last combat campaign came in 1991 in the First Gulf War, Operation Desert Storm. There, the A Company Mohawks flew signals and electronic intelligence missions and proved to be effective SCUD* missile hunters. They also performed several bomb damage assessment missions. They flew the latest D-model aircraft with improved

---

* SCUD. A highly mobile tactical ballistic missile developed by the Soviet Union. Used extensively by Iraq during the First Gulf War.

SLAR, IR, and photo capabilities as well as new electronic technologies. The aircraft and crews returned to Fort Hood in April 1991.[6]

Well-founded objections notwithstanding, the United States Army still decided to close down its OV-1 Mohawk units. They claimed modern developments would meet the requirement, cutting costs with joint systems that would serve every branch of the armed forces, all at the same time. The rationale fell short. There was nothing at the time that could satisfy the immediate intelligence needs of ground commanders. Nonetheless, the Army stuck by its decision. A Company, 15th Military Intelligence Battalion, turned in its OV-1 aircraft in 1996. The unit's storied Mohawk history—that so many of us lived as we dared to fly those dangerous missions with the 131st during the Vietnam War—came to an end.

That history had begun in the 11th Air Assault Division tests conducted from 1963 to 1965 at Fort Benning, Georgia. It saw the formation of the 20th Aerial Surveillance and Target Acquisition (ASTA) Detachment at Fort Riley, Kansas, on July 1, 1965; its deployment to Nha Trang, Vietnam on October 23; and its move to Phu Bai in early April 1966.

The 20th ASTA went to Vietnam with six airplanes. In their first six months, they lost five Mohawks with seven crew members killed or missing in action. The Army redesignated the 20th as the 131st Surveillance Airplane Company on June 1, 1966. They plussed the unit to eighteen Mohawks and increased manning. By year's end, enemy gunners downed four more Mohawks. Half the unit's airplanes were lost in one year, with thirteen pilots and observers killed or missing in action (remains never recovered). Only five crew members were rescued.

What of those brave Spuds I knew? What became of them after the war?

Gary "Mr. Clean" Alton, our commander, Spud 6, stayed in the Army after Vietnam. His next assignment put him in Washington, DC, where the family bought a home. He completed Command and General Staff College, but when selected for battalion-level command, he declined, deciding to finally settle down in one place with his family. After a career of service in and out of combat and qualifications as a paratrooper, pathfinder, and Army aviator; after serving with the Joint Chiefs of Staff in the Pentagon; after moving his family from home to home to home, driving across the country, packed into their station wagon, he felt it was time to stay in one place, raise his family in a stable environment, and let his eldest daughter finish in the same high school she had started. He retired from the military as a lieutenant colonel with twenty years of service.

Gary and his wife Ruth had a good life. He began a second career as a real estate broker. He found success and personal satisfaction in that work for ten years. Then dreadful news. Like nearly all of us at Phu Bai, Gary smoked cigarettes for many years and he'd been exposed to Agent Orange. The doctors diagnosed lung cancer. Treatment and surgeries followed. His doctor encouraged a less stressful job. Gary moved from broker to real estate appraiser. He did that for another ten years. After a second cancer diagnosis and more disagreeable treatments, he retired, spending more time with family, and helping raise his first grandson, Christopher.

Gary loved all who'd served with him in the 131st. He attended every reunion, proudly wearing his old Spud hat, embroidered with "SPUD 6" and "Mr. Clean." Each year on Father's Day, he began going to the Vietnam Veterans Memorial on Washington's National Mall. There, he'd place roses below the names of all the 131st service members carved upon its stone—red roses for those killed, yellow for those missing in action. His effort helped start a movement that grew into a national event that continues to this day. By 2018, three thousand roses were placed at the wall. More thousands continue to be left each year.[7]

As Gary became increasingly ill, with his health in decline, we Spuds made a visit to his winter home in Green Valley, Arizona. There, we spent time together, broke bread and drank, and shared old stories from the war that we'd already told a hundred times.

After his third diagnosis of lung cancer, Gary struggled for a time before passing away on March 17, 2010, age seventy-five. He left his wife Ruth, a large and loving family, and his beloved Mohawk brothers. He was laid to rest with honors at Arlington National Cemetery after a moving service at Fort Meyer's Old Post Chapel. Gary Alton's legacy lives on in three daughters, ten grandchildren, nineteen great-grandchildren, and one great-great-grandchild.

John "Buick" Bingham, master of Spud esprit, served two tours of duty with the 131st. After Vietnam, he separated from the service and joined the Plumbers and Pipefitters Union in Salt Lake City, Utah, a trade he'd learned before joining the Army. John struggled with alcoholism for several years before getting sober in 1981, which he maintains to this day. He and his wife, Raona, worked industrial piping jobs, traveling throughout the United States. John worked as a certified piping welder, foreman, general foreman, and purchasing agent. After retiring in 2001, he and Raona settled in the mountains south of Carson City, Nevada. Unfortunately, Raona passed away in 2008, after a lengthy battle with cancer.

After Raona's passing, a friend introduced John to Reine, a widow from Washington State. They became inseparable life partners. They explore the ghost towns and the back roads of Nevada. They record ancient Native American archaeological sites under the tutelage and direction of the Nevada Rock Art Foundation. Reine and John divide their time between homes in Nevada and Washington, playing golf as their mood and weather permits.

John has three children by his first wife, Susan. He also shares the love of his late wife Raona's two adult children and Reine's two grown kids. He is blessed with thirteen grandchildren. Mohawk blood still runs through John Bingham's veins, and he still carries his old nickname "Buick" with pride.

Tom Bratcher left Vietnam after commanding the Spud special flight detachment at the Royal Thai Airbase in Udorn. He moved his family to Fort Monmouth, New Jersey, where he attended the Signal Officers' Advanced Course. The family went on to Fort Rucker, Alabama, for Tom's assignment in the telecommunications directorate on the post. After two and a half years, Bratcher received a pleasant surprise with orders to graduate school at the University of Colorado, Boulder. On graduation, he moved on to a signal corps assignment in the 82nd Airborne Division at Fort Bragg, North Carolina. For his mid-career schooling, he went to the Air Force Command and Staff College at Maxwell Air Force Base in Montgomery, Alabama.

Tom filled out the rest of his career with assignments to Atlanta in the Georgia Tech University ROTC department, and to Heidelberg, Germany, for his work in telecommunications at the US Army Europe headquarters. After military retirement in 1984, he remained in Heidelberg as a civilian telecommunications contractor through 1989.

After finishing his second career, Tom moved his family back to the States. He always liked golf and skiing and taking runs with his wife, Elsie. In retirement, he found time to experience all that to the fullest. Tom and Elsie were deeply in love. Together they so enjoyed those years. Sadly, Tom Bratcher died from heart problems on December 8, 2015. He left us too soon, at seventy-three.

Henry "Hank" Brummett, who made me a gun pilot, had successful military and civilian careers after leaving Phu Bai. He attended the Army's Command and General Staff College and earned a master's degree in statistics before commanding a helicopter company at Fort Hood, Texas. That was followed by an assignment to the Army staff at the Pentagon before moving into the office of the Chief of Staff of the Army. He later commanded an aviation battalion in Korea, returned to the Pentagon, received his promotion to full colonel, and attended the Naval War College. He headed the Program Analysis & Evaluation Directorate for the Army Recruiting Command and capped his Army career as the installation commander of Fort Sam Houston, Texas. He retired from the military in fall 1989 with twenty-eight years of service.

Brummett's civilian career was no less successful. He served as city manager for two San Antonio suburban cities and taught math at the San Antonio College for fifteen years.

Hank married his wife, Judy, in 1961. They were happily married for forty-seven years until her untimely death in 2008. He met Sharon in 2009. They married and have been happy together ever since. His daughter, Kristan, sadly passed away. Hank now enjoys his retirement, spending time with family: his son, Michael, a retired Air Force lieutenant colonel;

his daughter-in-law, Jane; and their daughter, Hank's granddaughter and pride and joy, Nanne.

Max Davison, my OV-1 Mohawk instructor pilot and mentor, continued to whisper in my ear in every airplane I flew. I could hear his voice reminding me: "Stay ahead of the airplane," "You fly the airplane; don't let the airplane fly you," "Have a plan if x, y, or z happens," and on and on.

After Max came home from flying with the 131st in Vietnam, the Army assigned him to Fort Rucker, Alabama, as an instructor pilot in the OV-1 Mohawk qualification course. It was my good fortune to be paired with Major Davison as the man to teach me to fly the Mohawk and prepare me for war. Max went back to Vietnam in 1969. He returned to the States in 1970, to attend the Army Command & General Staff College at Fort Leavenworth, Kansas. He stayed there as an instructor for a short time after graduation. The Army could not leave an officer there for long who had such an in-depth knowledge of the engineering and flight characteristics of the OV-1 Mohawk.

He took command of the DCASPRO, the Defense Contract Administration Services Plant Representative's Office, at the Grumman Aircraft facility on Witham Field in Stuart, Florida. There, he oversaw Army acceptance of all the OV-1 Mohawks that Grumman delivered. He held a very high standard. Tragically, his wife Masako was murdered one night while taking a walk on the beach near their home in December 1981. Grief paralyzed Max and their two children, but he found strength in his responsibility, now as a single parent.

It took years, but Max met a wonderful woman named Edie. They fell in love and married in 1993. After his retirement, they lived in Jacksonville, Florida, spending time each summer in Max's hometown, Beatrice, Nebraska. They bought a motor home and traveled the country for weeks on end. In 1998, Max Davison died suddenly, but peacefully, sitting in his living room. He'd had a heart attack. He was only sixty-two.

I remember Max as a high-energy guy. His dear friend, John Pfeiffer, described him as "an eagle disguised as a banty-rooster." He was that, and more. His spirit will always be a part of my conscience.

Curt "Astronaut" Degner grew into the best infrared pilot in the United States Army. After our time together in the 131st, the Army sent Curt to the Mohawk instructor pilot course at Fort Rucker, Alabama, and to training at the Grumman Aircraft facility in Stewart, Florida. He became an expert in the newest version of the Mohawk, the OV-1D, being readied for delivery to units in the field.* Curt was one of the original members of the transition team that trained pilots, TOs, and support personnel on the new airplanes delivered to their units. The team's first assignment?—Return to Vietnam and facilitate aircraft delivery and pilot training for the 131st. Curt saw more combat flying on this second tour, including a near disaster when he struck a large bird one night, shattering the aircraft nose cone. That funneled two-hundred-mile-an-hour wind into the cockpit and caused an electrical failure. Curt recycled switches, getting the generators back on line and restoring electric power. He limped into Udorn Airbase, knowing it was the closest field with a long runway and crash rescue. He survived his second visit to the war zone and went on to transition other units in the United States and Germany.

Curt left active duty in October 1972, to take a full-time position as a Mohawk pilot and instructor with the Oregon National Guard. He suffered a heart attack in 1983, at the age of forty-two. He remained in the guard as a ground school instructor until retiring in 1988. He received one of the first waivers granted by the Federal Aviation Administration (FAA) after a major myocardial infarction and entered a post-military career as a corporate pilot for Payless Drugs. At the same time, he and his wife, Carolyn, purchased a small farm, raising peaches, cherries, and nectarines.

The FAA continued his waiver each year until inexplicably cancelling it in 1996. He was permanently grounded, forcing him into retirement. That lasted a year.

Itching to do something, Curt and Carolyn became the franchise owners of a Sears store they built in early 1998, in Woodburn, Oregon. They did that for nearly two years before finally retiring for good. They

---

* The OV-1D incorporated interchangeable mission pallets, allowing a single OV-1 airframe to perform any of the traditional Mohawk missions, photo, SLAR, or IR by changing system configurations in less than an hour. This dramatically increased the flexibility of the unit.

sold the business and bought a motor home. They spent time touring the country and enjoying trips overseas. They continue to enjoy life, living near Portland, Oregon.

Steve Easley only had a year to serve when he returned to the United States. The Army assigned him to Fort Bliss, Texas. With no aviation units there, he was detailed to the military police as the non-commissioned officer in charge of the post's stockade guards. Easley did not reenlist.

After his discharge in June 1970, he worked as a security guard at a copper mine in his hometown of Ely, Nevada, for a short time. He entered college at the University of Nevada, majoring in business management. While in college, he enrolled in a casino dealer's school in Las Vegas. The Fremont Hotel & Casino hired him as a dealer. Within two years he moved to management and found executive positions in several hotel-casinos on the Las Vegas Strip over the years ahead. He also helped open casinos in Detroit, Michigan, and Biloxi, Mississippi. Steve retired from the gaming industry after thirty-five years, and started his own business training hospitality workers.

Frank "Jinx" Griswold saved my life the day I was shot down. Our paths crossed many times after that, and we remained close friends for life. After Phu Bai, Frank joined me at the University of Nebraska at Omaha where we finished our college degrees under an Army-funded program. That's where I first met his lovely wife, Timmi. Their next assignment was to the Mohawk school at Fort Huachuca, Arizona. They went to Germany in 1974, where Frank commanded the Mohawk company at Hanau, later moving it south, to Stuttgart. After command, he became the aerial surveillance officer at the US Army Europe headquarters, responsible for staff oversight of all Army intelligence flights in Europe. Frank retired from the Army in 1976.

Frank and Timmi moved to Alabama where Frank started a distinguished career in the Alabama Department of Corrections, rising to deputy commissioner before retiring in 1999. After his second retirement, the couple enjoyed travel with grandchildren and hosting frequent family gatherings in their home. Frank was devastated on losing his beloved

Timmi to cancer in 2005. Three years later, he found love again with his second wife, Bobbi, who brought her large family into his life. Frank loved his two families, and they loved him. He was especially proud of his kids. His son Bill, is a retired college dean and Alabama National Guard colonel. His son Steven is a retired Air Force colonel. With their wives, Teresa and Mary Beth, they gave Frank two granddaughters and two grandsons. Sadly, Frank's daughter Tammy passed away in 2018.

Frank and Bobbi traveled the world, making great memories until Frank's death on Christmas Day 2019. He died from a brain tumor. He was eighty-two. I spoke with him days before he died. He believed a C-123 overflying his Mohawk in Vietnam, while spraying Agent Orange, may have caused his tumor. My good friend is missed.

Larry "Fox" Hower was one of the Old Gun Pilots leaving Phu Bai when I arrived. He returned for a second tour of duty with the 131st in time for Lam Son 719, the South Vietnamese invasion of Laos in early 1971. With no more armed Mohawks, he was happy to head home in January 1972. Fox left the Army and bought a thirty-acre farm on the coast of Maine and started flying commercially. He flew for Continental, JAL, and United airlines. He became a captain on all Boeing aircraft to include thirteen years on the 747. He met his wife Cyndy on the shores of Rhode Island, in 2006. They live in a village on the water and have a nice thirty-three-foot power boat. They spend as much time together as they can, cruising Cape Cod and the islands. He's come far from his days at Phu Bai.

Joe "Magnet Ass" Kennedy returned stateside to attend schooling at Fort Sill, Oklahoma before being assigned to Aberdeen Proving Ground, Maryland. On military retirement in 1977, he became a government civilian employee, continuing work at Aberdeen. He also joined the Maryland National Guard with duty as a part-time Army helicopter pilot. He retired from the National Guard in 1997 at their mandatory retirement age of sixty. He retired from civil service in 2009. Joe Kennedy defended his country for over forty-six years in military and government service.

Joe and his wife, Joyce, enjoyed scuba diving in the Caribbean, skiing all over the United States and Canada, traveling to Europe, and relaxing on cruises. Joe remained an avid golfer, bow hunter, and fisherman most of his life. He was proud of his daughters, Shawn, Trea, and Kristen, and loved his four grandchildren. In later years, the once proud and strong Mohawk gun pilot suffered memory challenges. He passed away in 2021 at age eighty-four. Joe was buried at Arlington National Cemetery, the resting place of several other departed SPUDs.

Joe "Sweet" Lowdermilk went from Phu Bai to Fort Huachuca, Arizona, where he instructed students on the Mohawk surveillance systems. The Army wanted Joe to learn to fly helicopters and qualify in the Cobra attack helicopter en route to a second tour of duty in Vietnam. Having completed his obligated service, Joe decided to leave the Army instead.

He moved to Florida in late 1970 and entered the automobile business as a salesman. Within ten months, he'd become general manager of the dealership. His son, Joe Jr., was born in 1971, but Joe's marriage dissolved shortly after. Years later, Joe reconnected with his high school sweetheart, Diane. They fell back in love and married.

Joe retired from the car business in 2010. He was proud that his dealership ranked in the top ten in the country during his time as general manager. He and Diane spend winters in Florida and summers in Indiana. Joe enjoys boating, fishing, and golf. His son, Joe Jr., is a medical echocardiogram technician.

Jon "Sour" Lowdermilk also went to Fort Huachuca, Arizona, after Vietnam. He continued to fly Mohawks while training new TOs bound for Vietnam. Jon was discharged from the Army in March 1970, and he moved to Naples, Florida. There he began a successful career in commercial real estate, specializing in commercial property management. He also met a lovely young lady named Sally. They married in 1971.

Jon retired in 2009. He and Sally now split their time between Florida and a home on Chatuge Lake, North Carolina. They have two children. Daughter Jeanne is an attorney and son TJ is director of legislative affairs for the US Department of Commerce.

John "Tree" Pfeiffer had served earlier in the 131st, establishing himself as a legend by the time I arrived. He left Phu Bai in October 1967, bound for Fort Rucker, Alabama, the home of Army Aviation. Frustrated as a non-flying classroom instructor, he left the Army in 1968 and founded an aviation memorabilia business that grew rapidly, supplying the post-exchange and base-exchange stores for the Army, Navy, and Air Force in the area. His core product was a wall plaque inscribed with the High Flight sonnet written by Royal Canadian Air Force pilot John Gillespie Magee in 1941, a few months before his death in aerial combat during World War II. That poem had moved John and inspired his business.

> Oh, I have slipped the surly bonds of Earth
> And danced the skies on laughter-silvered wings;
> Sunward, I've climbed, and joined the tumbling mirth
> Of sun-split clouds,—and done a hundred things.
> You have not dreamed of—wheeled and soared and swung
> High in the sunlit silence. Hov'ring there,
> I've chased the shouting wind along, and flung
> My eager craft through footless halls of air. . . .
>
> Up, up the long, delirious, burning blue
> I've topped the wind-swept heights with easy grace
> Where never lark, or even eagle flew—
> And, while with silent, lifting mind I've trod
> The untrespassed sanctity of space,
> —Put out my hand, and touched the face of God.

After running a successful company for five years, he accepted an invitation to join the Georgia National Guard and once more fly Mohawks. He sold the business and moved to Marietta, just outside Atlanta. While flying part time in the Guard, he began another career with a hotel management company. He was tasked to step in and turn around failing establishments. He did that until he was needed as a care-giver for both his ninety-year-old father and his sister who was fighting cancer. John moved back home to Allegany, New York, into a new family home that had been built on their old family farm.

John began volunteering his time in work with the Joint POW/MIA Accounting Command (JPAC), the agency charged with recovering the remains of missing American servicemen and women from all wars. After John's sister lost her battle with cancer and his father later passed away, John traveled to Southeast Asia to work with State Department officials and JPAC personnel to help, more specifically, pin down the locations of crash sites associated with the 131st. John lived in peaceful retirement, enjoying life and the views across the remaining acres of the Pfeiffer family farm until his death on May 11, 2024.

Burwin "Smuggler" Reed had various aviation and infantry staff assignments after finishing his command of the 131st at Fort Hood, Texas. He attended the Army Command & General Staff College at Fort Leavenworth, Kansas, with subsequent assignments to the Army Operations Center and the National Military Command Center (NMCC) in the Pentagon. He returned to Fort Hood to serve as the deputy inspector general before retiring from the Army as a lieutenant colonel in 1985.

He formed a debris management business in Virginia, recycling materials from the construction of homes, businesses, roads, and other projects. He owned the business for eighteen years and loved working for himself, being his own boss, and working in the outdoors. He closed shop in 2015, and retired. He enjoys life with Elizabeth, his high school sweetheart and wife of sixty years. He considers himself a poor but persistent golfer and an excellent hunter and fisherman.

Bill "Slidin' Seiden" continued flying dangerous Mohawk missions after I left. He also made a name as the 131st Beaver pilot. After Vietnam, the Army assigned him to Fort Hood, Texas. He left the service and attended the University of Mary Hardin-Baylor, graduating with a bachelor's degree in 1973. He became a civilian flight instructor in Napa, California, waiting for an airline opportunity. He moved up to chief flight instructor and the chief pilot with the local air taxi service.

His airline chance came with an interview with American Airlines. He got hired. Bill spent thirty years flying with American, accumulating more than twenty thousand hours. He rose to captain and spent his last seven years flying to Europe and South America.

Bill Seiden is active in community service organizations and his church in Vacaville, California. He loves his blended family with his wife, Karen, sharing two daughters from his first marriage and their two daughters together, along with a total of six grandchildren. Bill and Karen's firstborn is a child with Down syndrome. They find her a real joy, and she has helped them become more compassionate people.

Ed Shulda was the aerial observer with Joe Kennedy the day they took that horrendous hit in the tail of their Mohawk. After Vietnam, Ed left the Army and returned home to Renton, Washington. He used his GI Bill to go back to school, studying accounting and business while working odd jobs. He got married. Massive Boeing layoffs impacted the Washington State economy. In 1971, Ed decided to go back in the Army until things got better.

Over the next fifteen years, the Army sent Ed to some great places, including three tours of duty in Europe, one with duty at a Royal Air Force Base in England. He opted to stay in. He did well, advancing steadily to the rank of master sergeant, the second-highest enlisted grade in the Army. He was honored to go to Fort Hood, Texas, to help organize the new A Company in the 15th Military Intelligence Battalion, what would become the battalion's Mohawk company. Ed served as the operations sergeant and first sergeant, the top kick, the senior non-commissioned officer of the company. His superiors recommended him for promotion to sergeant major.

Ed retired in 1985, before his promotion. His father went blind and his mother needed help. He returned home to Washington, went back to school, and worked odd jobs. He found work with the post office where he worked until his retirement in 2006, so he could care for his wife after her diagnosis of amyotrophic lateral sclerosis (ALS), known commonly as "Lou Gehrig's disease." She died in 2013.

Ed found love again and remarried. He and Shirley enjoy family trips and the time they have with each other. Ed has three grown children and eight grandkids. He struggles with PTSD and medical effects from Agent Orange.

Mitch "Mad Bomber" Waldran was my good buddy in the 131st. We flew many a fantastic mission together, and we came home together on the same airplane. Mitch went on to make significant contributions through the rest of his Army career and later as a civilian contractor.

He commanded the first improved Hawk missile battery deployed to Germany. He became helicopter qualified and commanded an aviation company at Fort Bragg, North Carolina. We teamed up again as students at the Armed Force Staff College in Norfolk, Virginia. He went on to numerous key staff assignments, becoming involved in combat developments at Fort Monroe, Virginia. There, he helped plan and coordinate much of the aviation testing being done in the Army. After work on space and missile defense in Huntsville, Alabama, he moved back to Fort Rucker where he was the deputy director of tests and evaluation in the combat developments directorate.

Mitch Waldran retired from the Army in 1989. He continued contributing to America's defense as a civilian contractor. He supervised teams designing and testing airborne systems for the interdiction and eradication of illicit drugs, and he helped develop aircraft modifications used to detect drug laboratories in jungle terrain. For ten years, he worked for Science Applications International Corporation (SAIC) as the senior manager of projects related to US Army aviation. Mitch became a semi-retired gentleman in 2000, limiting his work to occasional consulting assignments. Among those, he performed analysis and technical evaluation for the Defense Advanced Research Project Agency (DARPA).

Waldran had a lifelong love affair with aviation. It seemed he always owned one or more airplanes after Vietnam. He enjoyed retirement in Ocala, Florida, and life with Mois, his wife of sixty-four years, along with frequent visits from his son, Mitchell Allen; his wife, Jennifer; and their two children, Mitch's cherished grandchildren. Mitch spent his last days in memory care. He passed away on October 10, 2023. He was eighty-three. The last thing he remembered was being a Mohawk pilot in Vietnam.

Steve "Drop Tank" Ward was assigned to Fort Lewis, Washington, after Vietnam. He served as a logistics officer in the support brigade but flew with the Mohawk Company on post. An aircraft from the company crashed into Hoquiam Bay on the Washington coast. Steve oversaw the recovery. He was able to find the pilots' bodies the first day. They were both his friends. Tough work. He used a barge and crane to recover the airplane, piece by piece. That took three days.

Steve stayed at Fort Lewis until his obligated military service ended in December 1972. He had strong family ties in Utah that pulled him back home. He left the active Army and moved to Ogden with his wife, Brenda. There he could help on the family farm and fall into a more settled lifestyle.

On arrival in Utah, he immediately joined the Army Reserve. He commanded the Aviation Detachment with six Huey helicopters, one Jet Ranger, a familiar U-6 Beaver, and a twin-engine Cessna 310. He enjoyed his time in the Reserve, achieving the rank of major. As years went by, he needed more time for his civilian work. He'd invested in substantial warehouse complexes that demanded his attention. He left the Reserve after seven years and has succeeded in several entrepreneurial enterprises since. He and Brenda now enjoy life in beautiful Saint George, Utah.

Bill "Lightfoot" Reeder (the author) I returned home from Vietnam with orders to the University of Nebraska at Omaha to complete my undergraduate degree in an incredible, fully funded Army program. It was a great opportunity to decompress after combat, study hard, and enjoy a relaxed two years before, I knew, I'd have to go back to Vietnam. It was grand. I found time to go fishing and, most of all, to do things with my three-year-old son, Spencer. I was thrilled with the arrival of my daughter, Victoria, a month before graduation.

I majored in political science and minored in history. I'd thought I might transfer to military intelligence since they'd just taken over the Mohawk program. I'd gone to Washington, DC, to talk to the MI career managers who expressed enthusiasm about me coming aboard. I'd pin on MI brass and be all set to go to the OV-1 instructor pilot course after graduation en route to my second combat tour in Vietnam. That would quite probably be back to the 131st.

Then, I heard the news. The Army had removed the guns from the Mohawks in Vietnam. There were no more armed OV-1s, not even among the Spuds. That hit me hard. I gave it careful thought for about a minute. There was no decision, really. As much as I tried to interject some form of logical decision-making analysis, the obvious glared right in my face. I was a gun pilot. I liked flying photo reconnaissance more than any other mission. The Mohawk was a special airplane to be sure. But most of all, I loved engaging targets with rockets. I loved shooting. I would not transfer to military intelligence. I made a call to my current assignment folks and asked if I could decline my Mohawk orders and ask for rotary wing transition to learn to fly helicopters.

"Sure, that's easy," they said.

"And how about a qualification in Cobra attack helicopters, right after?"

"Sure, that's easy."

I graduated from the university, learned to fly helicopters, and went back to Vietnam as a war-seasoned, senior captain, AH-1G Cobra gunship pilot. Another dream came true. I cover the twists and turns of that second tour of duty in my book, *Through the Valley: My Captivity in Vietnam* (2016).

In Memoriam

To the SPUDs Who Gave Their Lives in Southeast Asia

Specialist 5 Kenneth Ainsworth, February 2, 1968, vehicle ambush—South Vietnam

Captain Lawrence Booth, October 16, 1969, SLAR—Laos

First Lieutenant Jimmy Brasher, September 28, 1966, SLAR—North Vietnam

Chief Warrant Officer 2 Jack Brunson, May 31, 1971, VR—Laos

Captain James Gates, April 6, 1966, VR—Laos

Specialist 5 Dennis Giles, September 24, 1968, SLAR—South Vietnam

Captain James Johnstone, November 19, 1966, VR—Laos

Specialist 4 John King, November 2, 1970, IR—South Vietnam

Private First-Class Marshall Kipina, July 14, 1966, IR—Laos

Captain John Lafayette, April 6, 1966, VR—Laos

Captain Larry Lucas, December 20, 1966, VR—Laos

Major Glenn McElroy, March 15, 1966, VR—Laos

Captain Clinton Musil, May 31, 1971, VR—Laos

Captain John Nash, March 15, 1966, VR—Laos

Lieutenant Colonel Frank Newman, February 24, 1970, Training flight—South Vietnam

Captain Robert Nopp, July 14, 1966, IR—Laos

Private First-Class Robert Pittman, September 28, 1966, SLAR—North Vietnam

Specialist 4 Dennis Rattin, October 16, 1969, SLAR—Laos

Specialist 5 Daniel Richards, December 8, 1972, SLAR—South Vietnam

Chief Warrant Officer 2 George Rogalla, November 2, 1970, IR—South Vietnam

Chief Warrant Officer Russell Rowe, July 19, 1970, friendly fire—South Vietnam

Specialist 4 James Schimberg, January 9, 1966, IR—South Vietnam

Captain James Shereck, March 4, 1971, SLAR—South Vietnam

Specialist 4 Lawrence Smith, November 26, 1971, SLAR—South Vietnam

Captain James Spann, November 26, 1971, SLAR—South Vietnam

Major James Whited, KIA November 19, 1966, VR—Laos

First Lieutenant Thaddeus Williams, January 9, 1966, IR—South Vietnam

Specialist 4 Harold Wilson, February 19, 1967, IR—South Vietnam

Major Johnnie Wright, February 19, 1967, IR—South Vietnam

Author's Note

This is the story of the courageous young men who flew unusual airplanes in a special mission aviation unit. They flew into the perilous corners of Southeast Asia where no other US Army personnel or aircraft ventured. It is my memoir, a true story based on my memories and the recollections of those who served with me. I confirmed those facts, not resident in my head, through investigations into original source documents and a myriad of other reference materials. I spent hours in interviews and correspondence to get things as right as I could.

The dialogue I use in telling the story is obviously reconstructed. I did that according to what I remembered of those interactions and to the best recollections of those involved. The dialogue is faithful to the conversations that took place. The story is as factual and true to the events as possible. Even so, there are surely some errors that may be found. For those I apologize and can only promise that I will accept all criticism in the spirit of correcting those mistakes in any future editions of this book that might be published.

I am grateful to everyone who gave of their time to make this book possible, to those who spent hours sharing memories and answering my myriad questions, to those who found photos and other historic materials they willingly shared, and to those who simply cheered, helping me drive on enthusiastically throughout the project.

I owe thanks to so many, too many to list here. Some are included among my sources, but not all. There are a few, however, that I'll highlight. Above all, I must thank my wife, Melanie, my biggest cheerleader and principal editor. I am particularly grateful to Patty DiMaggio whose husband Joe was our Grumman technical representative at Phu Bai. She helped Joe go through the boxes holding his lifetime collection of stuff. They picked out relevant documents, manuals, and other materials that were tremendously helpful to me. That material allowed me to refresh my knowledge of the OV-1 airplane, inside and out. Next, I must single out John Pfeiffer. Our many hours of conversation helped me better understand the early days of the Mohawk, the evolution of the armed aircraft, and the development of the first gunnery training program. He also gave me insight into the unit's first year of operations in Southeast Asia. Terry Clark, the OV-1 Mohawk Association communications director, assisted immeasurably with fact check after fact check. Ian Baird, of the University of Wisconsin–Madison, helped me understand the indigenous tribal makeup of southern Laos and how cultural nuances played on the friendly and enemy actions in the region. I am indebted to Mickey Kappes and Thomas Briggs for helping me appreciate the role of the CIA case officers we worked with during the Laotian secret war. Finally, my thanks to the late Grant Wolfkill, a man I never met but whose book, *Reported to Be Alive*, weighed on my mind on nearly every mission I flew. His experience as a captive of the Pathet Lao later helped me survive my own ordeal as a prisoner of war when I was shot down and captured on my second tour of duty. The lessons I'd gleaned from reading his book gave me a strength of knowledge that bolstered me during my time in captivity.

Glossary

General Terms

AAA. Anti-aircraft artillery. *See* weapons.

ABCC (Airborne Command and Control Center). Cargo airplane specially configured with communications and radar pods in the cargo bay; manned with twelve to fifteen personnel responsible for controlling air traffic and the flow of fighter/bomber aircraft to forward air controllers for airstrikes. *See* C-130.

Ace. A military aviator who shoots down five or more enemy aircraft in aerial combat. The kills must be confirmed by a witness, photo, or film.

AGL. Altitude measure above ground level unlike the altitude shown on an airplane's altimeter that displays altitude above mean sea level (MS) calculated from barometric pressure.

Arc Light. B-52 strike normally consisting of three of the heavy bombers.

BX. *See* PX.

Covey FAC. *See* FAC.

DMZ. Demilitarized Zone. The area within five kilometers either side of a line roughly approximating the 17th Parallel, dividing North and South Vietnam.

Drop tanks. Large cylinders holding up to 150 gallons (over one thousand pounds) of fuel, each. One hangs under each wing. Larger 300-gallon tanks can be used for long-distance ferry flights.

ECM. Electronic Countermeasures. A system designed to give warning of surface-to-air missile launches or tracking by radar-guided anti-aircraft guns. In the OV-1 Mohawk, the components sat atop the instrument panel on the far-left side. They consisted of a round four-inch scope with a rectangular box lying across the top of it.

Ejection seat. Powered by an explosive charge to propel the pilot and right-seat observer from the aircraft. The seat mechanism initiates an automatic sequence, deploying the parachute and separating the crew member from the seat.

Ejection seat harness. Webbing worn by a crew member that allows attachment to the parachute risers (straps) on the ejection seat, connecting the crew member to their parachute.

FAC. Forward Air Controller. Experienced pilots flying O-1, O-2, and OV-10 airplanes who mark targets and give instructions to attack planes for airstrikes.

Firebase. A position, stripped of vegetation, fortified with trenches, bunkers, coiled razor-wire, and land mines, defended by a force ranging from platoon to battalion that often conduct combat operations outside the firebase perimeter. Artillery units often positioned their cannons on firebases.

FNG (fucking new guy). A common term used among American service members throughout Southeast Asia and elsewhere to refer to new arrivals.

G-force (Gs). The force of gravity exerted on an object (human body included). One G is what we feel as we go about our normal routine on earth. Two Gs is twice that force. In other words, if we weigh 180 pounds, at two Gs it is as if we weigh 360 pounds.

Most pilots lose consciousness at around five Gs. The Mohawk can handle seven Gs.

II (Imagery Interpretation). That element of the company intelligence section that analyzes mission photos and SLAR and IR imagery to find useful intelligence information.

Karst. Large protrusions of rock resulting from limestone erosion over millions of years. Towering formations thrust from the jungle floor in Laos and parts of Vietnam. Some are bigger than football fields rising vertically several hundred feet above the surrounding landscape. In some areas there are clusters of karst formations grouped together or running in long, impressive lines.

MACV-SOG. Military Assistance Command Vietnam—Studies and Observations Group. The MACV special operations command that ran highly classified, covert special operations across the borders into Laos and Cambodia.

MSL (mean sea level). The altitude of an airplane above the sea. This is how all elevations on earth are measured. *See also* AGL.

Nail FAC. *See* FAC.

PDJ. The abbreviation of the French, *Plain des Jarres*, referring to the Plain of Jars in northern Laos. An archaeological area covered with ancient chiseled stone cylinders of various sizes. A region of intense conflict during the Laotian civil war.

PX/BX (Post Exchange/Base Exchange). Department stores on military bases open only to military personnel and their families.

Raven FAC. Covert forward air controllers, flying O-1 Bird Dog airplanes in support of Laotian military operations.

Small arms. Smaller-caliber rifles and pistols carried by individuals.

Speed boards/speed brakes. Drag-increasing panels located on both sides of a Mohawk fuselage halfway between the wing and the tail. They were hydraulically activated using a thumb-switch on the power levers in the cockpit to rapidly reduce the aircraft's speed.

Survival vest. A netted fabric vest with pockets for our emergency radio and an assortment of survival gear including a compass, smoke grenades, pen flares, strobe light, signal mirror, fishing line, first aid packet, magnesium fire starter, and knife.

Tri-Border. The region where the borders of South Vietnam, Laos, and Cambodia come together.

Viet Cong (VC). From the Vietnamese, Việt Cộng, which translates to Vietnamese Communist. The term refers to the irregular guerrilla forces drawn from the local population inside South Vietnam, often led by cadre from North Vietnam. However, many often used the term VC indiscriminately to refer to regular North Vietnamese Army forces as well as the southern-based guerrillas.

Wing stores. Those items attached to the bottom of airplane wings. On the 131st Mohawks, those included rocket pods and external fuel tanks (and .50 machine pods, early on). The airplane could also drop bombs from those same attaching points. No Mohawk ever did that in combat.

AIRCRAFT
Fixed-Wing Airplanes

A-1E, Skyraider. Korean War era, single-engine, propeller-driving attack airplane.

A-26, Invader. A twin-engine propeller light bomber and ground attack aircraft built by Douglas Aircraft Company. The airframes used in Laos were upgraded with more powerful engines and improved propellers. Each mounted eight .50-caliber machine guns in the nose.

AC-130, Spectre. US Air Force four-engine, turboprop, cargo aircraft converted into a massive, capable gunship.

B-52, Stratofortress. Heavy bomber, capable of carrying loads of up to 108 500- and 750-pound bombs.

B-57, Canberra. A twin jet-engine attack bomber and reconnaissance airplane with night target acquisition and attack capabilities.

C-46, Commando. A twin-engine propeller airplane developed from a Curtis pressurized high-altitude airliner. Used as a military transportation aircraft by Air America and Continental Air Services throughout Laos.

C-130, Hercules. US Air Force four-engine, turboprop, cargo plane capable of transporting up to 124 passengers, eighty-eight paratroopers, over twenty tons of cargo, or some combination of each. A select number were specially modified as lethal Spectre gunships while others sported capable communications suites to become airborne command and control centers.

F-4, Phantom. US Air Force, Navy, and Marine all-purpose jet fighter-bomber. Used in both air-to-air combat and ground attack missions.

O-1, Bird Dog. Light, single-engine, propeller-driven, two-seat observation airplane.

O-2, Skymaster. Twin-engine, push-pull, propeller-driven, observation airplane used by US Air Force forward air controllers.

OV-1, Mohawk. Twin turbo-prop airplane built by Grumman Aircraft Company. It was produced as any one of three model types: OV-1A for photo-reconnaissance missions, OV-1B for side-looking airborne radar (SLAR), and OV-1C for infrared (IR) requirements. The OV-1A aircraft in the 131st were armed with 2.75-inch folding fin aerial rockets. In earlier years, they also had pod mounted .50-caliber machine guns fixed to their wings as well.

OV-10, Bronco. Twin turboprop, two-seat observation airplane used by US Air Force forward air controllers.

PC-6, Pilatus Porter. A Swiss-made, single-engine turboprop, utility airplane capable of short field takeoff and landing. Used extensively by Air America and Continental Air Services.

T-28, Trojan/Nomad. A proven trainer put to work as a capable attack aircraft.

U-6, Beaver. A Canadian-built, all-purpose utility transport airplane powered by a nine-cylinder radial engine. Capable of hauling six passengers or over two thousand pounds of cargo. Excellent short field takeoff and landing capability. Used by the 131st for supply runs and transporting unit members to and from the airbase in Danang for connections with commercial and military transport.

Rotary-Wing Helicopters

AH-1G, Cobra. US Army attack helicopter armed with 2.75-inch rockets, 40 mm grenade launcher, and 7.62 mm minigun. Some also carried a wing-mounted 20 mm Gatling gun. The only Cobras seen in Laos were there in support of MACV-SOG operations close to the Vietnam-Laos border.

CH-47, Chinook. A tandem-rotor, twin turbine engine, heavy-lift transport helicopter capable of carrying up to fifty passengers or ten thousand pounds of payload.

H-34, Choctaw. A piston-engine, medium-lift transport helicopter. Used extensively by Air America.

HH-3, Jolly Green. Twin-engine, all-weather helicopter used by the US Air Force for special operations insertions and search and rescue. Known famously as the "Jolly Green Giant."

HH-53, Super Jolly. A more capable follow-on to the H-3.

UH-1, Huey. US and Air America utility helicopter used for troop movement and resupply. Capacity up to twelve soldiers or over three thousand pounds of cargo. The workhorse helicopter of the wars in Vietnam and Laos.

MILITARY FORMATIONS

Squad. Eight to twelve men led by a sergeant.

Platoon. Twenty to forty men led by a lieutenant and/or platoon sergeant.

Company. Seventy to one hundred men led by a captain.

Battalion. Four hundred to seven hundred men led by a lieutenant colonel.

Brigade/regiment. Two to five battalions led by a colonel.

Division. Multiple brigades/regiments with artillery, engineer, and logistical support (sometimes armor). Eight thousand to twelve thousand men led by a major general.

Corps. Several combat divisions, along with supporting artillery, engineer, intelligence, and logistics commands, often with separate combat brigades and regiments also assigned. In Vietnam, the four Army corps were located in fixed areas of geographic responsibility.

WEAPONS

United States and Royal Laotian Forces

Claymore mine. Directional, command-detonated, anti-personnel mine with an effective and devastating firing range of fifty meters.

CAR-15. Colt Automatic Rifle, Model number 15. MACV-SOG preferred the short-barreled "Commando" carbine version of the weapon. Fires 5.56 mm x 45 mm ammunition. 7.5 pounds.

"Forty-five." .45-caliber semi-automatic pistol. Carried principally by officers and tank crewmen.

M-16 Rifle. 5.56 mm x 45 mm automatic rifle. US infantry weapon beginning in 1965. Issued to the South Vietnamese airborne starting in 1967, then the ARVN infantry in following years. 7.5 pounds.

M-60 Machine Gun. 7.62 mm lightweight machine gun used by both the US forces and the Army of the Republic of Vietnam.

M-79. Hand-held 40 mm grenade launcher.

Artillery and Mortars

60 mm Mortar. Lightweight, high-firing-angle weapon with a range of 3,800 yards. Crew able to fire up to twenty rounds per minute. Normally deployed at company level.

81 mm Mortar. Medium-weight, high-firing-angle weapon with a range of 6,500 yards. Normally in a battalion weapons platoon.

105 mm Howitzer. Fires a thirty-three-pound high-explosive projectile up to seven miles.

155 mm Howitzer. Fires a one-hundred-pound high-explosive projectile up to nine miles.

North Vietnam and Pathet Lao

AAA (Triple A). Anti-aircraft artillery. Any of the various anti-aircraft weapons ranging from the .51-caliber anti-aircraft machine gun through the 14.5 mm double and four-barreled guns, to the twin-barreled 23 mm and 37 mm guns.

AK-47. The principal individual weapon of the North Vietnamese Army. 7.62 mm x 39 mm automatic rifle manufactured by the Soviet Union and China.

Armor

PT-76. Soviet-manufactured amphibious light tank with a 76.2mm main gun.

T-54. Soviet-manufactured main battle tank with a 100mm main gun.

Artillery and Mortars

Mortars. Various caliber, short-range, high-firing-angle weapons from 60 mm through 107 mm.

122 mm rocket. Three-to-seven-kilometer range rocket with devastating high explosive fragmentation warhead. Utilized the Soviet-built single-round "Grad" launcher, though often fired less accurately from bamboo launching apparatuses crafted on sight.

130 mm gun. Soviet-manufactured, vehicle-towed field gun, firing a 73-pound projectile as far as seventeen miles, significantly farther than any South Vietnamese artillery.

NOTES

CHAPTER 2

1. James Wilbanks, *The Tet Offensive: A Concise History* (New York: Columbia University Press, 2006), 30–55.

2. Ibid.

3. President Lyndon Johnson, speech, October 31, 1968, New York Public Radio Archive Collections, accessed October 13, 2023, https://www.wnyc.org/story/president-johnson-halts-bombing-in-vietnam/.

CHAPTER 3

1. For full details of the Ho Chi Minh Trail network, see John Prados, *The Blood Road: The Ho Chi Minh Trail and the Vietnam War* (New York: Wiley, 1999); see also P.J. Schweitzer, *Description of the Ho Chi Minh Trail* (Arlington, VA: Institute for Defense Analysis, 1966).

2. A.W. Thompson, Project CHECO, *Strike Control and Reconnaissance in SEA* (Hickam Air Force Base, HI: HQ Pacific Air Forces, 1969), 48.

3. If you are open to some pretty foul and raunchy lyrics, some of these songs are in the *SPUD Hymnal*, available online at https://www.horntip.com/html/books_&_MSS/1970s/1971_the_SPUD_hymnal_(various)/1971_the_SPUD_hymnal_1st_edition_(mimeo)/index.htm.

L. Bowers, "The McConnell-Johnson Agreement," in *Tactical Airlift: The United States Airforce in Southeast Asia* (Washington, DC: Office of Air Force History, 1983), 673–74.

4. Author interview with John Pfeiffer, October 19, 2023.

CHAPTER 4

1. To view the source documents relating to roles and missions debates between the Army and Air Force, see Richard I. Ward, *The United States Air Force: Basic Documents on Roles and Missions* (Washington, DC: Office of Air Force History, 1987), 379–84.

2. For a full discussion of the 11th Air Assault Division tests and implications for the use of Mohawks in Vietnam, see James W. Williams, *A History of Army Aviation: From Its Beginnings to the War on Terror* (New York: iUniverse, 2005), 107–13. The earlier Army

study that set the stage for those tests is the subject of J.A. Stockfisch, *The 1962 Howze Board and Army Combat Developments* (Santa Monica, CA: RAND, 1994).

3. Ibid.

CHAPTER 5

1. Bernard C. Nalty, *The War against Trucks: Aerial Interdiction in Southern Laos, 1968–1972* (Washington, DC: Air Force History and Museums Program, 2005), 98, 130, 167. Melvin H. Porter, *Tiger Hound*, Project CHECO Report (Hickam Air Force Base, HI: Headquarters Pacific Air Force, 1966), 26, 30.

2. Arthur J. Dommen, *Laos: Keystone of Indochina* (Boulder, CO: Westview, 1985), 59–63. Adread M. Savada, ed., *Laos: A Country Study* (Washington, DC: Library of Congress, 1995), 29, 42, 44, 54.

3. Ibid.

4. Ibid.

5. Ibid. Jacob Van Staaveren, *Interdiction in Southern Laos, 1960–1968* (Washington, DC: Center for Air Force History, 1993), 147. Nalty, *The War against Trucks*, 98.

6. John Guilmartin, "Tchepone: Fighter Jock Song," Buffalo State University, accessed December 2, 2023, https://faculty.buffalostate.edu/fishlm/folksongs/tchepone.htm.

CHAPTER 6

1. For a complete discussion of "Night Owl" F-4 integration into C-130 Blind Bat missions, see Victor B. Anthony, *The Air Force in Southeast Asia: Tactics and Techniques of Night Operations, 1961–1970* (Washington, DC: Office of Air Force History, 1973), 36–45, 134–40,https://media.defense.gov/2011/Mar/24/2001330120/-1/-1/0/AFD -110324-027.pdf.

2. For 497th Tactical Fighter Squadron "Night Owl" support to AC-130 gunship operations, see ibid., 134–48, 158–63.

3. Ibid., 43.

4. Robin Olds et al., *The Memoir of a Legendary Ace, Robin Olds* (New York: St. Martin's, 2010), 247, 253–340.

5. See John Prados and Ray W. Stubbe, *Valley of Decision: The Siege of Khe Sanh* (New York: Houghton Mifflin, 1991).

CHAPTER 7

1. Jacob Van Staaveren, *Interdiction in Southern Laos, 1960–1968* (Washington, DC: Center for Air Force History, 1993), 137.

2. For further information on Air America, see Allen Cates, "Air America: A Histor-ical Synopsis from End to End," Air America, accessed July 17, 2024, https://www.air -america.org/air-america-history.html.

3. Ian G. Baird, "Obtaining the Nha Heun 'Culture' from the King: Considering a Sacred Script and Oral History in Southern Laos," *SOJOURN: Journal of Social Issues in Southeast Asia* 36, no. 2 (2021): 267–68. Personal correspondence with the author.

4. Ibid.

5. Ian G. Baird and Bruce Shoemaker, *People, Livelihoods, and Development in the Xekong River Basin, Laos* (Bangkok, Thailand: White Lotus, 2008), 17–18.

6. "Declaration on the Neutrality of Laos, 23 July 1962," United Nations Treaty Series(New York: 1963).

7. There are several good works on Laotian history, the Laotian civil war, and America's "secret war" that followed. The information I've highlighted in these next several paragraphs comes principally from two sources:Arthur J. Dommen, *Laos: Keystone of Indochina* (Boulder, CO: Westview, 1985), 9–47; Timothy N. Castle, *At War in the Shadow of Vietnam: U.S. Military Aid to the Royal Lao Government, 1955 to 1975* (New York: Columbia University Press, 1993), 14–61.

CHAPTER 8

1. For the full story and personal accounts of Raven FAC operations in Laos, see John H. Fuller and Helen Murphy, eds., *The Raven Chronicles: In Our Own Words, Stories by Forward Air Controllers from the Secret War in Laos* (Mesa, AZ: Chronicles Project, 2016).

2. Ban Thateng was an interesting place, a frequent combat arena between communist and loyalist forces. See "The President's Daily Brief, 13 January 1969," 19, Central Intelligence Agency, accessed July 17, 2024, https://www.cia.gov/readingroom/docs/DOC_0005976559.pdf; and Kenneth Conboy and James Morrison, *Shadow War: The CIA's Secret War in Laos* (Boulder, CO: Paladin, 1995), 221–23.

3. For more information about the Mk5 ejection seat and itsspecifications, see "Mk5 Ejection Seat," Martin-Baker, accessed July 17, 2024, https://martin-baker.com/products /mk5-ejection-seat/.

4. A very brief account of our rescue by "Pony Express" is included in "History of the 20th Helicopter Squadron," USAF Helicopter Association, accessed July 17, 2024, https://usafhpa.org/20poniesnew/aircommando20th.html.

CHAPTER 9

1. For a firsthand account of the group based at Phu Bai, see Rosemary Thunder Schwoebel, *A Vietnam Memoir: Adventures of an American Red Cross Donut Dolly, 1968–69* (Independently published, 2017).

2. Melvin Zais, "Battle of Dong Ap Bia" (Camp Eagle, Republic of Vietnam: Office of the Commanding General, Headquarters 101st Airborne Division, May 24, 1969)." Samuel Zaffiri, *Hamburger Hill: The Brutal Battle for Dong Ap Bia, May 11–20, 1969* (Novato, CA: Presidio, 2000).

3. Ibid.

4. Ibid.

5. Ibid.

6. See an account in Christopher Hobson, *Vietnam Air Losses: USAF, Navy, and Marine Corps Fixed-Wing Aircraft Losses in SE Asia 1961–1973* (Leicester, UK: Midland, 2001).

CHAPTER 10

1. Michael Clodfelter, *Vietnam in Military Statistics: A History of the Indochina Wars, 1772–1991* (Jefferson, NC: McFarland, 1995), 7.

2. Arthur J. Dommen, *Laos: Keystone of Indochina* (Boulder, CO: Westview, 1985), 27, 71–73, 82–91.

3. Karen Coates, "Plain of Jars," *Archaeology* 58, no. 4 (July/August 2005): 30–35.

4. Timothy N. Castle, *At War in the Shadow of Vietnam: United States Military Aid to the Royal Lao Government1955–75* (New York: Columbia University Press, 1993), 39–40, 79–81.

5. Ibid., 88–90.

6. For a full understanding of America's covert role in the Laotian civil war, see Thomas Leo Briggs, *Cash on Delivery: CIA Special Operations during the Secret War in Laos* (Rockville, MD: Rosebank, 2009; and Kenneth Conboy and James Morrison, *Shadow War: The CIA's Secret War in Laos* (Boulder, CO: Paladin, 1995).

7. Ibid.

8. A riveting and tragic story. See Dennis E. McClendon, *The* Lady Be Good*: Mystery Bomber of World War II* (Fallbrook, CA: Aero, 1982).

CHAPTER 11

1. Grant Wolfkill, *Reported to Be Alive* (New York: Simon & Schuster, 1965).

CHAPTER 12

1. This program has since been declassified. See "Photoreconnaissance of Cambodia," CIA Memorandum, April 2, 1970, approved for public release August 31, 2004 (copy in author's possession), Freedom of Information Act Electronic Reading Room, accessed July 17, 2024, https://www.cia.gov/readingroom/document/cia-rdp79b01709a001700060003-6.

2. Milton E. Osborne, *Sihanouk: Prince of Light; Prince of Darkness* (Honolulu: University of Hawaii Press, 1994), 151–84.

3. John M. Shaw, *The Cambodian Campaign: The 1970 Offensive and America's Vietnam War* (Lawrence: University Press of Kansas, 2005), 38.

EPILOGUE

1. Ray L. Bowers, "The McConnell-Johnson Agreement," in *Tactical Airlift: The United States Airforce in Southeast Asia* (Washington, DC: Office of Air Force History, 1983), 673–74.

2. The disastrous Lam Son 719 operation degenerated into chaos in the air and on the ground. A well-documented study is found in James H. Willbanks, *A Raid Too Far: Operation Lam Son 719 and Vietnamization in Laos* (College Station: Texas A&M University Press, 2014).

3. Headquarters Department of the Army General Order No. 5, February 5, 1973.

4. Army Regulation 600-8-22, *Military Awards*, June 25, 2015.

5. Mark W. Stephenson and Peter J. Bonner, "Nighthawks: Unit History of A CO, 15th MI BN" (Fort Hood, TX: 15th Military Intelligence Battalion, 1985).

6. Terry M. Love, "Mohawks over the Desert" (May 1991).

7. Meredith Tibbetts, "At Vietnam Wall, 3,000 Roses Mark Father's Day Remembrance," *Stars and Stripes*, June 17, 2018.

Sources

Primary Sources
Interviews and Correspondence
Ian G. Baird, University of Wisconsin–Madison

Lysle C. Barthlome, pilot, 131st Surveillance Airplane Company

Mark L. Bellamy, pilot, 20th Aerial Surveillance and Target Acquisition (ASTA)/131st Surveillance Airplane Company

Thomas L. Briggs, Central Intelligence Agency

Gary Brownworth, technical observer, 131st Surveillance Airplane Company

Henry Brummett, pilot, 11th Air Assault Division, 131st Surveillance Airplane Company

Charles E. Chauvin, pilot, 131st Surveillance Airplane Company

Theron O. Clark, pilot, 131st Surveillance Airplane Company

E. Rick Coleman, pilot, 131st Surveillance Airplane Company

George P. Davis III, pilot, 131st Surveillance Airplane Company

Curtis L. Degner, pilot, 131st Surveillance Airplane Company

Steve C. Easley, technical observer, 131st Surveillance Airplane Company

Daniel C. Fordiani, pilot, 131st Surveillance Airplane Company

Larry Hower, pilot, 131st Surveillance Airplane Company

Gabe L. Hudson, pilot, 131st Surveillance Airplane Company

William Jordan, intelligence officer, 131st Surveillance Airplane Company

Mickey Kappes, Central Intelligence Agency

Harold C. Lacy, technical observer, 131st Surveillance Airplane Company

Joe D. Lowdermilk, pilot, 131st Surveillance Airplane Company

Jon F. Lowdermilk, pilot, 131st Surveillance Airplane Company

Neil F. Ostgaard, pilot, 131st Surveillance Company

John L. Pfeiffer, pilot, 20th Aerial Surveillance and Target Acquisition (ASTA)/131st Surveillance Airplane Company

Burwin P. Reed, pilot, 131st Surveillance Airplane Company

J. William Seiden, pilot, 131st Surveillance Airplane Company

Documents

Government Documents

Central Intelligence Agency. "The President's Daily Brief, 13 January 1969." Accessed July 17, 2024. https://www.cia.gov/readingroom/docs/DOC_0005976559.pdf.

Defense Intelligence Agency. "Message 021952Z FEB 76, Subj: DIA Data Summary." Accessed July 17, 2024. https://tile.loc.gov/storage-services/service//frd/pwmia/PDS40/124846.pdf.

"Headquarters Department of the Army General Order No. 5." February 5, 1973.

United States, Military Assistance Command, Vietnam. *Command History, 1968, Annex F.* Military Assistance Command, Vietnam. Saigon, South Vietnam, 1969.

———. *Command History, Volume II, 1968.* Military Assistance Command, Vietnam. Saigon, South Vietnam, 1969.

Zais, Melvin. "Battle of Dong Ap Bia." Camp Eagle, Republic of Vietnam: Office of the Commanding General, Headquarters 101st Airborne Division, May 24, 1969. Accessed July 17, 2024. https://web.archive.org/web/20190515114632/https://www.vietnam.ttu.edu/star/images/1683/168300010494.pdf.

Other Documents

"Declaration on the Neutrality of Laos, 23 July 1962." UN Treaty Series. New York: United Nations, 1963.

Schweitzer, P. J. *Description of the Ho Chi Minh Trail.* Arlington, VA: Institute for Defense Analysis, 1966.

Books and Articles

Briggs, Thomas Leo. *Cash on Delivery: CIA Special Operations during the Secret War in Laos.* Rockville, MD: Rosebank, 2009.

Curry, Robert D. *Whispering Death: Our Journey with the Hmong in America's Secret War in Laos.* Lincoln, NE: iUniverse, 2004.

Davis, George P., III. *SPUD 19: A Vietnam Army Aviator's Battles with PTSD.* Parker, CO: War Writer's Campaign, 2016.

Fuller, John H., and Helen Murphy, eds. *The Raven Chronicles: In Our Own Words, Stories by Forward Air Controllers from the Secret War in Laos.* Mesa, AZ: Chronicles Project, 2016.

Naekel, Gerald. *Mohawks Lost: Flying in the CIA's Secret War in Laos.* Create Space, 2016.

Schwoebel, Rosemary Thunder. *A Vietnam Memoir: Adventures of an American Red Cross Donut Dolly, 1968–69.* Independently published, 2017.

Tallon, Joseph F. *100 Days in Vietnam: A Memoir of Love, War, and Survival.* Virginia Beach, VA: Koehler Books, 2016.

Wolf, Richard I. *The United States Air Force: Basic Documents on Roles and Missions.* Washington, DC: Office of Air Force History, 1987.

Wolfkill, Grant. *Reported to Be Alive.* New York: Simon & Schuster, 1965.

Speeches

President Lyndon Baines Johnson, October 31, 1968. New York Public Radio Archive
Collections. Accessed October 13, 2023. https://www.wnyc.org/story/president
-johnson-halts-bombing-in-vietnam/.

SECONDARY SOURCES

Anthony, Victor B. *The Air Force in Southeast Asia: Tactics and Techniques of Night Operations, 1961–1970.* Washington, DC: Office of Air Force History, 1973.

Baird, Ian G. "Obtaining the Nha Heun 'Culture' from the King: Considering a Sacred
Script and Oral History in Southern Laos," *SOJOURN: Journal of Social Issues in
Southeast Asia* 36, no. 2 (2021): 258–90.

Baird, Ian G., and Bruce Shoemaker. *People, Livelihoods, and Development in the Xekong
River Basin, Laos.* Bangkok, Thailand: White Lotus, 2008.

Bowers, Ray L. *Tactical Airlift: The United States Air Force in Southeast Asia.* Washington,
DC: Office of Air Force History, 1983.

Castle, Timothy N. *At War in the Shadow of Vietnam: United States Military Aid to the
Royal Lao Government, 1955–75.* New York: Columbia University Press, 1993.

Cates, Allen. "Air America: A Historical Synopsis from Beginning to End." Air America.
Accessed July 17, 2024. https://www.air-america.org/air-america-history.html.

Clodfelter, Michael. *Vietnam in Military Statistics: A History of the Indochina Wars, 1772–
1991.* Jefferson, NC: McFarland, 1995.

Coates, Karen. "Plain of Jars." *Archaeology* 58, no. 4 (July/August 2005): 30–35.

Collar, Dave. "The OV-1 Mohawk in Vietnam," *Trading Post* (a publication of the American Society of Military Insignia Collectors), Summer 1993, 13–15.

Conboy, Kenneth, with James Morrison. *Shadow War: The CIA's Secret War in Laos.* Boulder, CO: Paladin, 1995.

Correll, John T. "Arc Light." *Air Force Magazine,* January 2009.

Dommen, Arthur J. *Laos: Keystone of Indochina.* Boulder, CO: Westview, 1985.

Hobson, Christopher. *Vietnam Air Losses: USAF, Navy, and Marine Corps Fixed-Wing
Aircraft Losses in SE Asia 1961–1973.* Leicester, UK: Midland, 2001.

Kurlantzick, Joshua. *A Great Place to Have a War: America in Laos and the Birth of a Military CIA.* New York: Simon & Schuster, 2016.

Leary, William M. "CIA Air Operations in Laos: 1955–1974," *Studies in Intelligence* 43,
no. 3 (Winter 1999–2000).

Love, Terry. "Mohawks over the Desert." May 1991. Print copy in possession of the
author.

———. *OV-1 Mohawk in Action.* Carrollton, TX: Squadron Signal Publications, 1989.

McNease, Bill. *Honor Roll: The Story of Those Lost in SE Asia in the OV-1 Mohawk.* Independently published, 2016.

Montagliani, Earnest S. *Army Aviation in RVN: A Case Study. Project CHECO Report.*
Hickam Air Force Base, HI: Headquarters, Pacific Air Force, 1970.

Nalty, Bernard C. *The War against Trucks: Aerial Interdiction in Southern Laos, 1968–1972.*
Washington, DC: Air Force History and Museums Program, 2005.

Olds, Robin, et al. *The Memoir of a Legendary Ace, Robin Olds.* New York: St. Martin's, 2010.

Osborne, Milton E. *Sihanouk: Prince of Light; Prince of Darkness*. Honolulu: University of Hawaii Press, 1994.

Parker, James E. *Codename Mule: Fighting the Secret War in Laos for the CIA*. Annapolis, MD: Naval Institute Press, 1995.

Porter, Melvin H. *Tiger Hound*. Project CHECO Report. Hickam Air Force Base, HI: Headquarters Pacific Air Force, 1966.

Prados, John. *The Blood Road: The Ho Chi Minh Trail and the Vietnam War*. New York: Wiley, 1999.

Prados, John, and Ray W. Stubbe. *Valley of Decision: The Siege of Khe Sanh*. New York: Houghton Mifflin, 1991.

Savada, Adread M., ed. *Laos: A Country Study*. Washington, DC: Library of Congress, 1995.

Sexton, Richard R., and William M. Hodgson. *OV-1/AC-119 Hunter-Killer Team*. Project CHECO Report. Hickam Air Force Base, HI: Headquarters, Pacific Air Force, 1972.

Shaw, John M. *The Cambodian Campaign: The 1970 Offensive and America's Vietnam War*. Lawrence: University Press of Kansas, 2005.

Staaveren, Jacob Van. *Interdiction in Southern Laos, 1960–1968*. Washington, DC: Center for Air Force History, 1993.

Stephenson, Mark W., and Peter J. Bonner. "Nighthawks: Unit History of A CO, 15th MI BN." Fort Hood, TX: 15th Military Intelligence Battalion, 1985.

Stockfisch, J. A. *The 1962 Howze Board and Army Combat Developments*. Santa Monica, CA: RAND, 1994.

Sweetman, Bill, et al. *The Great Book of Modern Airplanes*. New York: Portland House, 1987.

Tibbetts, Meredith. "At Vietnam Wall, 3,000 Roses Mark Father's Day Remembrance." *Stars and Stripes*, June 17, 2018.

Warner, Roger. *Shooting at the Moon: The Story of America's Clandestine War in Laos*. South Royalton, VT: Steerforth Press, 1996.

Willbanks, James H. *A Raid Too Far: Operation Lam Son 719 and Vietnamization in Laos*. College Station: Texas A&M University Press, 2014.

———. *The Tet Offensive: A Concise History*. New York: Columbia University Press, 2006.

Williams, James W. *A History of Army Aviation: From Its Beginnings to the War on Terror*. New York: iUniverse, 2005.

Zaffiri, Samuel. *Hamburger Hill: The Brutal Battle for Dong Ap Bia, May 11–20, 1969*. Novato, CA: Presidio, 2000.

Index

Vietnam (MACV), 10, 52, 134,
154, 162, 164
Studies and Observation
Group (SOG), 29, 99
military intelligence (MI), 170–71
military payment certificates
(MPC), 57
Miller, doctor, 157–59
missing in action (MIA), 78
Misty (call sign), 26
Mohawks, 4, 27t
characteristics of, 7–9
checkout with, 7–11
closure of units, 172
first missions with, 45–63
types of, 49, 177
Moonbeam, 81, 144
mortality, confrontation with, 52,
105, 143
mountains, flying and, 70, 72
music, 39–40, 66–67
Musil, Clinton, 187

Nail (call sign), 26
Nakhon Phanom (NKP), 89, 99
Nash, John, 187
Negritos, 152
Newman, Frank, 162, 188
Nha Heun ethnic group, 97, 117
nicknames, 4, 41–43, 123–26,
149–52
night missions, 21–22, 80–81
Nopp, Robert, 96, 188
Nui Ba Den, 164

O-1 Bird Dog, 12, 26, 27t, 75, 109
O-2 Skymaster, 26, 27t, 89
O'Brien, Kevin, 76
officer candidate school (OCS),
78, 154
Olds, Robin, 84
101st Airborne Division, 13, 130
131st Army Surveillance Airplane
Company, 1–5, 41, 134, 136
personnel changes, 61–63,
147, 166, 169–86
Valorous Unit Award, 171
Operation Desert Storm, 171–72
Operation Lam Son 719, 170
operations officer, 106–7, 133, 141,
147–48
Ostgaard, Neil "Uncle Nils," 61
OV-1 Mohawk. See Mohawks
OV-10 Bronco, 26, 28t, 89
oxygen, effects of, 87
Oy tribe, 97

Paquette, Ed, 7–11, 14, 19, 58,
67–70
Parish, Jim "Traveler," 61
party suits, 39–40, 60
patches, 39, 60, 87
Pathet Lao, 65, 97, 100–101,
134–35, 153
PC-6 Porter, 28t
perforated steel planking (PSB),
11–12
Pfeiffer, John "Tree," 41–42, 176,
181–82

216

ABOUT THE AUTHOR

William Reeder Jr. is a training and leader development consultant living in the Pacific Northwest. He spends parts of each year in the education of NATO Special Operations Forces in various European locations. He was formerly an associate professor of social sciences and deputy director of the US Army School of Advanced Military Studies at Fort Leavenworth, Kansas. He retired from the US Army in 1995 as a colonel and subsequently earned a PhD in history and anthropology from Kansas State University. His military service included assignments in field artillery, cavalry, and aviation. He has extensive combat experience.

Reeder is a thirty-year Army veteran with two tours of duty in Vietnam, flying armed OV-1 Mohawk reconnaissance airplanes and AH-1 Cobra attack helicopters. He participated in deep reconnaissance and surveillance operations throughout Southeast Asia and supported the special operations missions of MACV-SOG (Military Assistance Command Vietnam—Studies and Observations Group). He has more than three thousand hours of flight time including more than one thousand hours in combat. During his second combat tour, he was shot down and captured by the communist North Vietnamese, spending nearly a year as a prisoner of war.

Subsequent military assignments included various Army command and staff positions and a stint at the US Air Force Academy. He commanded at all levels, platoon through brigade (including command of an AH-64 Apache attack helicopter squadron). His last assignment before retirement in 1995 was as the deputy chief of staff, de facto chief of staff, for the United States Southern Command in Panama.

His military awards and decorations include the Silver Star Medal for gallantry, Valorous Unit Award, Defense Superior Service Medal, Legion of Merit, two Distinguished Flying Crosses, three Bronze Star Medals, three Purple Hearts for wounds received in action, the POW Medal, Vietnamese Cross of Gallantry with Bronze Star, and numerous Air Medals (one with "V" device for valor). In 1977 he was named Army Aviator of the Year and was inducted into the US Army Aviation Hall of Fame in 2014. He was featured in the PBS documentary *The Helicopter Pilots of Vietnam*, as well as the "Attack Helicopters" episode of *Deadliest Tech* on the Military Channel. He has provided military commentary on CNN and the Discovery Channel.

Reeder is married to the former Melanie Lineker of Westminster, Maryland, who is also a retired Army colonel and retired in 2021 from her post-military career as the director of manpower (N-1) for the US Navy Northwest Region, headquartered at Bangor Submarine Base, Washington. They have four children and one grandchild.